STROM THURMOND:
The Public Man

STROM THURMOND

The Public Man

Joseph C. Ellers

Sandlapper Publishing, Inc.
Orangeburg, South Carolina

Manufactured in the United States of America

*Photos printed in this book were used
with the permission of Strom Thurmond
and come from the Thurmond Collection~
Clemson University Library.*

Book Designer: Janette K. Butler

Library of Congress Cataloging-in-Publication Data

Ellers, Joseph C., 1959–
    Strom Thurmond : the public man / Joseph C. Ellers
       p.   cm.
    ISBN 0-87844-116-6
    1. Thurmond, Strom, 1902– . 2. Legislators—United States—
Biography. 3. United States. Congress. Senate—Biography.
I. Title.
E748.T58E45   1993
973.9'092—dc20
  [B]   93–21384
                                     CIP

To my family

CONTENTS

Preface   ix

Chapter 1   Young Thurmond   1
Chapter 2   Thurmond at Law   15
Chapter 3   The Journey Begins   30
Chapter 4   The Judicial Thurmond   47
Chapter 5   He's in the Army Now   68
Chapter 6   A Soldier Becomes a Governor   76
Chapter 7   Thurmond and His Bride   95
Chapter 8   Thurmond for President   103
Chapter 9   Governor Again   124
Chapter 10   Thurmond at Large   144
Chapter 11   Thurmond Goes to Washington   166
Chapter 12   Back to the Senate   182
Chapter 13   A Personal Tragedy . . .
                and Moving On   195
Chapter 14   The Winds of Change   211
Chapter 15   Thurmond Becomes a Statesman   229
Chapter 16   The Public Man   250

Notes   253
Index   265

PREFACE

This book, *Strom Thurmond: The Public Man*, is about the career of James Strom Thurmond. Originally, I had intended it to be a more encompassing biography that described the interplay of his personal life with his professional life. The focus changed because reliable information on his personal life was not available, and also because I realized that the "story" is the public evolution of Strom Thurmond—and the South.

As I refined the focus of the work, I made a conscious effort to concentrate on the years from 1932 to 1968. One chapter deals with the time before those years—and one chapter after—but the balance of the book deals with that period. Again, there were two reasons: verifiable information was readily available for this period, and it was also what I considered to be the most exciting time. After his reelection to the U.S. Senate in 1966, this time as a Republican, Thurmond's brand of conservatism began to come into vogue so that his positions were not that far from the mainstream—and therefore required less courage.

This is an unauthorized biography. Senator Thurmond did not participate in the writing of this work. Almost all the information was gained through his papers, which he donated to the Clemson University Library in Clemson, South Carolina. I cited numerous newspaper sources because they were readily available and they support numerous points from a public perspective. Every key idea included here has published documentation of one kind or another, and most of that is available at the Clemson University Library.

Despite the "arm's length" nature of this work, I have had opportunities to work both for and with the senator. I was a volunteer in Pickens County for Strom's 1978 reelection effort. As a Republican party officer, as a delegate to state conventions, during work at the 1976 Republican National Convention, and in the course of my own government service, I have had numerous interactions with the senator. And in 1987, I wrote a manuscript on federalism with the senator.

I confess that I have been an admirer of Strom's and that my research into his life has only strengthened that admiration. This is not contradicted by the fact that there are many things about the South of Thurmond's past that I am ashamed of. There has never been any justification for policies, laws, and customs that separate the races, and those who tried to preserve them failed to understand a basic American ideal. My feeling, completely unsubstantiated by any hard fact, is that Thurmond's transition from one point of view to the other came about because he reached this same conclusion and acted upon it.

I describe myself as a "southernist." My intention is to present positive looks at southern institutions, southern people, and the South in general. To me, Strom Thurmond is a great southerner and a great American—both for his consistency in basic American ideals and his ability to change when necessary. South Carolina can be proud of one of its greatest sons and I am grateful to have had the opportunity to present his story.

In my efforts, I have been assisted by many. Jim Cross, the Thurmond archivist at Special Collections of the Clemson University Library, has lent considerable time and expertise to this project. Michael Kohl, the director of Special Collections, and his fine staff have also been of great help.

My publisher, Frank Handal, and all the fine people at Sandlapper also deserve special appreciation for their support.

Linda Benefield served as the editor and did an excellent job of tightening up my words and making the story more readable.

Finally, I want to thank my family and friends, especially my wife, Karen, and my daughters, Emily and Anna, who have supported me over the many years of this project's duration.

Despite the involvement of all of these interested people, I accept the full responsibility for the content and tone of this work. I fully recognize that it is a hybrid—not a scholarly work and yet not exactly intended for the general reader. It is a look at the important parts of the career of a man who shaped southern, national, and world history—and it is a labor of love.

STROM THURMOND:
The Public Man

Chapter 1

YOUNG

THURMOND

The spring of 1897 in Edgefield, South Carolina, seemed to be full of possibilities for J. William "Will" Thurmond. Although still a young man, Will had already begun making his mark on the community. He was an attorney, and had served in the state legislature until his election as solicitor in 1896.

Will was active in local politics and had made many friends—among them South Carolina's powerful populist U.S. senator, Benjamin Ryan Tillman. Tillman, like Thurmond, came from Edgefield, and the relationship between the two was mutually beneficial for years. This friendship, coupled with his own abilities, caused everyone in Edgefield to expect big things out of young Will Thurmond. Unfortunately, the same situations that bring opportunities may also bring setbacks.

On March 25, after a satisfying day's work at his law office, Thurmond left at about five o'clock in the afternoon and walked down Edgefield's dusty streets through the town square to the drug store of W. E. Lynch. Inside, Thurmond was accosted by Will Harris, a traveling salesman for the Murray Drug Company. Young Harris knew Thurmond and did not like him for several reasons. Thurmond had been instrumental in denying Harris's father a magisterial appointment. And then there was Thurmond's Tillmanism. In the South Carolina of the late 1890s Tillman was a watershed person—there did not seem to be any middle ground; you either liked him or you did not. And in South Carolina political passion has often resulted in bloodshed.

Harris used the chance encounter with Thurmond to vent some of his alcohol-induced steam. He threatened Thurmond and suggested that he (Harris) had a weapon. Thurmond withdrew to his

1

law office, assuming the confrontation was over. As he sat behind his desk, trying to finish up some last-minute details by the light from his oil desk lamp, he heard the drunken voice of Will Harris outside his office, accusing and threatening. Harris came inside Thurmond's office, still ranting, and reached into his pocket as if to draw a weapon. Will Thurmond was ready. Using his pistol, he shot Will Harris and killed him.[1]

Will Thurmond was arrested, charged with murder, and jailed. In his signed statement given on March 26, Will stated that he "fired under unquestioning conviction that instant action was necessary" for self-defense.[2] At his trial, the jury believed him, and he was found innocent of any wrongdoing. But it was still a blot on his record. Even in a state known for hot tempers, Will knew that many of his ambitions were stymied. He did not give up, however. He continued to pursue political power and wealth throughout his life, and he was successful in many ways.

And unfortunate as this incident was, it did nothing to prevent his marrying Eleanor Gertrude Strom. Their union would produce six children, three boys and three girls. Their second born was named James Strom Thurmond.

Edgefield Background

No story of the life of Strom Thurmond would be complete without some understanding of the place that nurtured him— Edgefield County in South Carolina. Located on a plain along the Savannah River, Edgefield County is in the part of the state known as the "midlands." Because of the rivalry between the aristocratic Charlestonians and the yeoman farmers of the upcountry, the midlands have produced many of South Carolina's leaders. And Edgefield County has provided more than its share of this leadership. So far, ten South Carolina governors have hailed from that small county. Joining them have been numerous U.S. senators and congressmen, among them the infamous Congressman Preston Brooks, best remembered for his caning of abolitionist Senator Charles Sumner in the days preceding the Civil War.

The history of public service is so strong here that William Preston (a U.S. senator from Edgefield) wrote that "The object of a Southern man's life is politics and subsidiary to this end we all practice law."[3]

But while politics may have been the object of life, there has always been room in Edgefield for the soldier—another form of public service. Edgefield has been notable for its "military ethos" because of its elite military academies and the antebellum requirement that all white males be part of the state militia.[4]

The deep commitment to military service goes back to the days of the American Revolution. When the call went out for volunteers, Edgefield men were quick to join the ranks of both Tory and rebel forces, and the conflict here was a civil war. The widespread participation in that cause is validated by the fact that the Revolutionary War produced some fourteen hundred widows and orphans in the Edgefield area.[5]

Edgefield men also saw action in the War of 1812, the Seminole Indian War, and the Mexican War. William Barret Travis and James Butler Bonham of Edgefield were among the 182 who died at the Alamo. And of course, Edgefield supplied its share of soldiers in the Civil War. (One of these was George Washington Thurmond who also saw action in the Mexican and Indian wars. He was with General Robert E. Lee when Lee surrendered at Appomattox, and Thurmond made the long walk home from there.)

An understanding of Strom Thurmond (and southern politics) requires some background on the reasons why southerners fiercely resisted the Republican party and efforts to introduce blacks into their social and political circles. These reasons began to develop immediately after the assassination of President Lincoln in 1865. With his compassionate voice silenced, radical Republicans took control of the federal government and implemented policies designed to punish the South—economically and politically. The federal troops that remained in the South after the Civil War did not act as a stabilizing force; instead, they treated much of the South as occupied territory. In the first election (held in June of 1868), outsiders (known as carpetbaggers) and freed slaves were placed in control. These people often identified themselves as Republicans, and white southerners quickly developed hatred for the groups that wrested control from them.

In Edgefield County, which had a black majority, blacks were routinely elected to posts such as county commissioner, sheriff, clerk of court, probate judge, and state representative.

To stem this tide, some southerners resorted to force and intimidation to try to reestablish control. Ex-Confederate General M. W. Gray appealed for guerrilla military response. His groups of armed night riders terrorized Republican sympathizers, most of them black. In July of 1876 another group of whites, led by ex-Confederate

General M. C. Butler, was involved in a pitched gun battle with a black militia unit in Edgefield County.

The tide began to turn against blacks in South Carolina in 1876. That year, Wade Hampton ran for governor as a Democrat. Through various intimidation tactics, he was able to obtain a small majority and was elected as the first Democratic governor since Reconstruction. While the outcome was still up in the air, presidential politics entered into the picture. Republican Rutherford B. Hayes was locked in a tight race with Democrat Samuel Tilden. South Carolina, and other southern states, cast their electoral votes for Hayes and he was elected. Then President Hayes fulfilled his end of the bargain by calling an end to Reconstruction and withdrawing federal troops from the South. With them went the end of Republican control of the state, and this signaled the beginning of a series of maneuvers—some violent and some political—that wrested control away from South Carolina's black citizens.

Although Hampton was not a radical racist, the situation for South Carolina blacks soon became very bad. Over the Christmas holidays in 1881, some four to five thousand blacks left Edgefield County for Arkansas. The final touches to locking blacks out of the political process were added at the request of Governor Ben Tillman. In 1890 Tillman had campaigned for governor on a populist agrarian platform that included large doses of racism. After his election, he had the state constitution rewritten to add literacy tests and property qualifications to prevent blacks from ever regaining any political power in South Carolina.

These events occurred just a few years before Strom Thurmond was born. The memory of occupying armies remained strong in the minds of many southerners for many years after the armies were gone. Almost all white southerners who were products of this age had the same idea; they hated the Republican party and were committed to barring blacks from any political power.

Strom Thurmond was a product of this age and because of this, a disproportionate amount of his time and energy were devoted to racial issues. Many times, his involvement in these issues has obscured real contributions to his state and nation. His early stands also served to stereotype him as a bigoted segregationist. This, too, is unfortunate because while many things have remained constant for Thurmond over the years, his position on racial issues has changed dramatically. Many do not give Thurmond any credit for his change of heart, instead attributing to him a political shrewdness he does not have. A study of the Thurmond record shows numerous instances when he has done things that were impolitic purely because he believed them to be the right thing to do. The reality is that the South of today owes much of its new character to the courage of Strom Thurmond. Instead of following the pack, there is much evidence that, in fact, he started the parade.

But the journey was a long one and the distance from Edgefield to Washington was much farther than any map would have shown. The Edgefield of Strom's past was far from the mainstream, and the shadow of South Carolina's past leaders such as John C. Calhoun and Ben Tillman often obscured the route. But with his ambition and dedication to hard work, Strom Thurmond would have a chance to lead on his own—and he chose to lead by serving.

The Thurmond Family

The December 28, 1898, marriage of John William Thurmond and Eleanor Gertrude Strom united two of the most prominent families in the area. Miss Strom's father was a physician, and he intended for his daughter to be educated. She attended the Colwell Private School, Edgefield Academy, and the Greenville Female College. Prior to marrying Will, Gertrude taught school. She was a small woman, "almost fragile in appearance," but she was described, along with Will, as a "forceful" personality.[6] Will Thurmond augmented his forceful personality by being physically imposing. Both traits served him well in the courtroom and in politics.

After the sensationalism surrounding the death of Will Harris, Will Thurmond had to scale back his personal ambitions, but he continued to work with candidates on the sideline. One of his constant associations was with Ben Tillman, and as Will was his personal attorney in addition to a political ally, their association was frequent and personal. For instance, it was Thurmond who telegraphed the news to Tillman that he had been unanimously elected as a delegate to the Democratic National Convention.[7]

Because of their association, Thurmond often visited Tillman at his Edgefield home. One of these visits was significant for young Strom—then only nine years old—who accompanied his father. When they arrived, Will told his son to go up and shake hands with the senator. Before Strom got up enough courage to step forward, Tillman boomed at him, "What in the hell do you want?" According to Strom, "It was enough to scare a young boy to death." But he replied, "I want to shake hands with you." And Tillman took his hand and said, "What do you want to do? Shake hands? Well why in the hell don't you shake then?" "I started shaking and I've been shaking hands ever since," Strom remembered.[8]

Strom often accompanied his father on political trips, and one of them was to have a profound impact on his life. That same year, 1912, found Will Thurmond managing the gubernatorial campaign of Judge Ira B. Jones against Cole Blease. In those days in South Carolina, political candidates traveled to just about every county seat, debating face to face with their opponents. It was at one of these stump meetings that young Strom decided that, some day, he would be governor.[9]

In 1913 Senator Tillman decided enough time had passed and he could secure a political appointment from President Woodrow Wilson for his old friend Will Thurmond as the federal district attorney for South Carolina. Requests from senators are not necessarily granted by presidents, so Senator Tillman had Will working in South Carolina to secure as much local political support as he could. Will wrote to Tillman reporting that he had testimonials of support from four members of the state supreme court, a number of circuit judges, four presidential electors, the unanimous endorsement of the lawyers in his judicial circuit, and "quite a number of the [Democratic] State Executive Committee."[10]

Despite Will's local support and the vociferous support of Senator Tillman, President Wilson was reluctant to appoint Thurmond, preferring to appoint Francis H. Weston, whose "alleged incompetence . . . was given less weight by Wilson than the conviction that the chief enforcer of Federal law in South Carolina should not be a man who had killed a fellow citizen."[11]

Tillman continued to be loyal to his friend, however, and refused to give up. He was so determined that he had Congress split the state into two judicial districts in March of 1915, and after much badgering of President Wilson, Will Thurmond was appointed to the district attorneyship. In addition to his duties as the U.S. district attorney, Will also operated a successful law practice in Edgefield. His skill at law was well recognized, and S.C. Supreme Court Justice Eugene S. Blease described Will as the "ablest all-around lawyer who ever appeared before the Supreme Court of South Carolina."[12] Will also wrote a law casebook that was widely read by lawyers of the state. When times got tough in the early 1930s, Thurmond was moved to remind several attorneys that they owed him money for the purchase of the casebook.

Will Thurmond was both ambitious and talented—and so was his wife, Gertrude. That they also had well-recognized family names was another plus. The most important thing they passed on to their children, however, was self-confidence. All the Thurmond children were launched with the belief that they were achievers—as both their father and mother had been. That kind of background almost always breeds further success. In the case of John William and Gertrude Strom Thurmond, this proved to be especially true. Strom's brothers, John William and Allan George, were physicians. Their sister, Gertrude, received an M.A. degree, participated in a labor conference during the Roosevelt administration, and was employed by the War Manpower Commission during World War II. The youngest children in the family, twins Mary and Martha, were active in their local communities. Strom's achievements may be the best known in the family, but they were not the only ones. The accomplishments of this family are a testimony to the upbringing provided by Will and Eleanor Gertrude Strom Thurmond.

The Early Years

James Strom Thurmond, the second of the six Thurmond children, was born on December 5, 1902. Strom was born in a house the Thurmonds owned in Edgefield. When he was four, the family moved to the outskirts of town because, as his mother recalled, "Their Pa wanted them to learn to work on the farm and wanted them to live on a farm."[13] The Thurmonds' new home was a large white frame house, filled with late-Victorian furniture that indicated the family was "substantially successful" during the time the children were growing up.[14]

As a youth, Strom enjoyed life on the farm, especially the animals. His mother recalled that, "From the age of two, Strom began to ride—horses, ponies, goats, and even bulls about the place. Sideways, standing up in the saddle—any way—he can ride any kind of horse. But he never was afraid of animals—seemed to have a way with them." Strom continued to enjoy animals for a long time after he left the farm. Once when Strom was in his thirties, he challenged someone to a mule race—and won. According to his mother, Strom knew how to pick them.[15]

His mother also remembered that Strom had a dramatic way of avoiding punishment. One day Strom had committed an offense that carried the maximum punishment—switching. By the time his mother had cut a branch suitable for a switch, Strom had run upstairs and climbed out the window onto the roof where his mother could not reach him. The punishment was still waiting on him when he eventually climbed back inside. [16]

For the most part, Strom behaved well and did not receive much punishment of any kind. Days on the farm allowed little idle time for getting into trouble. The day began with chores; after school, there were more chores and study at night. And, of course, there were Sunday school and church services at the Baptist church every Sunday.

Schooling began early, and Strom's first education came as a pupil in Miss Mary Butler's private school, where he won a prize for being the best speller. A short time later, he entered the public schools of Edgefield, where he played sports, debated, and won oratory contests. At Edgefield he was something of an athlete, and his sisters remembered that Strom could "run faster than anybody."[17]

Long before jogging was in fashion, Strom included running in his exercise regimen. Throughout his life he has paid attention to physical fitness—and in this area, as in many others, he owes much to his father. Will Thurmond routinely walked to work, was reportedly an "enthusiast on the subject of eating correctly," and regularly stressed these virtues to his family.[18]

Young Strom did not devote all his time to school, chores, and sports. His ambition, even as a youth, needed additional outlets and so Strom worked at various odd jobs (including one at a textile mill) and saved his money. By the time he was fifteen, he had saved the huge sum in those days of $600. When a neighbor left to join the service during World War I, he had to leave his crop in the field. Strom used his money to buy the crop, harvested it, and made a handsome profit.[19]

In 1919 Strom completed the tenth grade in the Edgefield schools (the highest grade at that time) and entered the Clemson Agricultural College (now Clemson University) in the fall. The college in those days had only three curricula: agriculture, engineering, and textiles. With Strom's upbringing, agriculture was the logical choice.

Life at Clemson was much like life at a military academy. As a land-grant institution founded under the provisions of the Morrill Act of 1862, Clemson was required to offer military training to its students. Reflecting these guidelines, the Clemson of 1919 was an all-male, all-white military college where all the students were members of the cadet corps. The activities available to the cadets were limited to intramural and intercollegiate sports, various literary societies, agriculture societies, county clubs, and dancing clubs for sophomores, juniors, and seniors.

Strom's first year at Clemson was a standard plebe year. He suffered through the hazing and concentrated on his first-year studies. His only activity was to join the Edgefield County Club, which was composed of other students from Edgefield County.

Strom returned to Clemson in the fall of 1920 determined to be a larger part of campus life, and he threw himself into it with vigor. That year, while serving as a private in Company B of the First Battalion, he joined the Calhoun Literary Society and the Sophomore Dancing Club and was elected vice president of the McCormick/Edgefield Club. He also won a spot on the second cross-country track team that year. That he did not make the first team was a frustration for him, and he resolved to make it the next year. Over the summer, Thurmond worked hard on his running. Early in the morning and late at night, he donned his running clothes and did his roadwork. While this may not seem extraordinary today, in those days no one jogged, and Strom's running caused quite a stir. On one occasion, a neighbor asked Will Thurmond about reports that there was some "crazy boy running down the roads in his shorts." An amused Will explained to the upset neighbor that it was his son, Strom, who was on the track team at Clemson.[20]

When he returned to school that fall, Strom made the varsity track team, where he earned his letter and was a member of the Block C Club. Part of the training for the track team regularly involved distance runs of five to ten miles. On one occasion, Strom and five of his companions decided to run eighteen miles to the neighboring city of Anderson. Since they could not use the spike-soled running shoes common in those days to run on the road, they wore tennis shoes instead. Strom's shoes were new and not broken in. Some five miles into the run, Strom realized his shoes were rubbing his feet badly but refused to quit. He completed the entire eighteen-mile run, but as a result of the problem with his shoes, he lost all his toenails and had to receive medical treatment for weeks. When asked why he did not just stop—it was, after all, just a training exercise—Strom replied, "If I'd stopped when my feet began to hurt, we wouldn't have set a record."[21] This kind of perseverance in the face of adversity is a trait Strom has exhibited throughout his life.

Membership in the cadet corps gave Strom other opportunities for leadership. By 1922 Strom had risen to Sergeant of Company H of the Second Battalion. As a member of the corps, Strom was also part of the Army Officers Reserve Corps training program. Between his junior and senior years, he attended summer camp at Camp McClellan in Alabama. (He received his commission as a second lieutenant in the Army Officers Reserve Corps in 1924.)

The year 1922–23 was his final year at Clemson. Strom's entry in Clemson's annual, *Taps*, reads:

> Four years ago, a young, unsophisticated lad alighted at Cherry's Crossing. He, too, was contemplating a plunge into the "sea of knowledge." Little did any one dream that this same person was to write his name in indelible print on the records of this institution. Nor did any one think that this handsome young man was to become a ladies' man of the "first water" and was to provoke so many extra heart beats from the "fairer sex."
>
> Strom's athletic ability found expression on the cinder path. Although having to work hard, he proved to be a good point winner and a fair representative of the purple and gold.
>
> May success ever be yours, Strom, old boy.

Under his picture was the legend, "One cannot always be a hero, but one can always be a man."

On May 16, 1923, Strom was one of 133 graduating seniors. Armed with his new diploma and his self-esteem, and with his ambition intact, Strom set off to live the legend. But rather than strike out into new territory, he returned to the part of the world he knew best—part of the world that also knew him—McCormick County, next door to Edgefield.

Beginnings in Education

An agricultural degree is not an essential part of being a farmer. Strom had no intention of returning to Edgefield to become a gentleman planter, despite his genuine interest in the farm way of life. Strom appears to have been genuinely committed to a career in education. When he started teaching, it was not something he did while he was waiting for something better to come along. The first four years of his professional life were devoted to educating young people. His first assignment was at McCormick High School, where he taught vocational agriculture. In those days, South Carolina had only a few scattered textile mills in the upstate as an alternative to agricultural employment. Because of this, agriculture was viewed as one of the basic components of a young man's education (in the same way that home economics was part of a young woman's education). When the new agriculture teacher arrived with his degree from Clemson, it was assumed that he knew all the latest techniques in scientific farming and that knowledge would be money in the pocket of the young men and their parents.

While at McCormick, Strom also coached the basketball and football teams. His coaching provided him with some public exposure, and very early in his profession he was called on to defend the sport of football. His defense came in a letter to the editor of the November 28, 1923, McCormick *Messenger*. In this, one of his first "public" statements, Thurmond exhibited all the formalism and platitudes of the newly educated. He defends football as a game that "promotes from necessity, clean living, self-restraint, and a good physique. . . . We must ever be willing to learn even from condemned or rejected practices, scientific and skillful principles—hold fast to that which is good, and reject that which is bad." This a far cry from the Strom Thurmond who developed the art of communicating with people on whatever level was appropriate.

While Strom was new to the community and new to his position, he had no qualms about throwing himself into the local issues of the day. When the American Legion Auxiliary asked for assistance in teaching adults, Strom responded through another letter to the editor, this time on January 17, 1924: "I shall be glad to teach any white adults who have had poor opportunities for an education, the fundamental principles, even the alphabet itself . . . without remuneration."

Later that year, Strom contributed a series of articles that advised readers as to the best ways to grow vegetables and fruits, the spray schedule, and the "income and outgo" of plants. This was in line with his service as an agricultural teacher, but it was also presumptuous; he was treading on the toes of the agricultural extension service, which was supposed to answer questions of that nature.

After a year of teaching, Strom had an opportunity to return to his home county of Edgefield to take a similar position. When his resignation was made public, it was clear he had favorably impressed the people of McCormick County. The May 14, 1924, Augusta *Herald* reported that Thurmond had "been very popular . . . and his presence in the community will be missed."

When Strom began his duties as agricultural teacher for Ridge Spring and Edgefield High School, he also did duty as a member of the board of education. His return to Edgefield also signaled a growing involvement in all facets of his community. Over the next few years he was involved in many organizations, among them the Junior Order of United American Mechanics, the Knights of Pythias, and the Masons. He was a senior member of the American Red Cross Lifesaving Service, a deacon of the First Baptist Church, and a teacher in one of the Sunday school classes. Strom also worked with young people at the Summerland Farm School near Saluda, and he organized the Edgefield Baptist Association on June 4, 1927, and was elected its president. (His vice president was Joe Frank Logue, who would figure prominently in an important event in Thurmond's future. Logue, like Thurmond, was a member of one of Edgefield's premier families).

Along with his school duties and his civic involvement, Strom still found the time to act like the young man he was. He recalled that several times he had raced over the rough, red clay roads on his motorcycle—driving over eighty miles an hour—with his hands off the handlebars on his way to and from work.[22]

Superintendent of Edgefield County

By 1928, Thurmond had decided to pursue a higher level in his career. He could have sought a post as a principal or moved to another school district where there was more opportunity. Instead, Thurmond sought the position of county superintendent of education. This was a fateful decision because the county superintendent was an elected post. This was Strom's first try at public office. He faced an aging incumbent who was simply no match for Strom's youthful vigor. Thurmond won easily, thereby making his entrance into public life and also bolstering his already established self-confidence. Taking on incumbents is almost always a ticket to political obscurity; thus, Thurmond's first victory may have encouraged him to take steps later that were to prove almost disastrous. No matter—this time he had won and he made the most of his opportunity. Due to South Carolina's constitution, which embodied a deep distrust of executive power, most of the political power in the state resided with the state legislature. Even local affairs were mainly in the hands of the legislators. Despite these kinds of limitations (which Thurmond was to face again), he set out to use the authority that he did have to improve the quality of education and life in Edgefield County.

Thurmond persuaded local physicians to provide all Edgefield students free medical examinations. In the face of the onset of the Great Depression, Thurmond also instituted tight-fisted money management programs that would enable him to take better care of pupils and teachers alike. A little-known fact about Thurmond's early career was his empathy with teachers and his long struggle to provide them with better pay and more job security. The Edgefield *Advertiser* complimented Strom on his work in this area and noted, "Teachers in this county are far more fortunate than teachers in some counties where they have been paid only two months since last September."

Throughout those difficult years, Strom kept his schools open and kept his employees paid. This was an especially difficult challenge because it meant getting taxes from people who had little or no money. He not only collected the money but maintained the goodwill of the people while he did so—a real feat during those times.

At some point, the realization dawned that this was not the arena where he was truly at home. It was not the administrative challenges of the school district that got his blood boiling—it was the political process. With that realization came an understanding that he could not go much further in education. He was already at the top of the pyramid. What he saw in front of him was an endless parade of teacher contract renewals and juggling to meet payrolls. He knew that he had to get into politics, but there was always the chance of failure. And besides, a person in politics needs a career of some kind to fall back on. You could not be a teacher and hold public office. Farming was not a good option either. With this in mind, Strom acted along the lines of Senator Preston's observations. It was obvious—he could practice law and enter upon a career in public service.

Soon after his election as county superintendent, Strom Thurmond began studying law. He could not go to law school and maintain his position as county superintendent, so Thurmond resorted to the old way of learning law. He "read" law from one of the ablest attorneys in the area—a man who loved him and nurtured his ambitions—his father. Before his work day began and well into the night, Strom read assignments carefully thought out by his father. His readings included various landmark cases and interpretations of the basic aspects of civil and criminal law. After a scant year's preparation, Strom was ready to sit for his bar exams. The examination lasted three days and after it was over, Strom was pulled aside by the examiner and told that he had tied for the best score with a graduate of Harvard Law School.[23]

Thurmond was admitted to the South Carolina Bar on December 13, 1930. He immediately entered his father's firm and the name was changed to Thurmond and Thurmond. He also continued to serve as county superintendent of education. Will's guidance had helped Strom enter the legal profession. After his admission to the state bar, Will intervened again, this time to help Strom off to a good start in his legal career. In January of 1931, just a month after becoming an attorney, Strom was unanimously elected as the town attorney for Edgefield. In his telegraph telling him the good news, Will advised Strom, "important matters for your attention."

Strom was well launched in his legal career and, as an attorney, he was ready to pursue a political career as well. His term as county superintendent ran through 1932. At that point, he would have to decide whether to seek reelection or to pursue another office. If he decided to run for another office, he had the option of running for a seat in the state house of representatives or a more powerful position as a state senator. When he made up his mind, he left education forever.

Chapter 2

THURMOND
AT LAW

As a profession, the law has always been a haven for politicians. It puts them in the public eye and allows them to hone their communication skills, while not demanding all their time.

Compare even today the number of attorneys in elective office versus any other profession—attorneys fill the halls of Congress (and the legislatures of most states). The law is also clannish—perhaps not so much as the medical profession, but it is still like a club. Stories abound of opposing attorneys almost coming to blows in court and then meeting later to share a laugh. The legal profession requires some level of acting skill, and this, too, fits in neatly with politics.

In the 1930s in South Carolina, this clannishness was even greater than it is today. Most attorneys came from the elite families of the state. They were all white and mostly male, and so were the judges and juries. It was a closed club, still very much run by an unwritten set of rules that included rituals and formalities.

Outgoing mail still carried references to *instant* and *ultimo*—Latin designations noting when letters were received ("Yours of the 10th inst" meant that it had been received in the current month, while "Yours of the 10th ultimo" meant it had been received in the previous month). While these were common business designations in the 1800s, they had almost disappeared by the early 1900s except in the legal profession.

The advent of the telephone was an added convenience, but law offices still relied primarily on written responses to almost every kind of inquiry. The Thurmond and Thurmond office was blessed by the presence of Jenny Pattison, a reliable clerk, stenographer, and typist who handled the voluminous correspondence for years.

The Great Depression hit the South harder than most parts of the country because of its already depressed economy that depended almost solely on agriculture. Business was so bad that lawyers were reduced to taking all kinds of lawsuits, many of them on a contingency basis. Today, this is a common practice, but during those trying times, people came to view the law as a sort of lottery in which you could invest some time and "win" a big settlement, especially from large corporations and the government. One of Strom's more outlandish cases was a lawsuit against the R. J. Reynolds Tobacco Company on behalf of a man who claimed that a can of tobacco had made him ill. Strom demanded $135 for his client, and when the tobacco company offered a lesser settlement Strom invoked some powerful scare tactics. He informed R. J. Reynolds that the juries in Edgefield County gave "reasonable verdicts." And he added, "I secured two $20,000 verdicts in cases last week and another verdict in a third case and am confident if this case is tried that we can secure a reasonable verdict." Needless to say, the tobacco company settled.[1]

Some aspects of law remained the same in good and bad economic times. With the closed judicial system in which only white men served on juries, it was possible to get to know the jurors and how they would be likely to find on a given issue. Some men were called repeatedly for jury duty because the pool was relatively small. In these cases, attorneys from neighboring counties were always asking for information on jurors. Whenever an outside attorney came into town to try a case, he would look up a local attorney and get his opinion on the jurors drawn for the trial. The attorneys often used a kind of shorthand that said what they wanted to say without actually stating it. If, for instance, one attorney described a potential juror as "conservative," it might mean that he would not be likely to vote for a large cash award. If the attorney requesting the information represented a client who was going for a large settlement, he would try to strike that man from the jury.

Another regular practice that kept the attorneys in close contact with one another was that of "associating" on various cases. This is how it worked: if an attorney in Charleston had to try a case in Edgefield, he might contact an attorney he knew in Edgefield and associate him on the case. It was hoped that the local attorney would not only know the jurors better but might also understand the temperament of the judge a little better. Normally, the associate attorney received between 40 and 50 percent of the collected fee. On one occasion, an attorney from Pickens who desired to associate Strom noted: "If the case is settled though before trial even after suit is filed I think you should have your fifty percent on account of the fact that if the case is settled it will be done largely upon your influence in the particulare (sic) section of the state."[2]

This practice not only kept everyone in touch, it kept some of the lesser attorneys in business through tough times. These men understood the connected nature of their profession and did what they could to protect one another. Camaraderie of this kind is not often found today, but it was the cornerstone of South Carolina's legal system in the early part of the twentieth century. It not only helped Strom get started in law but helped him in his political career. Among Strom's fellow attorneys in those days were James F. Byrnes, Donald Russell, George Bell Timmerman (Sr. and Jr.), Edgar A. Brown, and Sol Blatt. These men and many others were to play various parts in Strom's future—and through the law they all knew one another and had worked together.

So it was that early in 1931, Strom Thurmond really began the practice of law. It was not his only job; he was still serving as the Edgefield County superintendent of education. And initially, as an attorney at least, Strom was in his father's shadow. Will Thurmond had guided his son to this point in his life, and he still had one or two things to teach him. As always, Strom was willing to learn from his father. And learn he did—Strom Thurmond became an outstanding attorney in a very short time.

Thurmond and Thurmond

Some people get their law degrees, pass the bar exam, and strike out on their own. They set up their own firm—"hang out a shingle"—and hope for the best. Most attorneys take another path. They join an established law firm where they can learn from more experienced attorneys and where a client occasionally gets passed their way. This is the most prudent way to enter the business of law, especially when you can enter a firm owned by your father— one where your name is immediately added to the title and you are made a partner. This is exactly what Will Thurmond offered Strom, and Strom accepted it without hesitation.

Will Thurmond had a reputation as being a good attorney, and when Strom joined the firm, he accepted instruction because he trusted the source. Will was a tough taskmaster but his affection for his son came through even when he was teaching. In his letters, he routinely addressed Strom as "My dear Boy" and signed off with "Affectionately, Dad."

In between, however, were explicit instructions regarding how various matters were to be handled. In one case, Will told Strom to "go right in and see McKay & Manning and get them to consent to an order dismissing their appeal in the two cases above named. If they will not consent to dismiss these cases, then go up to Mr. Tompkins' office and prepare a notice and affidavit in each case. Set out in your affidavit that they gave notice of intention to appeal in the case but did not within thirty days thereafter perfect their appeal or serve a proposed case with exception and have taken no further steps in the appeal."[3] Will's instructions had a way of actually doing the work. In the early days, Strom was not left on his own to decide the right course of action. Will provided the guidance, Strom accepted it and grew rapidly in stature as an attorney.

Strom's willingness to learn and his father's confidence in his son's abilities were demonstrated by the fact that in September of 1932, less than two years after joining the firm, Will Thurmond was able to write, "I do not examine witnesses or try cases now." Strom was now doing the work.[4] A factor in Strom's growing workload was Will's declining health. Despite this, Will remained active in the firm, and he evidenced some admirable qualities toward his clients. In one instance, when he and Strom had helped to secure a sizable settlement for a widow, he took time to write her, urging the importance of "using that money in the purchase of a home for you and the children. You should be able to buy over there [McCormick] a good little farm for that amount, $2,000.00, and I advise you by all means to do this whether you move to the farm right now or not. Money is hard to make and it is very important that when you have it to invest it wisely."[5]

Unfortunately for Will, his ill health forced him to become more concerned about his own financial security, and that of his family, as time passed. In April of 1934 he had a severe heart attack, and on May 23 he wrote to a client thanking him for a payment of $25 and explaining, "I have been quite sick a bit lately and am hard pressed for funds at this time and do not wish to inconvenience you but it will be necessary for you to send us a check for the balance of $125.00 or send a note for this amount payable in the fall so that I may have it discounted and secure the money for it. It is unnecessary to remind you that we saved thousands of dollars by winning the Pipkin case for you at McCormick. It was an extremely close and hard case and the fee we charged you was much smaller than we would normally charge in a case of this kind since I have always considered you a close friend."[6]

Will was happy when the University of South Carolina voted to confer an honorary degree on him at their June 13 commencement, but his health continued to fail. On June 17, 1934, Will Thurmond died. His death was felt deeply by his entire family but especially by Strom. Strom admired and respected his father in an old-fashioned way. With good reason, Strom had always seen his father as a strong man. Will's death left a void in Strom's personal and professional life. It also imposed on Strom the burden of fulfilling some of his father's dreams—dreams that had been denied Will Thurmond because of his past.

As would be his lifelong custom, Strom reacted to the sadness of this event by redoubling his efforts. He dedicated himself to becoming more than a capable attorney—he worked to be one of the best—and his efforts were to be rewarded.

Strom's Law Practice

In the best sense of the word, Strom Thurmond was a country lawyer. His practice did not involve setting up multimillion-dollar business deals, nor did he spend his time representing celebrities. Most of his clients were rural people—a few local merchants but mainly farmers and farmhands who worked the land in Edgefield County. These people were not rich, but they had problems and when they did, they were likely to come to the county seat and get themselves a lawyer who could straighten things out.

The income for country lawyers was somewhat limited during the Great Depression, but there were several sources from which they could make a decent living. Most attorneys made their money by representing people or organizations involved in lawsuits—that is, one person sues another, generally for an amount of money. In civil cases, attorneys often receive a percentage of the amount collected as a result of the suit. Another way for attorneys to make money is to handle real estate closings, wills, and domestic matters such as divorces or marriage annulments.

A second source of income, although generally not as lucrative, was to defend persons charged with criminal conduct. Then as now, this work was dramatic and involved opportunities to demonstrate Perry Mason–like oratory skills to juries. Unfortunately, many of those brought to trial did not have much money to pay their attorneys.

Some of these local attorneys, the ones with political connections, might be hired as a city or county attorney or maybe even as a city judge. Not much money was made in these positions, but it helped pay the bills.

Other attorneys, again with political or even family connections, might be retained by one of the few big corporations that operated in the South prior to World War II. In Louisiana, it might be a big oil company; in West Virginia, a coal mine; and in many places, the railroad. In those days, the railroads were important as sources of commerce, travel, and communication. The railroad retained an attorney for each county it passed through because people were always suing it for one reason or another.

Because of Thurmond's connections, skills, and hard work, his legal practice included every one of these aspects. As a bachelor, he had the extra time to devote to business that other family-oriented attorneys might not have, so he took every opportunity that came his way. From the beginning, Strom had a healthy legal practice. But it did not happen accidentally. He pursued clients from a wide range of sources; some of his efforts were successful and some were not.

One of his earliest attempts to stir up business was in June of 1931, only six months after he had begun his practice. A military veteran came to Thurmond seeking to secure some bonus money that was due him. Strom wrote to M. L. McHugh, a field examiner for the newly created Veterans Administration, asking him what fee an attorney was allowed to charge for this service. McHugh advised Thurmond that under the World War Adjusted Compensation Act, "you are precluded from charging any fee."[7]

Another early effort to generate clients also went poorly, this time involving the Federal Land Bank. In November of 1933 Thurmond sent the following advertisement to the local newspapers: "Persons wishing to borrow money from either the Federal Land Bank of Columbia or the Land Bank Commissioner may apply to the undersigned. Thurmond & Thurmond."[8]

By putting this ad in the paper, Thurmond hoped to encourage local people to apply for loans so he could charge them a fee. When the Federal Land Bank of Columbia was advised of his efforts, they took a rather dim view. On May 24, the assistant counsel of the Land Bank wrote Thurmond: "We believe that the average man will receive from your notice an implication of agency which does not exist and, therefore, we ask that you discontinue publishing this notice or any other notice of this kind in which the name of the Federal Land Bank . . . is used."[9] Their position was that Thurmond and Thurmond's ad implied that the firm was authorized to accept applications, which was not the case.

One noteworthy aspect of these two instances is that both involved the federal government. In the Depression in the 1930s only the government and the big corporations had any money, so a lot of time was spent trying to get some of it. Thurmond had no problem with suing the State of South Carolina, either. A regular target was the state highway department—its huge budget and daily interaction with the public made it a natural target. In one instance, an Edgefield man requested $100 from the highway department for "dirt unlawfully moved from his premises and used in a fill during the grading and construction of Dixie Highway slightly over one mile from the Town of Edgefield."[10] That amount of money would have bought an acre of land or better in those days, so there was a punitive nature to this request. However, in his closing, Thurmond wrote that he felt "kindly toward the Highway Department and wish. . . . to avoid bringing a suit against it in this matter."[11]

While he was trying to drum up business with various government agencies, Thurmond was defending others against unreasonable attacks as the city attorney for the towns of Edgefield and Johnston and the county attorney for Edgefield. In one of his first major cases, and one of his larger early fees, Thurmond was involved in securing a right of way for highway purposes over the land of one of Edgefield's citizens. When a lower court had granted the right of way, the citizen had appealed to the state supreme court. When the mayor of Edgefield became anxious about the outcome, he called S.C. Supreme Court Justice Eugene S. Blease, a friend of the Thurmond family. Blease had difficulty in explaining the situation because Edgefield's mayor was not an attorney, so Blease appealed to Strom to explain it to him.[12] Whether Strom was ever successful in explaining the situation to the satisfaction of the mayor is not known but Strom was able to bill the town $350 for handling the matter.[13]

On another occasion, Thurmond's efforts resulted in a savings of $10,745.73 to the town of Johnston on a debt it owed to the Bank of Western Carolina. Through expert negotiations, Strom was able to reduce their indebtedness, and the bottom line of these efforts was that his firm could bill the town 12 percent of the amount saved, $1,289.48.[14]

Collecting debts was also a good way to make money in those days. Almost everyone owed someone money, and since money was scarce, people were less lenient with delinquency than they might once have been. This resulted in a constant parade of collection opportunities, but it also posed a dilemma. In 1933, when things were at their worst, Thurmond and Thurmond accepted some collection work. In one of their efforts for the People's State Bank of South Carolina, the firm had demanded payment of $1039; "otherwise our instructions from the Bank are to foreclose the mortgage and sell the land to pay the debt."[15]

Yet the law firm also accepted clients who owed money to various banks. In an impassioned plea, Will Thurmond wrote on behalf of one client, "The agent of the plaintiff should realize that these times and conditions are unprecedented in this country and that it is impossible to raise money now for any purpose."[16]

If the argument was true for one case, it was certainly true for the other. And this perhaps played a role in the lessening of collection work as time passed. But there was another reason, and Strom stated it plainly in a letter. In 1936 J. Russell McElvee wrote to Strom asking him to serve as his collection agent. Strom thanked him for the opportunity but added, "As you know, too, I am in politics and it might be embarrassing for me to handle these collections."[17] Of all the arguments for not taking collection work, this was the strongest. Men in politics had no business harassing citizens about overdue bills, especially when there really was no money to pay them.

In 1933 Thurmond's leniency was even stretched to cover an incident in which a client was owed money as the result of a traffic accident. The client, an Augusta, Georgia, physician, was involved in a collision with a black professor employed by the South Carolina State College in Orangeburg, South Carolina. After the collision, the professor had acknowledged that the wreck was his fault and agreed to make full restitution. Because of the agreement, no lawsuit was filed.[18] The professor made a few payments but as of August 1939, six years later, he still had an outstanding balance and Thurmond was still trying to collect it. Collections in any form were just not good politics, it seemed.[19]

Some of Thurmond's other civil work was interesting because it reflected the nature of things in South Carolina at that time. In addition to drafting wills and settling estates, most attorneys were called on to handle an occasional domestic issue. It was not as prevalent then as now, but such issues did come up, and when they did, the cases were more complicated than they are today. In those days (and lasting until the late 1940s), South Carolina had no laws that permitted divorce. The only options were annulment (not easily obtained) and securing a divorce in another state. In 1935 a young lady came to Thurmond asking that her husband either live with her or pay for her support. When Thurmond wrote to the errant husband, he pointed out, "As any lawyer can tell you and as most people already know, the law of this state requires a man to support his wife. He is not forced to live with his wife but he is required to support her, and if he fails to do so, she can issue a warrant and have him placed in jail and prosecuted for non-support. We are writing to know if you intend to live with your wife and if you do not, then we wish to hereby make a demand on you to support her, and we feel that $25.00 per month is a very reasonable amount."[20]

In another instance Thurmond was able to arrange an annulment only to have his fee questioned. He was asked if he would "make any adjustment on the bill which you rendered."[21] Thurmond defended his bill but stated, "It is not my wish to work a hardship on anyone and I am willing to deduct 10% from my fee which will reduce the same by $50.00, so you may forward me a check for $450 for my fee."[22]

While most of his civil cases involved whites, Thurmond took on black and white clients without any apparent discrimination between the two groups. In one of these cases, he represented three black women injured in an automobile accident. This incident provided one of the few humorous incidents on record in his legal career. The item in question was ladies' hosiery. Thurmond sent an itemized account of damaged clothing to be replaced to another attorney, John E. Johnston. Johnston replied, "The writer does not feel that Lilla Anderson should need anything if she is able to wear the $2.25 hose as you state. I certainly cannot afford to pay that much for hose for my wife, and if you are married I seriously doubt if you pay that much."[23] Strom's response was, "I omitted after the word hose 'and other parts of clothing' in my letter to you. I do not have a wife but, if I did, I certainly agree with you that $2.25 is a high price to pay for hose, especially for a lawyer's wife to wear."[24]

In this instance, as in many others, Thurmond took cases from black clients in the same way that he accepted them from whites. In civil suits, he stood to make the same percentage from his black clients as from his white ones. But criminal cases were another story entirely. When Thurmond took a criminal case for a black or white client, payment was often small and sometimes he was forced to take some sort of trade-out rather than money. Although these cases did not pay very well, some were interesting, and they portrayed a different side of Thurmond—one that is not well known.

Thurmond for the Defense

A black man sat in the hot, stuffy Edgefield Courthouse, charged with murder. His glance took in a sea of white faces—Judge Greene in his high-backed chair peered down at him; T. C. Callison, the solicitor, shuffled papers at his desk right next to him. His glance over at the jury gave him no comfort either: twelve white men, not exactly his peers in this dusty southern town. But this black man had confidence because he had one of the best attorneys in the area. The attorney was white, too, but he had already earned a reputation among blacks by working just as hard for them as he did for his white clients. When the jury gave its verdict, the defendant's confidence was justified; he was found not guilty of murder. He turned to thank his attorney, Strom Thurmond, who congratulated him on his freedom.

This story may not ring true to those who hold a stereotypical view of Strom Thurmond (and the South), but this is exactly what happened. In this instance and others, Strom Thurmond defended black clients and won acquittal in an all-white, mostly male judicial system. For this particular defense, Strom was paid $75.[25]

It is important to understand, however, that there was a double standard involving blacks in South Carolina courtrooms. For his defense of this particular defendant, Strom gave instructions that clearly demonstrated the difference. He told his client, "It is important that you have some good white gentlemen testify to your good character and the three you suggested will be good witnesses, to wit, Mr. Will Timmerman, Mr. Ben Sullivan and Mr. Bryan Williams. It is important also to have one or two other white men testify to the bad character of [the other man], any two good white men will answer for this purpose." Strom understood that white testimony counted for more than black testimony. That it did is an indictment of South Carolina's judicial system, but that Thurmond used it for the benefit of his clients is to his credit.[26]

The only other advice Thurmond offered to his client involved money. He told him, "Tell your father to be certain to bring the money to pay us on the day of the trial, unless he brings it up before that time."[27]

But even as Thurmond understood that blacks had to be treated differently in the courtroom, there was no evidence to suggest that he withheld any portion of his efforts in their defense. One case demonstrated that clearly. It involved a young black man who had been sentenced to three years in prison for the accidental death of a black baby. After the verdict was rendered, Thurmond did not cease in his efforts for his client, and on July 12, 1932, he petitioned then-Governor Ibra C. Blackwood for a pardon.[28] Pardon requests were not unusual, but they were very unusual for Thurmond. In fact, his sentiment against the governor's power to pardon became a major issue several times later in his life. His efforts in this instance to secure something he disapproved of for one of his black clients speaks volumes in his behalf.

In all, Thurmond handled over fifty criminal defenses during his first stint as an attorney. Of these, more than twenty were murder cases. His record in freeing accused murderers is surprising, especially under the circumstances he worked in. Of the recorded verdicts, fifteen of his clients were found not guilty, four were convicted of lesser offenses, and three were found guilty.[29]

Getting paid for these criminal defenses remained a problem throughout Thurmond's legal career. In a later case, he managed to gain an acquittal for a client charged with murder. This time the defendant had no money, so Thurmond resorted to another tactic. He reminded his former client, "When you were down here a few days ago you stated that you could not pay me any money but would come and work for me. I discharged a hand yesterday and would like for you to start at once. Please plan to move immediately, and I suggest that you run down and get my wagon and mules if you do not have a way to move so that there will be no delay."[30]

In fact, getting paid at all for anything remained a struggle. Two checks, representing two separate actions on behalf of the Federal Land Bank of Columbia, demonstrate the low wage scale for attorneys in South Carolina at that time. For assisting in the collection of a rent payment, Thurmond was paid a 5 percent commission on $50 or a total of $2.50.[31] And on another occasion, he received a check for $50.08—$50.00 for handling a foreclosure and ".08 advanced by me for the bank in this matter."[32] When bills include eight cent charges, it is indicative of hard times indeed.

Given the difficulties in everyday business, a country attorney could always use a steady source of income. As was noted previously, Thurmond's steady source of income came from one of the biggest landowners in the South—The Southern Railway System.

Strom—Working for the Railroad

When Will Thurmond died, Strom fell heir to his father's legal practice. Possibly one of the most important things Will passed along to his son was the position of local counsel for the Southern Railway in Edgefield County. Will Thurmond had held the post for years, and on his death, the logical person to fill the slot was his son and law partner.

Two weeks after Will's death, Strom received the offer to serve from Frank G. Tomkins, the division counsel for the railway. In this position, Strom would be expected to serve in the role of trial counsel for any cases in Edgefield County, to assist in any lawsuits brought in Saluda County, and to "protect the interest of this company and its subsidiaries in all litigation arising in said boundaries."[33] Strom kept this position for as long as he was a practicing attorney.

Pay for this position was quite handsome. Strom was to receive $53.34 per month, equal to the pay for one foreclosure. And he received an additional $35 per month to pay a stenographer (who might not spend the entire time on railway business). Another perk was that Strom was to receive annual Southern Railway passes enabling him to ride at no cost anywhere the Southern went. This privilege was extended to include members of his family, as well.[34]

Overall, it was a nice job that did not demand much time and paid reasonably well. After a month of service, Thurmond felt compelled to report that he had done something so he wrote to Tomkins and told him about an ordinance regulating trains that he had previously suggested should be repealed by the town council of Johnston. On July 24, 1934, the town followed his recommendation and repealed the ordinance.[35]

Law and Politics

Thurmond's success as an attorney did not hurt his political aspirations in any way. In fact, he was helped by his interaction with other attorneys in the state, most of whom were politically active and many of whom held some sort of political or governmental office. He corresponded with James F. Byrnes, then a U.S. Senator from South Carolina (on his way to being a U.S. Supreme Court justice and "Assistant President" under FDR). He also corresponded with the men who took over Byrnes's law practice in Spartanburg—Cecil C. Wyche and Donald Russell. Wyche was later to serve as a federal judge; Russell served South Carolina as both governor and U.S. senator before becoming a federal judge.

Among the other attorneys of the day who were also active in politics were state Senator Edgar A. Brown and house Speaker Solomon K. Blatt, members of the "Barnwell ring," who held significant political influence. Others were L. Marion Gressette, later to become a powerful member of the state senate, and John Bolt Culbertson, South Carolina's lone liberal voice during much of the century, who was destined to become Thurmond's personal nemesis.

Another attorney who was counted among Thurmond's acquaintances was George Bell Timmerman, Sr., an attorney in Lexington, South Carolina. Timmerman was politically active and had served as chairman of the powerful S.C. Highway Commission. Thurmond and Timmerman were associated on a case for which they were able to split a fee of $160 ($75 each and an additional $10 to Thurmond for expenses).[36]

Timmerman and Thurmond's involvement was strengthened in 1937 when Thurmond ran into some legal trouble in Lexington and decided he needed local counsel. He chose Timmerman to assist him in a defense that involved one of Strom's outside business investments, a gas station.

The Town of Lexington, South Carolina
v. J. Strom Thurmond and Hugh R. Corley

In the summer of 1937, Thurmond and a business associate, Hugh R. Corley, decided to move a shed that sat on the lot containing their gas station in Lexington, South Carolina. After the relocation was complete, the town of Lexington went into court and requested a ruling that would forbid Thurmond and his partner from changing any aspect of their property. The town opposed moving the structure because it violated municipal ordinance and increased the risk of fire. A local court granted the town's request on July 25, 1937.

Naturally, Thurmond did not appreciate this attempt to curtail his freedom. With Timmerman acting for him as local counsel, Strom responded that he had not been in violation of the town ordinance because he was not erecting a new structure, merely moving an old one. Further, he argued that by moving the structure they actually decreased the risk of fire. As a parting shot, Strom suggested that the town ordinance was unconstitutional and, besides, the building had already been moved when the injunction was placed on him.[37] On August 7, 1937, with

Timmerman's assistance, an order was prepared vacating the earlier injunction and the issue was dropped. This was Thurmond's only personal contact with the legal system during his time as an attorney.

This interaction with Timmerman had gone well. Political ambition has a strange way of tossing people together, however. Their next meeting would place them as adversaries. And Thurmond and Timmerman would not meet in the structured environment of the courtroom; instead their mutual ambitions would later collide on the floor of the state legislature. But Strom had other mountains to climb before he could take on the powerful George Bell Timmerman, Sr.

Thurmond and Buzhardt

Over the period from 1930 to 1938, Strom was an active participant in the law. He was admitted to practice at all levels of federal jurisdiction, including the U.S. Supreme Court, so his legal skills were never in question, despite his lack of a formal legal education. He experienced success in all phases of his legal practice, from his handling of civil suits and criminal defenses to legal matters for local government and the Southern Railway. But through it all, Thurmond remained an active part of the political system. And as time passed, he devoted more time to the pursuit of political objectives. This led him to bring another attorney into the firm.

In 1935 Strom chose as his new associate young J. Fred Buzhardt of McCormick County. The arrangement was for Fred to remain in McCormick while Strom retained his lucrative practice in Edgefield. Adding Buzhardt to the firm allowed Strom to spend less time in the practice of law, which proved fortuitous because he needed more time and energy to devote to politics.

Long after Thurmond and Buzhardt parted ways, Thurmond maintained a friendship with Buzhardt and even appointed him to a state government post. The friendship continued to the second generation: Fred's son, also named Fred, received an appointment in the Nixon administration, courtesy of Strom Thurmond.

Thurmond rewarded those loyal to him by being loyal to them. This is not to suggest that there was any impropriety in remembering old friends—that was just good politics. But Strom learned his lessons in loyalty at an early age, from an old friend of the family, and he never forgot them.

Greneker Smoothes the Way to the Senate

In 1930, when Thurmond was still a county superintendent of education and just beginning the practice of law, one of the attorneys who took him under his wing was Thomas B. Greneker. Greneker was not only an excellent attorney but also Will Thurmond's friend and a political ally. At that time Greneker was the state senator from Edgefield County, and he had been elected partly because of the assistance given to him by Will Thurmond. When Strom began his law practice, he often worked with Greneker because, as he once wrote to another attorney, "when we [Greneker and I] are both on the same side we usually get a larger verdict."[38]

In 1932, several local offices would be up for election, but Thurmond did not want to face an incumbent. At that time, Greneker laid aside whatever ambitions he might have had and decided not to seek reelection for his state senate seat. That meant the way was at least partially clear for Thurmond to begin his climb. As it turned out, he was to have only one obstacle—young Ben Tillman. Summers are always hot in Edgefield, and with a contested primary to fan the flames, the summer of 1932 promised to be hotter than most. For the first time, a Thurmond was squaring off with a Tillman in Edgefield County.

Chapter 3

THE JOURNEY BEGINS

From the late 1800s to the mid-1900s, political rule in South Carolina (and the South, in general) was by one political party, the Democratic party. Beginning in the days of Ben Tillman, the Democratic party of South Carolina had assumed the mantle of guardian of white supremacy and effectively locked the state's blacks out of the electoral process. Racial identity was so strongly associated with the Democratic party that it was referred to as the "white man's party."

Even in the 1930s, Republicans in the state were limited to a few blacks, who were basically disenfranchised, and a few affluent, "country club" whites, many of whom had moved to the state from another part of the country. The dominance of the Democratic party is amply demonstrated by the results of the 1932 presidential contest between Republican Herbert Hoover and Democrat Franklin Delano Roosevelt. Roosevelt received 102,347 votes to only 1,978 for Hoover.

Because of this dominance, the Republicans never even bothered to field a candidate at the local level—there was just no hope of winning. So anyone interested in pursuing public office ran as a Democrat. This does not mean that the politics of the state resembled a dictatorial one-party rule. The Democratic party was divided along many different lines. In addition to the previously mentioned rivalry between the Low Country and the uplands, there were also problems between rural and urban areas. Other "isms" and schisms constantly divided the party to the point that the only thing it could agree on was that blacks and Republicans were never to be allowed any political power.

The diverse elements of the Democratic party were constantly battling each other for control, and this meant there had to be a mechanism that would allow the people to decide on their leadership. In some states, nomination for public office was handled by convention. A handful of delegates could decide from among several candidates for any given post. With nomination on the Democratic ticket almost tantamount to election, this nominating method would not have been sufficient. The answer was to conduct a primary that would allow the voters to select the Democratic nominees. The situation that resulted is exactly the opposite of that which exists today. In South Carolina during the early portion of this century, many more people voted in the primaries than in the general elections. This meant the real elections took place in June when the Democrats held their primaries.

When Strom Thurmond and Ben Tillman campaigned late in 1931 and early in 1932, they realized they had to capture the votes of Edgefield's rural white population. To this end, both men directed their efforts.

State Senate Campaign

In primary contests, political parties tend not to play favorites. The official line is that once a person becomes the party's nominee, the person can receive help. Of course, there are always times when party officers pitch in to help a candidate, either because one particular candidate is truly outstanding or because the alternative is an embarrassment to the party.

Edgefield County's Democratic party had been dominated by Tillmans and Thurmonds for years. In a case like this the party would have been expected to pursue a neutral course between these two powerful families. But in the primary election of 1932, Thurmond received some significant support. While he was campaigning vigorously for the senate seat, he was also campaigning for the position of delegate within the Edgefield Democratic party. To help kick off his campaign, the county Democratic party elected him as a delegate to the state convention. Then the state Democrats honored him by electing him as a delegate to the Democratic National Convention in Chicago, the first time Strom had received this honor. So, in its way, the power structure had voiced its approval of Strom Thurmond.

This had to be disappointing to his opponent, Ben Tillman. Despite his name, Tillman did not have his father's head (or desire) for politics. Tillman had planned to campaign primarily upon his name and any goodwill that name might inspire.

Strom Thurmond, however, was out constantly beating the bushes—talking with people on Edgefield's town square and going out to see them on their farms. Unlike Tillman, who made no serious attempt to develop any issues, Strom had a platform of sorts that he publicized throughout his campaign. Strom's issues were twofold: legislator pay and education.

One topic that aroused great unhappiness among Edgefield's rural population was the ability of the state legislature to vote itself money. Every time the legislature decided it needed a special session or an additional session, they were able to draw additional pay. To farmers who were constantly facing bankruptcy, this practice was irritating. Strom made it clear he would not accept any extra pay. His position was that people knew the salary when they were elected; they should work for that and no more.

His second issue was education. Strom had been a teacher and had administered an entire school district, so this was a natural issue for him. It also played into the Tillman tradition because "Old Ben" had achieved his initial fame by advocating the establishment of an agricultural school at Clemson to give farmers the information they needed to be successful. By emphasizing education, Strom not only played to his strong suit but also took away some of his opponent's strength.

Thurmond did more than acknowledge the importance of education. In a rural area where it had less value than in other places, he took a stand that the state should make efforts to increase its support for public education. At that time, the state supported only six months of the school year, and as a result many schools were open for only six months. Strom advocated that the state should underwrite a full nine-month operation.[1]

As the June primary neared, it became clear that the contest was really no contest. Tillman's name was just no match for Thurmond's energy, ideas, and the support he had garnered from party regulars. When the votes were counted, the results were anticlimactic: Thurmond had received 2,350 votes, Tillman a mere 538.

With the nomination for the senate seat won and no Republican opposition, Thurmond assumed the title of senator-elect. He had little time to celebrate, however, because he had to leave for Chicago to serve at his first national convention. At age twenty-nine, he was probably one of the youngest delegates at the convention, and going at that relatively young age made an impression on him.

Strom remembered walking down the streets of Chicago with a group of other delegates, particularly a banker from Hampton, South Carolina, who wore a big panama hat. Strom watched as the group was approached by beggars. "The rest of us were not bothered so much," Strom said of that incident. "We didn't look so prosperous or rich."[2]

Nationally, the Democratic party was at a crucial point. For years, the Republican party had controlled the national government. Grover Cleveland and Woodrow Wilson had been the only Democrats elected president since the Civil War. Now, with the national economy in shambles, the presidency was again within their grasp. The only issue was whether Franklin D. Roosevelt (FDR), New York's aggressive governor, could unite the party. For the South Carolina delegation, the issue was clear. Thurmond remembered, "I think our whole delegation was impressed with Roosevelt. He had a grasp of what needed to be done for the farmers and at that time farming was the main industry in South Carolina. I was impressed with FDR because he was a man of action and I felt he would get things done."[3]

Roosevelt was selected as the party's nominee to face President Hoover, and Thurmond returned to Edgefield to do what he could to get him elected. One of Strom's jobs was to serve as the finance chairman of Edgefield County's Democratic National Campaign Committee. Even though the vote in South Carolina was not really in doubt, the party raised funds for two reasons: the money could be used in other areas where it might do some good, and the fundraising gave the local people the sense of being a part of the national effort. In those days, money for presidential campaigns was raised by selling election medallions; Strom urged "every white citizen in the county, man and lady" to purchase one. Times being what they were, these medallions cost a dollar.[4]

In the general election in November, FDR swamped Herbert Hoover to become the nation's new president, and in South Carolina, the political career of Strom Thurmond was officially launched. Before moving on to the business of state government, however, Strom paused to thank the people of Edgefield County for allowing him to serve as their superintendent of education—and he reminded them of the good things he had done for education in the county. He was pleased to note that some $33,000 in expenses had been eliminated from the education budget and that twenty of his twenty-eight school areas had been able to reduce taxes accordingly.[5] Later he acknowledged that he was driven by two factors:

"a duty to the children of the county" and "a duty to the tax payers of the county."[6]

His hardheaded fiscal conservatism had accomplished both factors by keeping his teachers paid and keeping his schools operating while others had closed. This aspect of Strom, coupled with his progressive move to ensure proper medical attention for his students—at no cost—favorably impressed the people of the county.

With his education days coming to a close, Thurmond turned his attention to state matters—specifically, what he intended to do as state senator. So that there could be no doubt about where he stood, Strom wrote another letter to the editor, outlining the goals he intended to accomplish during his term in the state senate. This list was expanded slightly from his original two points, but it continued along the same lines and combined the same interesting mix of fiscal conservatism and progressivism he had exhibited as a county superintendent of education.

The first major item involved limiting the legislative session to thirty days with a maximum pay of $200. He felt even then that less governing was better, especially when additional days of the state legislature tended to be expensive, both in terms of increasing the size of state government and extra pay for legislators. His second major item was a call for a reduction in state expenditures because "our people are simply not able to pay high taxes," coupled with an acknowledgement that "we cannot fail to run government," especially the courts and the schools, so people would have to pay the taxes they owed.

His final pledge was to work for a reorganization of state government (a recurring theme of his), but he coupled this with a desire to expand the educational opportunities for the young people of the state. Strom hoped that reducing state expenditures would enable local school districts to collect more money and better serve their students.[7] With these objectives clearly established, Thurmond prepared to begin his service as the state legislature convened in January of 1933.

Columbia, the capital city of South Carolina, escaped the wrath of General William Tecumseh Sherman when his troops made the first half of the "march to the sea" from Atlanta to Savannah during the Civil War. But on Sherman's return journey, he swung through and torched it. Included in his assault was a barrage of cannon fire directed at the partially completed state capitol building. Only ten shots struck the building—little damage was done because the cannons were not large. But there remains to this day brass markers that show where each shell hit.

Memories of other kinds also cast their shadow over the dim interior of the capitol. Even though he never presided there, John C. Calhoun's influence could still be felt. As a chief proponent of the concept of states' rights—sharing credit only with James Madison and Thomas Jefferson—his influence was pervasive. (As an aside, Calhoun's initial defense of states' rights came about as the result of his opposition to some tariffs that unfairly punished southern planters. The arguments, as originally presented, had nothing to do with the preservation of slavery.)

Thurmond's entrance into the state government of South Carolina placed an obligation on him to keep the faith—Calhoun's faith, in a manner of speaking. This obligated him to defy federal intervention at every turn and to defend the institutions of the South as Calhoun had done so often many years before. In this obligation, Strom was not alone. The extent to which some of his contemporaries defended southern institutions varied, depending on their temperament. In the 1930s some of Strom's fellow legislators listed among their affiliations membership in the White Supremacy League. Thurmond himself had no such affiliation. [8]

It is also important to understand the dynamics of South Carolina state government. As a people, South Carolinians have always had a distrust of centralized authority. This distrust began during colonial times and continued through the period after the Civil War when abuses in executive power deepened it. By the time the state constitution was rewritten in 1895, this distrust was incorporated into the constitution by ensuring that the governor had almost no power. Power was decentralized into the hands of the state legislature. This imbalance of power not only had an impact on state government, it also affected local government. Until the 1970s, there was almost no "home rule," as local autonomy is known. The legislative delegation for each county ran the county and the chairman of this delegation—and therefore the most powerful person—was almost always the senator.

While many legislative bodies have rigid seniority systems where older hands hold the power, the political situation in South Carolina served to somewhat dilute that as well. Party discipline is important only if you have opposition. In South Carolina's legislature, the only party represented was Democratic. Issues were not debated along party lines but instead along various other lines. Coalitions would often form around single issues and later disband when their purpose had been accomplished. In this kind of environment, even a young senator can assume a leadership role. For a man like Thurmond, already self-confident, the situation was tailor-made.

If the political realities were such that freshmen senators could step forward, some unwritten rules suggested that they not do so. Characteristically of Thurmond, if he knew about those unwritten rules, he ignored them. Scarcely had the legislative session begun when Strom found an opportunity to make a speech, something most new senators put off at least for a little while. The issue that raised his hackles was a proposal known as the Mill Bill. This legislation would prevent employers from locking employees in the mills. (This relatively common practice was used by mill owners to keep employees on the job—and to keep others away from them. It had been tolerated because the textile mills provided one of the few alternatives to cotton growing as a way to earn a living.) Strom was opposed to the practice, and in his speech he declared he was a "friend to capital but more a friend of labor." Few who have followed Strom's career would expect to find that statement or any of the other pro-labor stances he continued to take during his early years. [9]

As the session progressed, Thurmond had a chance to act on several of the issues on which he had campaigned. In line with his desire to reduce expenditures, he sought to remove the fertilizer inspection service from his alma mater, Clemson College, and transfer it to state government—along with the revenues generated by the service. This proposal would have been frowned on by "Pitchfork Ben" Tillman, as it was Tillman's hard fight that had placed the service and fees at Clemson's disposal. Thurmond was unsuccessful in this effort.

A second Thurmond effort was to attempt to cut salaries of elected officials, a proposal he made to the state senate. When Senator H. Kemper Cooke of Horry County asked Strom sarcastically if the salaries of the governor and judges were to be subject to cuts, as well, Thurmond snapped, "I will answer your foolish question when I'm through." So much for apprenticeship. [10]

Later in the year when Thurmond was confronted with the "extra pay" issue, he honored his campaign promise by refusing to accept the $260 offered to him. In a letter returning the voucher to state Comptroller A. J. Beattie, Strom advised him, "I was handed a voucher tonight in the sum of $260.00—being opposed to extra pay and having voted against providing for the same—refuse to accept it and will return said voucher."[11]

Other issues that came up during that year serve to highlight the conditions of the day and also one of Thurmond's great inconsistencies. One of his proposals that was not approved was a provision that only white people be hired to work in the capitol building. And on April 20 he voted to exempt Ku Klux Klan property from state taxation. While these acts are in keeping with the caricatured image of Strom Thurmond, they were not repeated during the balance of his years in the senate. And by way of contrast, on April 13, he voted in favor of admitting women to the freshman and sophomore classes at the University of South Carolina. On one hand, Thurmond's voting reflected a continued need to defend one southern institution, segregation, but on the other hand, he voted to expand opportunities for women. This has been a fairly consistent pattern of Thurmond's, and some of his later actions in this regard will be even more surprising. [12]

A final aspect of Thurmond's early career was shown in a proposal he put forward late in his first year: the proposal was to reduce property taxes while increasing income taxes, with the additional $1 million going to the public schools. This plan was a clever attempt to take from the rich and give to the poor. In South Carolina, most state income-tax revenue came from the rich, while property taxes were hardest on the poor. Strom's plan would make a lot of people happy and a handful unhappy—especially in Edgefield County—while supporting education at the same time. This plan was not adopted, but Strom kept plugging for more income for the schools throughout his service in the state senate.

Thurmond's second year in the senate, 1934, was less active than his first year. His first major thrust was populist in nature. His proposal to reduce auto inspection fees—originally sponsored in 1933—was approved in 1934. The effect of this action was to reduce inspection fees from $16 to $8.

Another issue was a proposal that would have enabled local newspapers to publish the names of drunk drivers. As a "dry," Thurmond had no use for drinking (a position he has maintained throughout his life). Thurmond favored the proposal: "A person is killed on South Carolina highways every 48 hours. With such a high rate, we should publish the names of drunken drivers." [13] But Thurmond did not want anyone to be singled out for ridicule; he insisted that the names be published without comment.

The other major issue in the state that year centered on electric power, and Thurmond adopted this issue as his own. It occupied his energies on and off for twenty years. One proposal before the state was the construction of a public power project known as the

Santee-Cooper project. Strom was a major proponent of the project because it would provide electricity and jobs to the people of Edgefield County. Because of his vociferous support, Strom was appointed to a special committee to meet with the governor and was instructed to "expedite appointment of a committee authorized by resolution passed by the House and Senate."[14] This committee was to lobby members of South Carolina's congressional delegation to see that federal monies were available for the project. This was the beginning of a long, drawn-out effort to bring electricity to large rural sections of the South, and Thurmond's interest, then and later, helped it to come into being.

The end of the 1934 session of the state legislature really signaled the end of Thurmond's initiation into public life. He had established himself as an outspoken maverick, of sorts, but not to such an extent that he could not get things done. The game of politics was in his blood, however, and bigger opportunities were out there to beckon someone of his abilities. One of the catalysts in this process was his service during 1935 as state councillor of an organization known as the Junior Order of United American Mechanics. The Junior Order was an interesting group, and Strom's leadership position within it helped prepare him for the future.

Strom and the Junior Order

The Junior Order of United American Mechanics was not a labor union, even though the name implies it. Instead, it was an organization founded in reaction to the flood of immigrants that flowed into the country during the 1800s. The motto of the Junior Order was "Put none but Americans on Guard." Their creed was "One language, One school, One country, One flag." It was a fraternal organization in which members addressed one another as "Brother." In his messages to the members, Strom signed off as "Fraternally yours." [15] Insight into their beliefs can be found in a speech Thurmond delivered as the state councillor. In it, he laid the blame for many evils at the feet of aliens: "A large portion of crime is due to illegally entered foreign born and those that have no other reason to be in this country than to accumulate a competence and go back to their native lands." Later in his career, in another capacity, Thurmond would make a similar observation. One essential aspect in understanding Thurmond is that in almost every area of his life—public and private—he has exhibited a remarkable consistency.[16]

As to its reason for existence, the Junior Order was active in some education issues, but its main focus was immigration laws. In one message, Thurmond urged the Juniors to "encourage our Senators and Congressmen to oppose any Bill to lower the gaps of immigration." He mentioned the "disturbance and discord growing out of the Communistic propaganda among the ignorant and unthinking people" and blamed the aliens for the propaganda Here, as in the case above, Strom established an idea early and held to it. His anticommunistic stance of the 1950s and 1960s was not invented to take advantage of some bubble in public opinion—it was well established by the mid-1930s.[17]

The most important aspect of Strom's association with the Junior Order was the enlarged perspective it gave him of his own potential future. At an early age, he had expressed the desire to be governor. When he went to Clemson and majored in agriculture, he seemed to move away from that ambition only to get back on track with his election as school superintendent and state senator. The election to a state post in the Junior Order really set him on the road to bigger things. As councillor, he had a legitimate reason to travel around the state and make speeches. The nature of the times meant that every speech he gave would receive coverage—occasionally his talks were even broadcast on radio. As always, Strom sought opportunities and then worked hard to make the most of them. With his broadened perspective as state councillor and a growing following, Strom began looking around for other mountains to climb.

Back to Columbia

When the state legislature reconvened in January of 1935, Thurmond's primary emphasis was on increasing funding for education at the state level. On January 16, he introduced a plan that would divert all the monies collected from beer and wine taxes into the public schools. In this way, he killed two birds with one stone—he supported education and made it a little more expensive to drink in South Carolina.[18]

Strom's proposal was amended along the way, but its final form was a major step forward for education in South Carolina. Chief provisions included:

1.   Sixty-five percent of all taxes collected on alcoholic beverages were to be channeled directly to the schools.

2. The state guaranteed to support the local districts seven months of the year (as opposed to six).

3. Teacher salaries were to be raised to an average of $75 per month for seven months of the school term.

4. Teachers were further protected because the law mandated that enrollment and attendance were to remain the same. This prevented local school districts from increasing class size and hiring fewer teachers.

5. The proposal also included an "anti-chiseling" clause that prevented the local school districts from using the money outside of the specified seven-month period. Further, teachers were to be paid their regular salary for any month they were employed in excess of seven months.

This proposal, passed in May of 1935, was a giant step forward for South Carolina—and Strom Thurmond had been the driving force. The entire education profession, especially teachers, was grateful to Thurmond for his part in making this happen. He had been one of them and he had fulfilled one of his campaign promises.

Another issue that came before the state legislature that year serves to highlight previous illustrations regarding the depth of feeling that continued to exist in the South long after the Civil War ended. The central issue was a labor question revolving around a practice, employed by cotton mill owners, known as the "stretch-out." In a stretch-out, mill employers required workers to continue to work after their shifts had ended with little or no additional pay. In a way, this amounted to involuntary servitude practiced by mill owners—most of them from the North—against southern labor. That year, the state legislature addressed the issue when an "anti-stretch-out" bill was introduced. At its introduction, Senator Jeff D. Parris of Cherokee County declared that he was "sick of Yankees coming down here and working our people to death." The state senate agreed with these sentiments but did not want to force employers out of the state, so it killed the legislation. Senator Thurmond took to the floor to demand a federal investigation into the unfair labor standards practiced by mill owners.[19]

One final issue confronted by Thurmond that year was not a legislative issue but a constituent service issue. State senators do not have the volume of constituent requests that federal legislators do, but there are issues that must be addressed. In the Depression era, one of those issues was jobs, and as the federal government was actively creating jobs, state governments sought to gain federal projects. And within each state, legislators fought over which area was to have federal work programs such as the Civilian Conservation Corps (CCC). The CCC was a quasi-military organization that employed people on public works projects. Many miles of sidewalks and roads in use today have a CCC background.

In 1934 the CCC had announced plans to open a camp in Edgefield County. The CCC camps were segregated, and upon the announcement, Thurmond and Edgefield House member M. Hanford Mims (and all the elected officials in the county) appealed to Congressman John C. Taylor for the CCC camp to be "composed of white personnel rather than negro."[20]

The CCC administration did not honor this request, and the camp was designated for blacks. In October of 1935, however, plans were announced to close the camp. When the news broke, Thurmond immediately appealed to J. C. Kircher of the U.S. Forest Service to keep the camp open.[21] Unfortunately for Edgefield County's black citizens, the CCC camp was closed because it "could be closed with the least damage to the general work program in the National Forest Area in South Carolina."[22]

Thurmond often worked hard for the black citizens he represented even though laws such as the poll tax prevented them from voting. In 1935 the General Election Board (GEB) of the federal government controlled millions of dollars worth of grants for educational purposes. That year, Strom lobbied Jackson Davis, the field agent for the GEB, for $10,000 to build an additional building at the black Bettis Academy. Strom wrote, "It gives me pleasure to say that Bettis Academy is performing a great work in training young colored people of this section of the state . . . this institute is a great asset not only to Edgefield and Aiken Counties but to the State." Strom added that "both the white and colored people of this section have full confidence and faith in [Bettis Academy] President [A. W.] Nicholson."[23]

Perhaps, though, the most interesting news to come out of South Carolina that year was not directly related to Thurmond. But it does demonstrate the political environment within which he operated and, indirectly, the incident played a role in shaping his future. The parties involved were Governor Olin D. Johnston and the powerful state highway department headed by Ben Sawyer.

In South Carolina the highway department has always had a disproportionate share of political power. One reason was that farmers depended on getting their produce to market, and this required a system of "farm-to-market" roads. Another reason could be the large budgets that were controlled by this department. For whatever reason, the highway department had a large power base. Olin Johnston had been elected governor in 1934, and he began his term by trying to break the power of the S.C. Highway Commission and its chief commissioner, Ben Sawyer. At one point, Governor Johnston demanded the entire commission's resignation, and on October 28, 1935, when they did not resign, he ordered troops into their offices and installed machine guns to keep them out. When the battle moved into the courts, the commissioners were reinstated, which not only affirmed the power of the highway department but also reaffirmed the power of the state legislature because it had approved the appointments.

Obviously, the highway issue was a watershed one, at least for Governor Johnston. Votes for the highway department could be construed as anti-Johnston votes and vice versa. The question of which side the legislature would take would have to wait until the next legislative session opened in January of 1936. Meanwhile, Thurmond had some issues of his own to deal with—particularly, what he would do that year. His future would include involvement with both Governor Johnston and the highway department.

The Political Pot Begins to Heat Up

Throughout 1936 Strom Thurmond widened his political circles. With his year as state councillor of the Junior Order behind him, he saw larger vistas and began to actively seek out a more ambitious future. One of his goals was to again serve as a delegate to the Democratic National Convention in 1936. He succeeded, and in writing "thank you's" to those who had elected him, he took the opportunity to prophesy that "President Roosevelt will be renominated in the most harmonious Democratic Convention the nation has witnessed in many years and that he will be overwhelmingly reelected in the general election in November." Thurmond was correct, of course. FDR easily swamped the Republicans' sacrificial lamb, Governor Alf Landon of Kansas.[24]

Early in the legislative year, Thurmond went to Washington to speak with officials there to get information needed to instigate a social security-type system in South Carolina. As he envisioned it, the state of South Carolina would implement a program to assist the "blind, aged, dependent children and handicapped" people. This progressive measure was later adopted and Strom was a guiding force in its passage.

In April Thurmond was elected to fill the unexpired term of W. L. Riley on the board of trustees of Winthrop College. At that time, Winthrop was primarily a women's college that educated teachers. Strom's election to this post placed him in the position of holding two separate public offices—the issue of dual office holding was to surface later in his career.

As the session drew to a close, Strom became embroiled in another clash between Governor Johnston and the S.C. Highway Commission. (Actually it was a continuation of the earlier clash, but the particular incident revolved around a disbursement provision for the highway department that had been vetoed by the governor.) When the measure was returned to the state Senate, twenty-five senators voted to override the governor's veto. Strom Thurmond was among the twenty-five who had voted to override but he noted that his decision was consistent with previous votes on similar issues that had nothing to do with the highway department. "We have set a precedent, we must stick to it," he said.[25]

Governor Johnston took the override personally, however, insinuating that the legislature was siding with the Highway Commission against him. The governor then urged the people to oust those who had voted for the highway department on the disbursement issue. That meant that Strom Thurmond was on Governor Johnston's hit list. In Strom's case, though, it was less damaging than it might have been—of all the state senators up for reelection, he was the only one with no opposition. But this one issue began to divide the men, with consequences to come later.

The only other important incident of that year occurred after the legislature had gone home. That winter, Sol Blatt, a young Barnwell County house member (and son of a Russian Jewish immigrant) decided to seek the position of speaker of the South Carolina House. In his bid to gain this powerful position, he called on Strom Thurmond, asking him to speak with two particular house members. Blatt noted, "They both think a great deal of you and if you keep after them I am satisfied that we will get both of these votes."[26]

With Thurmond's help, Blatt was elected speaker. Ironically, this set up a chain of events that made it seem that much political power was centered in Barnwell County. In addition to Blatt, Senator Edgar A. Brown, also of Barnwell, wielded considerable power in the state senate. In later years, this group would come to be known as the "Barnwell ring," and it would come under intense criticism from Strom Thurmond—one of those who had helped, in a sense, to create it.

The November general elections merely confirmed the already-known fact of Thurmond's reelection to the state senate. He could, if he chose, spend the next four years serving the people of Edgefield County. But his patience with local office was beginning to wear thin—1937 promised to be a year that would open new doors, and Strom was poised to stride boldly through them, no matter what the cost.

A Fork in the Road

In South Carolina, one of the paths from obscurity to political prominence begins with the lieutenant governor's position. The position itself has relatively little power—the main function of the lieutenant governor is to preside over the state senate. But it is a statewide office and, as such, can provide a base for higher office. Numerous lieutenant governors have gone on to become governor, and the position of governor is almost a prerequisite for election to the U.S. Senate in South Carolina. Therefore, many aspiring people seek the post.

As 1937 began, one young state senator had his eyes on that position. In 1938 both the governor and lieutenant governor positions would be up for grabs. The timing would be perfect for a state senator, who could retain the senate seat while seeking the other position. At the beginning of that year, Strom Thurmond was leaning very strongly toward making a race for lieutenant governor. The first public hint of this desire was in May of 1937 in Edgefield County's newspaper, which reported that Strom would not confirm or deny that he was seriously considering a run for the post. The story added that Strom's wide acquaintance over the state would prove a great advantage if he should decide to run.[27]

As the summer wore on, stories continued to circulate that he would be a candidate. On July 20, Thurmond was prominent at a Young Democrats meeting. By that time almost everyone in politics in the state assumed he was in the race. His friends were encouraged by the fact that he had not denied the rumors, although he had been pressed publicly to do so. By all accounts, he was poised to throw his hat in the ring.[28]

Meanwhile, he continued to attend to his duties in the state senate. He began the legislative year as chairman of the Public Buildings Committee. Early in the session, he introduced legislation to build a new state office building. He also saw to it that Winthrop College had a new classroom building and auditorium.

And his activities did not stop there. In education, he sponsored legislation raising pay for first-grade teachers to $595 per year, and he was able to secure passage of legislation that increased state support of local education to eight months per year (up from seven).

Thurmond's legislative diligence went even further that year as he sponsored legislation to create Soil Conservation districts in the state. His efforts also included provisions to increase benefits payable to workers under the state's Workmen's Compensation Act and a resolution inviting Mrs. Franklin D. Roosevelt to address the General Assembly in February 1937.

In all, Thurmond's hectic pace (and the overall success of his efforts) established that he was coming into his own as a legislator. Further, by the end of the 1937 legislative session, Thurmond had set an admirable standard for all public officials. He had addressed almost all the areas he set out to when he entered the senate, and by doing so, he had fulfilled his campaign promises. Unlike some politicians, Thurmond never proffered the excuse that he was only one of many—he made his presence felt.

With all this activity at the state level, it is important to remember that Thurmond also had a large say in the affairs of Edgefield County. At the end of that year, he was able to point out with pride that he had abolished local government positions, built and refurbished school buildings, provided the county with a recreation building, refinanced bonds and notes, paved roads, reduced county tax millage from 12.5 to 5, and eliminated the need to borrow money for county operations.

Thurmond's effectiveness as a state legislator was evident. No wonder the people of Edgefield held him in high regard. In Strom Thurmond, they had a capable, honest public servant who did what he said he would do. If he had ambitions for higher office, the people were determined to support them—Edgefield County's loyalty to its sons was high. So Strom's rumored ambitions did not detract from his standing in any way. As the months wore on, the people of Edgefield were preparing to make the sacrifice and send yet another of their sons to serve the state of South Carolina.

Then something happened that threw the political community into confusion: the sudden death of Eleventh Circuit Judge C. J. Ramage in August of 1937. No one expected Strom Thurmond to have any interest in this position. It was completely outside the career path he was on. A judgeship was tantamount to political retirement. Once elected to a judgeship, a person lost much political power and exposure. And the position was most certainly not a stepping stone to higher political office.

Yet, upon Ramage's death, Thurmond decided to follow the fork in the road that led him away from political ambition. And the path was not easy. Though he had many friends, he had made enemies as well. Some of these men had positions of prominence in state government. Others were powerful in the state legislature. And in this election, oratorical skill and public opinion were not important. This election would take place within the statehouse. Only 170 votes would be cast: 124 house members and 46 state senators would decide who would be the next circuit judge. In a battle like this, Strom would need the powerful people on his side. Unfortunately, he soon learned that some of them would not be. But, as always, Strom was confident. He set out to beat them convincingly—to win for himself a position no one had known he even wanted. In his attempt, he established patterns that would stay with him for the rest of his life.

Chapter 4

THE JUDICIAL THURMOND

B y the time Strom Thurmond was thirty-four years old, he had achieved success in many endeavors. He had been a competent teacher, an outstanding education administrator, an able attorney, and a popular elected official. During those years Strom had a "Midas touch" that turned nearly everything he touched into gold. He appeared to be well along the path of his chosen ambition, a path destined to lead him to the governorship of his native state and perhaps even greater honor as a U.S. senator. His interest in the Eleventh Circuit judgeship was notable mainly because it was inconsistent.

If his decision to take up the law as a career came relatively late (while he was a school superintendent), his decision to become a judge came relatively early. His interest, coupled with his youth and brief service as an attorney, only served to reinforce the generally held belief that Thurmond was a brash young man. Once again, though, he backed up his brashness with thoroughness. And, as has always been the case, once his mind was made up, Thurmond pursued his objective with single-minded determination.

The Judicial Campaign

August in South Carolina can be unpleasant. High temperatures and humidity combine to create sticky, stagnant days known as "dog days." Occasionally, a hot political contest will raise the temperature even higher. The sudden death of Judge C. J. Ramage in August 1937 set off an intense scramble that involved just about everyone remotely connected with politics in the state. Unbeknownst to most of the participants, the consequences of this intraparty squabble would be felt in South Carolina for the next fifty years. Partially congealed alliances would gel as a result of this contest, and the nucleus of a formalized opposition had its beginnings in the struggle between Strom Thurmond and the "Barnwell ring."

Immediately after Ramage's death, the Edgefield newspaper carried a story that listed Ramage's possible successors: T. C. Callison (the circuit solicitor), T. B. Greneker (a Thurmond ally), George Bell Timmerman, Sr. (a Lexington County attorney), and Strom Thurmond. The article went on the speculate that Callison and Greneker seemed to be the "most available" candidates and that Thurmond, "just 34," seemed to have his sights set in a different direction. (By this, the article's author meant Strom's plan to become lieutenant governor.) Strom was still undecided at this point: so much so that he suggested to Timmerman that he enter the race.[1]

No doubt Thurmond himself was surprised to find his name on the list of Ramage's potential successors. He was probably both pleased and surprised to find that several prominent attorneys around the state also felt that he could be elected. He learned this through a series of letters encouraging him to seek the position. One of these came from Greenville attorney Joseph R. Bryson, who wrote: "Several members of our Bar here were expressing the hope that you would offer to succeed [Ramage]."[2] Another kind letter came from a Bennettsville attorney, George W. Freeman: "I should like very much to see you offer for this position and feel confident that you could be elected."[3]

On August 10 the Edgefield County Bar Association also climbed on the bandwagon by endorsing their favorite son. In their endorsement, they noted that "J. Strom Thurmond is . . . a man possessing great strength of character, outstanding ability, and excellent judicial temperament and an accurate knowledge of the law."[4]

Thurmond may have been indecisive, but he was not idle. While still not committed publicly to entering the race, he made the rounds of legislative leaders, seeking assurances of support. In the few days after the Edgefield County Bar endorsement, he found a great deal of support—and some opposition. One source of opposition came from the Barnwell County delegation, House Speaker Sol Blatt and Senate leader Edgar A. Brown.

Thurmond had called Blatt seeking his support and at first had been assured he had it. On August 10, however, Blatt wrote Thurmond and qualified his support, saying he had "overlooked a letter that I had written . . . and if the party that I have in mind runs I will have to support him. . . . I am of the opinion, however, that the man that I wrote this letter to will not become a candidate. If he does not run I want you to know that I will go down the line for you."[5] The unnamed "party" Blatt referred to was George Bell Timmerman, Sr. Interestingly, Thurmond received a letter from Timmerman, thanking him for his suggestion that he "become a candidate for judge" and telling him that he had decided to enter the race.[6]

Immediately after receiving word of Timmerman's decision, Thurmond wrote to Blatt again, asking for clarification of his position. On August 16, Blatt wrote that, indeed the person he had pledged to support was George Bell Timmerman and he would have to stick with him. "I am grateful to you for the many fine things that you have always done for me and I regret very much that both you and George Bell are in the race at this time. I want you to know that I have the highest regards for you."[7]

Still later, after Blatt had begun actively campaigning for Timmerman, Thurmond wrote him again, accusing Blatt of attempting to scuttle his candidacy. At that charge, Blatt responded with real emotion: "I want you to know that I have no ill will towards you and have no objection in God's world to your being elected Judge. You have been kind and courteous to me and I am grateful beyond words."[8] These emphatic words notwithstanding, Thurmond did not have Blatt's support, and that lack could have been fatal to his campaign.

The other dig at Thurmond came from Blatt's Barnwell counterpart, state Senator Edgar A. Brown. Brown and Thurmond had never been politically close. Perhaps their age and mutual ambitions caused them to collide more frequently as members of the same legislative body. And unlike Blatt, Brown seemed to enjoy needling Thurmond. In his August 17 letter, he told Strom he was going to support Timmerman, while noting, "I thought your ambition ran in another direction." Brown ended his letter with the hope that "something may clear up the water so that I won't be forced to vote against you."[9]

The root of Thurmond's long-term disagreements with the leaders of Barnwell may be found in these exchanges. How could Blatt have forgotten a pledge to support Timmerman? Why would Brown support a nonlegislator for the judicial post? Strom had grounds for feeling that the opposition was personal. Eventually, both Blatt and Brown would pay a high political cost for their opposition.

But Thurmond did not allow the opposition of these men—even though they were powerful—to keep him out of the race. Their opposition was notable, but by August 14, he sent letters to twenty-two state senators and fifty-six house members thanking them for their support.[10] Only eighty-six votes were needed to be elected and Strom had already locked up seventy-eight votes— before making a public announcement of his candidacy.

By August 16, Strom felt confident enough to make a public announcement. On August 17, the *State* newspaper noted that the announcement had "upset the belief of many that he was looking into a political career." The same article stated that T. B. Greneker had received the endorsement of the Greenwood Bar Association and speculated correctly that Strom's announcement meant that Greneker was not in the race.[11]

At the same time Thurmond was publicly announcing his decision to seek the judgeship, the Lexington County Bar Association was endorsing its favorite son, George Bell Timmerman, for the post. As it turned out, these two men were the only ones seeking the judgeship—so the contest pitted Lexington County against Edgefield County. This distinction proved to be the cornerstone of Timmerman's campaign. In an August 21 letter to James R. Bryson (that was dutifully forwarded to Thurmond), Timmerman outlined his credentials for the post and then added, "Lexington County, my home county, is one of the oldest counties in this state and . . . has never had a democratic judge and many of our good people feel that, other things being equal, Lexington County is entitled to some consideration in the selection of a successor to Judge Ramage."[12] This thought was publicly expressed in an editorial in the Lexington *Dispatch*, which declared that the "people of this county believe we are entitled to this judgeship."[13]

Timmerman and his friends were never able to define the issues of the election solely on those terms. A look at Timmerman's campaign shows that he neglected to point out his strong suits— his legal career and his experience in state government. Timmerman was a graduate of the University of South Carolina and a former president of its alumni association; he had also been a past district governor of the Lions. These two posts had been much what the Junior Order was for Thurmond—a statewide platform. Timmerman's greatest exposure had been with his service as chairman of the S.C. Highway Commission. When Timmerman entered the race, he hoped he could count on the many friends of the highway department in the state legislature to support his candidacy.

Timmerman's hopes ran straight into the path of the Thurmond juggernaut. Immediately after announcing his decision to seek the judgeship, Thurmond embarked on an exhaustive campaign, putting maximum pressure on every potential voter from every conceivable angle. He began with direct contact with the legislators and expanded that contact outward to include attorneys, influential people, and even people who might have known someone who could influence someone else. One example involved a Thurmond acquaintance, Katherine Anderson, who had written Strom from her home in Florida upon hearing that he was in the race. Strom immediately wrote back and requested that she get her "Mother and Father to speak to the members of the General Assembly from your County in my behalf."[14]

By mid-September Thurmond was able to report to Donald Russell (a Spartanburg attorney and future governor and U.S. senator) that he had the votes of "about two-thirds of the Senate . . . and over one-half of the House." This added up to about ninety-three votes, more than enough to win, but Strom was not content. He admitted to Russell, "I am about as weak in Spartanburg County as any county in the state and am wondering if something can be done to help me up there." He then asked Russell and "some of my other friends up there" to secure additional votes, if possible.[15]

On the same day, Thurmond was corresponding with W. L. DePass, Jr., in Camden, regarding the charge that he was too young to be a judge. Thurmond acknowledged that he had heard the arguments but stated flatly that "this contention amounts to nothing." He concluded his letter to DePass, "If there are any lawyers over there who are particularly active for Mr. Timmerman I should appreciate you informing me who they are as it might be possible that in some indirect method I might be able to have some friends of mine to contact them and get them to take no part in the race." This was consistently a part of Thurmond's strategy: those he could not get to support him he at least wanted to be neutral.[16]

In another instance, Thurmond sought to turn the age question to his advantage. He wrote to Greenville attorney John Bolt Culbertson: "A great many of the lawyers in this state, especially the young lawyers feel that we should fill the judgeship with the younger lawyers rather than select old ones."[17] This was an indirect attack on Timmerman, who was Strom's senior by many years. The appeal fell on deaf ears since Culbertson had already decided to support Timmerman.[18]

Thurmond continued his frantic pace of letter writing and personal visits for the rest of the year. In December, one month before the election was to take place, he broadened his appeals to include people on the fringe of power. A letter to Mrs. C. Fred Lawrence, an officer of the Federation of Women's Clubs, asked for her support, "not as an officer . . . but as an individual. You have lots of friends over the state and a strong influence and your active interest in my behalf would be of great influence."[19]

In late December Thurmond benefited from the support of his old organization, the Junior Order of United American Mechanics, and their state councillor, Lewis H. Gault. Gault had been actively lobbying for Strom, and he brought him what should have been especially good news regarding Governor Johnston (a fellow Junior). Gault relayed that he had mentioned Strom's candidacy to the governor and that "everything is O.K. and if there is any doubt about any Johnston men [in the legislature] let me know in time. Keep this quiet and I will do likewise and so will the Gov."[20] This seemingly fantastic bit of news had no impact on Strom. He did not even acknowledge it; instead, he asked Gault to put in a good word for him with the mayors of Columbia and Charleston.[21] By that time, Thurmond felt that he had no need of support from the "Gov." And there was no love lost between those two anyway. There was no way Strom could count on Johnston's support—or could he?

Thurmond's efforts and letter writing continued unabated throughout the holiday season and into the new year. His supporters continued their labors as well. As late as January 7 (five days before the voting was to take place), Kathleen B. Watts (superintendent of education in Kershaw County) was working actively for him. Her form letter to other education officials said, "Knowing Mr. Thurmond as I do, I feel that all school people owe him more than one obligation for the many things that he has done for us." Throughout the campaign, Strom had used his education connections to support his candidacy, and their support was almost unanimous.[22]

When the legislature convened on January 11, the upcoming race between Thurmond and Timmerman (backed by the Barnwell group and the highway department) was the hot topic. Little groups swirled around the desks of various powerful legislators, attempting to get a feel for how the race was going. In the middle of the activity was Strom Thurmond, confident but still working hard at rounding up last-minute votes. He knew that promises made in the heat of summer might not hold up in the cold reality of the statehouse. Other power players could be seen moving from group to group: House Speaker Sol Blatt cajoling his colleagues and Senator Edgar A. Brown buttonholing any senators who were not committed. Indeed, this was Timmerman's only hope—that Blatt and Brown could somehow pull off a miracle when everyone got together for the new session.

Then, incredibly, Thurmond received a final bit of help from an unexpected source. Governor Johnston took to the platform to denounce the highway department. Without naming Timmerman, his speech had the effect of pulling the rug out from under his candidacy. After huddling with Blatt, Brown, and others, Timmerman made a decision. He withdrew from the race, leaving Thurmond in sole possession of the field. On January 12, Strom Thurmond was unanimously elected to the Eleventh Circuit judgeship and took his place as one of the youngest jurists in the state.

There can be no doubt that Thurmond had the votes to win the election, with or without the Johnston speech. This fact was confirmed when the legislature got together. In reality, this contest was between and man who felt he was owed a judgeship and one who went after the position with every weapon at his disposal. Thurmond just outhustled Timmerman and Timmerman knew it.

The aftermath of the race was interesting. One state newspaper, the Anderson *Independent,* called Thurmond's victory a "political upset of major proportions which stunned even those who usually feel they know what is going on."[23] There was even a suggestion that the power of the highway department was diminishing as a result of this contest. Among insiders, the issue was not Thurmond's victory but how it had been achieved. To win in a contest was one thing—to be so powerful that your opposition fled the field was quite another. Thurmond was certainly a man who bore watching.

Among the congratulatory messages Thurmond received, four stand out. One was a letter from former S.C. Supreme Court Justice Eugene Blease to Strom's mother. He congratulated her on the election of her son and added, "I wish that your fine husband could have lived to see his boy win this honor. Mr. Thurmond was so proud of Strom"[24] Here, perhaps, is an insight into why Strom sought this post. Will Thurmond had been a good lawyer, a young solicitor who could have held a prestigious judgeship—until he killed a man and put a wrench into his own career. As Will molded Strom, perhaps he put a subtle duty on him to achieve a position that Will could never attain.

The second letter came from Professor L. R. Booker of Clemson College, who said he was glad for Strom because he was a "Clemson man." And he added that he hoped he could someday "greet you as Governor."[25] This letter held out some hope that Thurmond could someday make the transition from jurist to governor, but in reality, he had removed himself—at least temporarily—from political consideration.

The third letter, from J. P. Coates of the S.C. Education Association, congratulated Thurmond and thanked him for his contributions to education. Thurmond replied that he was grateful for their support and it was his sincere wish that "South Carolina will continue to make progress along educational lines."[26]

The fourth letter came from Sol Blatt. In the aftermath of Thurmond's unanimous election, Sol had tried but been unable to congratulate Strom personally. He wrote his congratulations instead, adding, "I have always been a great admirer of yours and am appreciative of your friendship. I am proud of your election. I know that you will make an able judge."[27]

Despite these attempts at fence mending, relations were strained with the leaders from Barnwell County. For the next thirty years, with occasional lulls, Thurmond would feud with both Blatt and Brown—and for the most part Thurmond would walk away the clear winner. But for now, Strom had entered a kind of political retirement in which he could sit back and take it easy. Or could he?

Thurmond on the Bench

On January 20, 1938, Strom Thurmond was sworn in as the Eleventh Circuit judge. Another young attorney, Lanneau D. Lide, was sworn in as the Twelfth Circuit judge. Lide had defeated W. Marshall Bridges of Florence to capture his judgeship. On the same day, Thurmond resigned his seat in the state senate. (W. P. Yonce, a car dealer from Johnston was elected to fill that vacancy over M. Hanford Mims.)

Thurmond was less enthusiastic about resigning his seat on the Winthrop College Board of Trustees. He enjoyed his work with the women's college and was reluctant to give it up, especially since it gave him continued visibility in the education community. Representative Wilbur Grant of Chester had other ideas, however. He served notice on Strom that he would have to resign the Winthrop seat or face some political unpleasantness. Under increasing pressure to eliminate this instance of dual office holding, Strom did finally agree to resign his board seat on March 1 of that year. (W. B. Davis of Pickens was elected by the legislature to succeed him.)[28]

With this distraction removed from his life, Thurmond was ready to settle down to the life of a judge. His first bench service was not as a judge but as an observer in the trial of six convicts who had murdered a corrections officer. Sitting with Judge C. C. Featherstone, Thurmond received his formal introduction to the judicial process.

As the office existed at the time, the circuit judge was responsible for hearing civil and criminal cases in county courts. Although Thurmond was elected to fill the Eleventh Circuit vacancy, all judges were expected to travel throughout the state, riding circuit and dispensing justice. By the time Strom completed his judicial service, he had held court in almost every county in the state, which proved to be a powerful tool in the hands of a master campaigner because of a judicial procedure known as the jury "charge."

The court system operates in layers. Before an arrest warrant is issued, law enforcement officers have to go before a judge and demonstrate that valid reasons exist for making an arrest. Before an accused offender actually comes to trial, a grand jury decides if there is enough evidence to warrant the trial. If the grand jury feels that there is sufficient evidence, they issue a true bill and the case comes to trial. At the beginning of each session, the presiding judge will issue a "charge" to the grand jury. Normally, these charges are procedural in nature and may suggest methods for investigating the cases that come before the court. In Thurmond's hands, these charges were used as a means of making public (and sometimes political) speeches.

Thurmond was to hold his first court term in Laurens County on February 7 but on February 6, while he was traveling in a rain storm, the driver of Strom's car lost control and the car plunged into a ditch. Strom said of the accident: "I received rather severe injuries but think the wors[t] was a badly shattered nasal bone."[29]

When Thurmond arrived in Laurens on February 21 to open his first session of court, he received a formal welcome from the Laurens County Bar Association through its spokesman, Ralph P. Wilson. A Clemson College cadet, Joe Anderson, presented Judge Thurmond with a gavel modeled after the one used by John C. Calhoun. Thurmond then took full advantage of his first opportunity to make a charge. He instructed the Laurens County Grand Jury to investigate all institutions in the county, not with the idea of finding fault but in the spirit of helpfulness. He also reminded

the grand jury of the new school attendance law (which he had helped to write) and then reminded them it was their duty to see than equal justice was done.[30]

The first major case to come before Judge Thurmond in Laurens County was that of a black man accused of murdering another black man. After the evidence was presented, Thurmond addressed the jury and gave them a directed verdict of guilty—with mercy. In a directed verdict, the judge asks for the verdict he feels is appropriate for the case. In this instance, Strom's directed verdict saved the man from execution. The defendant was given life imprisonment rather than the death penalty because of extenuating circumstances.

When Thurmond moved to Greenwood County to hold court, he broadened his charge to the grand jury somewhat by stating that they were to "inquire into affairs of all officers . . . a good officer welcomes inspection." He added, "There is no quality to be admired more than honesty."[31]

Thurmond never shied away from that kind of intense scrutiny—and he also viewed his role as a judge in a philosophical light. In several instances, he was called upon to comment on various aspects of the legal system and its operations. He always had an answer ready, and often the answer went beyond the prescribed routine.

As was mentioned previously, Thurmond was elected to a judgeship at the same time as his acquaintance Lanneau D. Lide. As the two newest (and youngest) judges, Lide and Thurmond corresponded regularly during the first few months after their election. Lide confided that the part of the job that bothered him most was imposing sentences that were at the "discretion of the court," meaning the judge's discretion. In the same letter, Lide directed some praise at Thurmond's father, Will: "I take your father's book with me everywhere I go, and I believe it is the most valuable book I have. It was a fine contribution which he made to the bench and bar of the state."[32]

For his part, Thurmond was effusive in his praise for Lide and he acknowledged that he, too, had difficulty in imposing discretionary sentences. In response to Lide's query regarding his methods, Strom replied that he had "been careful to consider each case individually, taking into consideration the past record of a defendant, his demeanor, his schooling, his reputation, his family background and other points in order to arrive at a sentence that would be fair and just and accomplish the desired result under the law."[33]

Thurmond's intention was always to remain as true to the spirit of the law as he could. Often, if there were questions, Thurmond would seek out the author of a particular law to ascertain its best meaning. In correspondence with Orangeburg attorney Julian S. Wolfe, Strom remarked, "I shall always keep in mind that justice is the goal to be arrived at by a judge."[34]

Even when he gained additional seniority, Thurmond maintained his desire to ensure that his actions as judge were consistent with the intent of the law. In one instance, the verdict in a lawsuit had gone against state senator B. E. Nicholson and his client. Nicholson's earnest pleas for a new trial, based on Thurmond's handling of the case, caused Thurmond to seek counsel. This time, the situations were reversed as Thurmond corresponded with Judge Lide, presenting him with a record of the trial and telling him, "don't hesitate to suggest that a new trial be granted if you determine there is proper ground for same."[35] Despite his outward confidence, Strom occasionally faced self-doubts.

In this instance, though, Lide's response was reassuring. After examining the records of the case, he agreed with Strom's handling of the case and added, "While no one can forecast with certainty the view the Supreme Court might take of the matter, I am very much of the opinion that they will feel that your charge was full and fair, and that the criticisms are hypertechnical and without substantial merit."[36]

While Thurmond grew in judicial experience, he continued to cast glances toward the political arena. Under his sedate black robe beat the heart of a political man. In May 1938 he was elected to the Credential Committee of the national Democratic party. And he did not shy away from getting into the thick of local races, either. In January of 1939 the term of Governor Olin "Machine Gun" Johnston would expire, and at that time, a governor could not succeed himself. That meant there would be a primary battle for the seat—there always was. Two of the hopefuls to succeed Johnston were Neville Bennett and Charleston's charismatic mayor, Burnet Maybank. Rather than stay out of the race, Thurmond chose to take sides—and he did so in characteristic fashion. In a letter to Robert McC. Figg, Jr., Strom related: "I frankly told Neville at Jolly Street [political meeting area] last Saturday that I intended to support Burnet Maybank. I think he had expected my support and did not wish him to be misled. I am for Burnet 100%."[37] In this case, Strom picked the right horse—Maybank was elected—but his decision created some enemies.

In addition to his work as a judge and his political activities, Thurmond had time to pick up two honors. The first of these was the presentation of an honorary law degree from the University of South Carolina. This honor mirrored the one given his father only five years before. The second was that Thurmond and his law partner, J. Fred Buzhardt, were admitted to practice before the U.S. Supreme Court. Their applications were sponsored by Jared Hartzog, an attorney with the Bureau of Internal Revenue.

Strom's first year on the bench was not without turmoil, however, and usually this turmoil was created when the political scene spilled over into the halls of justice. Two instances demonstrate the kinds of difficulties faced by Thurmond that year. The first occurred in Horry County (which contains the Myrtle Beach area). When he arrived there in June to preside over their court, he was told by the foreman of the grand jury that irregularities had occurred in the preceding court. When asked what kinds of irregularities, the new foreman complained about the conduct of the old foreman—specifically, that procedures had not been followed. Thurmond was then told that the previous foreman had gambled. His greatest sin, however, was that he was a "Republican." In some parts of the state, even in the 1930s, the epithet "Republican" was the worst that could be used. Judge Thurmond responded that in the current session of the court they would not be looking to the past—instead they would be "looking to the future."[38]

The second instance occurred in another coast county, Charleston, and the potential for dramatic consequences was even greater. The Charleston area was the first site of European settlement in the state. Throughout its history, much of South Carolina's wealth and power was centered there. Even after the balance of power moved into the midlands of the state, the city remained important because of its commerce and large population. All candidates for statewide office tried to woo Charleston's voters, and there were many attempts to buy elections. As a result, Charleston politics was often characterized as rough and tumble—in sharp contrast to the city's general image of courtly manners. Its political reputation was deserved, however, and as a result, a close watch was always kept on the ballots.

In the 1938 Charleston Democratic primary, irregularities were suspected. In a decisive move designed to clear the air, Judge Thurmond ordered the ballots impounded and locked up to prevent further tampering. A joint meeting was set up with representatives of the Charleston County Grand Jury and members of the

Democratic Executive Committee. When the grand jury arrived to begin reviewing the ballots, they were immediately terrorized and intimidated by members of the Executive Committee. The grand jury reported to Judge Thurmond that they were certain irregularities existed, but that the tactics of the Executive Committee had filled them with "fear for their lives . . . and the Grand Jury had good reason to suspect that these men were carrying concealed weapons."[39]

Thurmond was incensed over this attempt to pervert justice and the will of the people. In addition to doing what he could to change the Charleston situation (an uphill battle), he also took to the stump to protest this kind of activity. In a speech to the Greenwood Lions Club, he referred to corrupt politics as "public enemy number one." In the same speech, he returned to the subject of patriotism. By the end of 1938 the international situation looked bleak, and Thurmond made the most of it. He warned his audience of the dangers of communism, fascism, and Naziism and added that many people would "welcome the opportunity to overthrow" our government.[40] Like many others, Strom saw the threat of war on the horizon, and he began including war rhetoric in his speeches.

A Second Year on the Bench: 1939

By the end of Thurmond's first year on the bench, he had moved beyond crime itself to the underlying reason for crime. His experience holding court had made an impact on him. As his second year began, he was searching for ways to combat the reason for crime.

In February of 1939 Strom gave a speech in Anderson which indicated how far his thoughts had come in regard to the root causes of crime. He asserted that schools were the principal bulwarks against criminal behavior: "If we spent more time on education, we would have to spend less to combat crime." And he continued, "We can't expect much of the boys and girls who are reared in homes where the father and mother live apart and there is drinking on the part of the elders."[41] His observations had convinced him that crime had to be combatted proactively, with prevention, and not just reactively, with punishment.

Thurmond found the opportunity to back up his thoughts with actions early that year. In April he attended a temperance rally and contributed $5 to the cause. Rev. Albert D. Betts thanked Strom in a letter for his contribution and expressed the hope that "the progress of our work will tend to make your burdens lighter as you administer justice."[42] Later that year, Strom donated $1,000 to establish a loan fund for home economics students at Winthrop College. (In return for his efforts on behalf of the college, Thurmond Hall was named for him that year.)

The spectrum of cases that come before a circuit court judge may be aptly demonstrated in two cases tried by Judge Thurmond in 1939. One involved chicken thieves in Oconee County. They pled guilty and received a five-year sentence. The other case was Thurmond's first brush with constitutional questions, although in this case, the constitution was South Carolina's, not national. The issue was a hot potato politically—as Thurmond would find out.

The constitutional issue took the form of a challenge to the state licensing law for coin-operated machines (vending and entertainment). The law was challenged as being both confiscatory and unconstitutional. When Strom returned from holding court in Conway, he found this case and a letter from newly elected Governor Burnet Maybank awaiting him. Governor Maybank wrote that he was not a lawyer and he had no notion of whether the law was "right or wrong, legal or illegal, but it does involve between $100,000 and $200,000 which is quite a sum for us to consider one way or the other."[43] Obviously, the Governor was pressuring Strom for a decision. It was a unique situation for Thurmond. He reminded the governor that the state supreme court had never decided any similar case and that therefore "precedent [will] be set in such matters in our State." The balance of his response demonstrated his uneasiness: "The case deserves serious consideration, and a hasty decision would be unwise. I do not expect to delay deciding it any longer than necessary, but a matter of this importance deserves the most careful attention, and I must give it the consideration it deserves. I have been giving the matter much consideration, and shall probably render a decree in approximately two weeks."[44] This kind of rambling apology is uncharacteristic of Thurmond, who rarely offered explanations for anything.

Not only does his reply suggest some uncertainty, but it also suggests an inner turmoil between doing something politically expedient and doing the right thing. He could have eliminated the law (and reduced taxes) by stating that it was unconstitutional. That course would certainly have won him some friends—but in the end, the force of law had to triumph over political considerations. Somewhat anticlimactically, Strom ruled in favor of the state and the license law was upheld.

Also of interest that year was Strom's interaction with one of South Carolina's first resident female attorneys, F. Mildred

Huggins, who tried several cases before him beginning in 1939.

Thurmond ended the year firmly entrenched in the judicial system, with plums of that nature within his reach. Earlier that year, an early Thurmond supporter (who later turned against him), Wilton Hall, publisher of the Anderson *Independent*, had written Strom commending him and added, "Keep pitching—and we'll make it read 'Associate Justice' one of these days."[45] After two scant years on the bench, Strom could have been headed for the S.C. Supreme Court.

Another Year on the Bench: 1940

The year 1940 began with storm clouds of war hovering above the nation. In South Carolina, clouds of a different nature were threatening the state. There had been an increase in the activities of the Ku Klux Klan, and responsible citizens were concerned about the possible consequences. One such citizen, Greenville attorney Stephen Nettles, wrote Judge Thurmond requesting that he "say something about the Klan when you charge the grand jury here next week. Unless this business is stopped, we are going to have trouble right here in Greenville. There is no question in my mind that local public sentiment is strongly against the illegal action of the Klan."[46]

Thurmond did as he was asked. In his January 8 charge, he strongly condemned the violent activities of the upstate Klan masked riders. "I am not in sympathy with any such doings." he said. "Any one convicted need expect no mercy at my hands." He further characterized the activities of the Klan as the "most abominable type of lawlessness."[47] There can be no doubt that Strom was personally opposed to the activities of the Klan. He risked some personal popularity by speaking out on the issue—whatever the political risk, Thurmond felt compelled to uphold the law.

On January 11 of that year Thurmond was reelected to his position as Eleventh Circuit judge without opposition. This term would allow him to remain as judge through 1944.

Later in that month, he caused a minor flap with the military because of his efforts to spare two youthful offenders from serving time in jail. The incident began when Thurmond agreed to suspend their jail sentences if they could produce evidence that they had secured jobs or been accepted by either the Civilian Conservation Corps or the army. The adjutant general of the War Department (now known as the Department of Defense) heard of this offer and wrote to Thurmond, complaining of his approach. "The instructions governing recruiting are explicit in requiring that only men of good moral character be enlisted and the Department naturally objects to suggestions being made that men with criminal records or those who have been imprisoned in jails or similar penal institutions are being sought by the Army."[48]

Thurmond responded to this letter by defending his actions and sharing his philosophy regarding crime and punishment. "Evidently, you misconstrued the matter relative to the boys referred to in your letter . . . but two young boys were before me in Greenville for receiving parts from a stolen bicycle and pleaded guilty in this offense which is a misdemeanor (not a felony). It has been my policy since being on the bench to try to redeem young boys of tender years and I feel that a great many of them can be led into a path of rectitude if placed in the proper environment. . . . It was because of my high regard for the CCC and the Army that I agreed to suspend their sentences."[49]

Strom's concern with youthful offenders was expressed by word and deed many times during his service on the bench. Later that year, he called for the creation of homes of detention (as an alternative to prison) for men aged 17 to 25. "When we send a young man to the chaingang or penitentiary, we don't know whether he will come back a better citizen or a criminal."[50] This was progressive thinking for its day—and Strom was a chief proponent in South Carolina's justice system.

Throughout that year, Thurmond continued to call for alternative methods of punishment. By the end of the yar, he had begun to promote the idea of a probation and parole system in the state. At that time, prisoners either served their entire time or they were set free without any kind of supervision. And according to Strom, "In many instances I think it is preferable to parole a man rather than send him to the penitentiary or chaingang, but under our state law we have no such action possible." He added that he sometimes took matters into his own hands; "Occasionally I have suspended the sentence of a prisoner and required that he report to some officer or leading citizen in the community and have found that this policy has worked satisfactorily in quite a number of cases."[51] Partly due to his urgings, the state eventually adopted the beginnings of a probation and parole system.

That year also saw Thurmond sitting for the first time as a temporary justice of the S.C. Supreme Court. On May 13 he replaced Associate Justice A. F. Carter. It is the practice of the supreme court to tap circuit court judges when temporary vacancies occur, but Thurmond's selection after only two years on the bench was an honor. And not only did he sit with the court and review cases, he was asked to draft several of the opinions. Obviously, he was held in high esteem by his peers on the court.

One of the opinions Thurmond drafted is especially interesting because it involves a labor union question. The case was *Pacific Mills v. The Textile Workers Union of America*. The union wanted permission to deduct union dues from the employees' pay checks. Pacific Mills objected to being asked to support a labor union. Thurmond's opinion, which had the concurrence of Justice Edward L. Fishbourne, supported the labor union. In his dissent, Justice Gordon Baker noted that "it would amount to . . . permitting the employees, members of the Union and the Union to make Pacific Mills their and its agent against the will of Pacific Mills to collect and pay these dues."[52]

To Thurmond, the issue was not whether he supported labor unions or not, but whether the action was lawful. Lawful actions had his support, regardless of his personal preferences. This incident may surprise those who have viewed Thurmond as doctrinaire. His dislike of some of the practices of organized labor is well known, yet he supported their petition because it was lawful. Throughout his service on the bench, Thurmond made the "right" decision even when it was in contrast to his personal beliefs.

One of the games historians play is "What if?" What if Thurmond had remained on the bench? What reputation would he have had, especially in regard to civil rights? If he had been forced to compare the practice of segregation with the ideals of the American way of life, what would his response have been? With more time on the bench and his already-demonstrated predisposition to progressive thinking, Strom could well have gone down as one of the best-remembered jurists in the nation. Of course, "what if?" speculations are just that. When Thurmond decided to rejoin the political world, the "ivory tower" approach had to be tempered by the cold facts of political life.

A Final Year on the Bench: 1941

The 1940s saw stirrings of racial tension. The growth and rejuvenation of the Klan dominated the first few days of 1940 in the upstate, and when Thurmond journeyed to Georgetown County on South Carolina's coast, he found another racial tinderbox awaiting him. This time, a black man was accused of raping a white woman. In South Carolina, conviction on these charges meant an automatic death penalty.

The case had aroused considerable local controversy, and Thurmond was at great pains to protect the defendant and provide a fair trial. On January 18, before the trial was to begin, he wrote to solicitor J. Reuben Long requesting that all forms be followed as he was "very anxious for everything to be carried out in the proper manner so that no technicalities can be raised that would upset the trial." Among the items Thurmond covered in his letter were the appointment of the defendant's attorneys (unless he was to be represented by an NAACP attorney) and proper protection for the defendant. Strom suggested additional police coverage and added, "I think it is preferable not to have a military company around the courthouse during the trial."[53]

After all the precautions had been taken, the trial produced anticlimactic results. The defendant survived the trial but received the expected guilty verdict and was executed. There were no protests as to the fairness of the trial.

Later in the year, Thurmond handed down one of his most unusual sentences in a criminal case. The incident that sparked it was a fight between two women in which the conflict escalated, and when one of the women went to phone for help, the other shot her three times (not fatally). When the case came before Judge Thurmond, he sentenced the shooter to three years in prison—one year for each shot that struck the victim.[54]

As the year wore on, the nation prepared itself for war. The National Guard had been mobilized and placed with the regular army. In Edgefield County, a Home Defense Force (HDF) had been established to replace the Guard, and Thurmond enlisted in the HDF as a second lieutenant. While the country tensely awaited international events, events much closer to home were heating up. A long-simmering feud between two Edgefield families erupted into bloodshed, and Strom Thurmond strode boldly into the middle of the crisis.

The Logue-Timmerman Feud

In the annuls of feuding families, Shakespeare's Capulets and Montagues may be the most famous; perhaps the Hatfields and McCoys rank up there as well. But for sheer violence, the Logue-Timmerman feud demands a place in feuding history because the facts are common knowledge and well reported; myth and mystery do not surround the events. Further, this feud occurred in this century in a community generally known for its courtliness.

Both Logues and Timmermans were known to Strom Thurmond. As school superintendent, he had hired Sue Logue as a teacher (in conflict with unwritten rules that generally prevented married women from holding teaching positions). And Sue's son, Joe Frank Logue, had been Strom's vice president in the Edgefield Baptist Association in 1927. Timmermans had also been Strom's friends and acquaintances—if you lived in Edgefield, you knew at least one Logue and one Timmerman, and you probably knew several of each.

Difficulties between the two families had simmered for years with only minor clashes until 1941. The straw that broke the camel's back fell in the autumn of 1940 when one of Davis Timmerman's mules got through a fence and kicked one of Wallace Logue's prize bulls to death. Logue went to Timmerman's store and demanded restitution for the death of the bull. When an argument ensued over the worth of the bull, Logue reached over the counter and grabbed Timmerman by the shirt. Timmerman picked up a pistol kept beside his cash register and shot and killed Logue. Timmerman was acquitted of all charges on March 2, 1941, when a jury found that he had acted in self-defense.

At that point, Sue Logue (widow of Wallace Logue) and her brother-in-law, George Logue, began planning their revenge, along with a trusted sharecropper, Fred Dorn. A few weeks later, one of Timmerman's black laborers was shot and killed. His murderer was never identified but suspicion centered on the Logues and Fred Dorn.

The second phase of revenge began with the enlistment of Joe Frank Logue (then a member of the Spartanburg Police Department). Using his contacts, Joe Frank hired Clarence Bagwell to kill Davis Timmerman. Logue hid in the backseat of a car while Bagwell went into Timmerman's store and fatally shot him, in an organized crime-type execution.

At that point, three people had lost their lives, but the killing was far from over. A reward offered for information on the Timmerman killing produced information that led to the arrest of Clarence Bagwell. Bagwell identified Joe Frank Logue as the man who hired him. When Joe Frank was arrested, he confessed his part and implicated Sue Logue and George Logue.

On Sunday morning, November 16, Edgefield County Sheriff Wad Allen (a Logue kinsman) and his deputy, W. L. Clark, drove to the Logue farm to arrest Sue and George Logue. Someone let the two officers into the house, whereupon they were ambushed by George Logue and Fred Dorn. Sheriff Allen was killed instantly, but Clark was able to kill Dorn before escaping outside, wounded.

Clark made it to the roadway and was taken by a passing motorist to an Augusta, Georgia hospital where he died—but not before telling what had happened at the Logue farm.

The ambush of the two officers had eliminated Edgefield County's law enforcement personnel: there was no one else left. When he left church in Edgefield that morning, Judge Thurmond was apprised of the situation, and as the ranking law enforcement officer in the county, he agreed to go out to the Logue farm immediately. When he arrived he found it in chaos—defended by armed Logue friends and surrounded by a group of well-armed citizens. Violence was imminent.

In Strom's words, "There was a large crowd gathering and I thought that there was danger of mob violence at any moment. I went up to the house and . . . opened my vest to show that I was unarmed." Once inside, Strom convinced Sue Logue to submit to arrest.[55]

George Logue had already escaped when Strom entered the house but was later captured. George Logue, Sue Logue and Clarence Bagwell were convicted of murder and received the death sentence. Joe Frank Logue received a life sentence.

While Thurmond modestly downplayed his role in the resolution of this crisis, it was the act of a brave man. When he arrived on the scene, he was confronted by two camps of armed people and the knowledge that two police officers had already died.

On December 7, 1941, just a few days after the resolution of the Logue incident, the Japanese attacked Pearl Harbor and war was declared against the Axis powers. When he heard the news, Thurmond immediately telegraphed President Roosevelt and offered his services in the regular armed forces.

Many years later, while reminiscing about his days as a judge, Thurmond recalled, "The position of circuit judge is one of the nicest positions I've held in my career. The people respect a judge and in travelling over the state, I had the opportunity to meet many fine people. The romance of the courtroom is unexcelled and [the excitement of being a judge] is exceeded only by being a lawyer in a case." Another advantage was the free time available to a judge."About half the time, when I wasn't holding court, I could study and read and travel and ride horseback and play tennis and do the things I wanted to do."[56] Somehow, though, one can't imagine Strom Thurmond spending the rest of his life as a judge.

If he had chosen that route, he would have retired around 1967. Even his remembrances of the quiet life do not exactly jibe with the hectic schedule the records show that he kept. This is not to say he did not have time to enjoy himself—he did. But he kept up a rigorous schedule throughout his time on the bench. Even his involvement in the Logue-Timmerman feud is suggestive: this was the response of a man of action. A man of action chafes at sitting behind a desk and dispensing sterile justice; a man of action wants to make things happen. Strom Thurmond can most certainly be characterized as a man of action.

It is safe to say that no matter what the world situation had been, Thurmond would have found a way to a more rigorous form of life. As it was, whatever plans he might have had were mothballed. He had volunteered his services to Uncle Sam, who has a habit of accepting such offers. Strom was preparing to trade his black judicial robes for the camouflage of military fatigues and the action of the courtroom for the action of the European and Asian theaters of war.

Chapter 5

HE'S IN
THE ARMY NOW

I n 1924, when Thurmond received his commission as a second lieutenant, he joined the Army Reserve Officer's Corps. From that time until 1937, when he had resigned from the group, there had been no sign of trouble. His military career—tranquil as it was—was over. With the automatic deferment that came along with his judgeship, no one would have expected Thurmond to play any role in World War II. Some men were already doing their best to avoid military service; all Strom had to do was sit back and do nothing. But anyone who thought he would take that approach did not know Strom Thurmond.

When Thurmond telegraphed President Roosevelt volunteering his services on the day the Japanese attacked Pearl Harbor, his patriotism was real. This was not a publicity ploy, a show of seeking to serve by someone secure in the knowledge that he would be turned down. When there was no immediate response to his offer, Thurmond persisted. And once in uniform, he took every opportunity to press for positions that were not "cushy." Some well-connected volunteers did their war duty stateside, commanding supply depots or other such assignments. Strom constantly sought opportunities to get closer to the fighting.

The state of South Carolina did make it a little easier for Strom to volunteer, however. In the 1941 session of the legislature, Act 255 was adopted. This act provided that "any State officer or employee serving in the Army, Navy, or Marine Corps, [the Air Force was part of the Army then] for the purpose of National Defense, shall be granted a leave of absence and that his absence in such service on account thereof shall not create a forfeiture of or vacancy in such office or position." Thus Strom could serve his country without giving up his judgeship—at least until 1944 when his term expired.

When he volunteered, Thurmond thought he would be mustered in at once, and so he began shifting his workload almost immediately. In a January 10, 1942 letter to one of his former senate colleagues who had petitioned for a hearing before him, Strom outlined his activities. By that time Strom had been to Atlanta "to see about getting in the Army." He had been given forms to fill out and had passed his physical exam, administered at Daniel Field in Augusta. Strom had applied for immediate duty, "and if I am accepted, I may receive a call any day to report for active army duty." In view of this, Thurmond requested that Senator Williams should have either his presiding judge or resident judge hear his case.[1]

Despite his desire to get started, Thurmond was not called immediately. On March 12, 1942 he received written confirmation of his leave of absence from the state and at last, on April 8, he received orders to report for active duty at Governor's Island, New York. He was officially excused by Chief Justice Milledge L. Bonham on April 13 for the duration of his term.[2]

The newspapers were very approving of Strom's voluntary enlistment. The Yorkville *Enquirer* praised Thurmond's actions while attacking those "scores of men who are trying to bring all manner of pressure on draft boards for deferred classification."[3]

Thurmond arrived at Governor's Island on April 17 and began his service with the provost marshal general's department with the rank of captain. His initial assignments were far from the combat he sought. After processing at Governor's Island, Strom was assigned to the 713th Military Police battalion stationed in Albany, New York.

One of his first assignments with the military police was to deliver a speech to the graduating class of the Bethlehem Central High School in Albany. Another of his early efforts in the army put Thurmond back in the role of defense attorney. At the request of the Red Cross, he agreed to defend Catherine Piazza Galluccio, whose husband, Private Louis Galluccio, had purchased some furniture prior to being drafted. The furniture company sought to repossess the furniture, and Thurmond was defending the wife's right to keep it under the federal law that prohibited the seizure of property belonging to men in the armed services. The local newspaper made a great deal out of the defense by the southern judge (and of his accent).[4]

Strom could not get entirely away from his judicial career in South Carolina, either. He received word that on July 6, the S.C.

Supreme Court had found that Judge Thurmond "fell into revers-
ible error" in his charge to the jury in the case of Sammie Osborn
(a black youth convicted of murder) and granted Osborn a new
trial.[5] In September of that year, Thurmond had occasion to write
the S.C. Probation and Parole Board regarding the request of an
inmate convicted of manslaughter. Strom recommended that the
man be paroled after serving four years, "if his record as a prisoner
is good and if he meets the other requirements of the Board in such
manners."[6]

By July of 1942 Thurmond was settling into the military. He
began by serving as a plans and training officer with the military
police battalion and then as the executive officer of the unit. But he
continued to chafe under these assignments because he wanted to
be part of the "real" army. He was allowed a brief visit to Edgefield,
but he was summoned back early to his unit—and a short time
later he got what he wanted: a transfer to a combat unit.

His first assignment was at headquarters of the Eastern Defense
Command and the First Army at Governor's Island, New York. His
commanding officer was Lieutenant General Hugh A. Drum. In
this position, Thurmond had at least a chance to see combat, but he
had to wait it out stateside for a time. He plugged away at his
duties, and in July of 1943 was promoted to major. His specific
duties as major, GSC, chief of department were in personnel. He
was responsible for "selection, procurement and assignment of
personnel for Army, Corps and Division Staffs" as well as handling transfers, personnel records, special and letter orders, pro-
motions, decorations, and awards. Not very exciting duty, but he
kept at his task.[7]

Thurmond was, of course, still very aware of the outside world.
Being stationed in New York was not the same as being in Europe
or the Pacific. By mid-year 1943 he knew that jockeying would
begin back in South Carolina for judicial seats, and his judgeship
was up for reelection. Thurmond decided that he would seek
reelection. He enlisted J. B. Westbrook, the clerk of the S.C.
Supreme Court, in his effort. Since he would not be able to personally campaign for the post, he needed someone to at least ensure
that his name was placed in nomination.

His second (and most important) consideration was what the
army would have to say. Strom petitioned for permission to seek
reelection, and it was granted on October 7, 1943, with the following stipulations: "Neither his candidacy for, nor his incumbency
in office will interfere with the discharge of his military duties;
that he will not campaign for reelection or be active in promoting
it; and no leave will be authorized for the purpose of promoting his

candidacy or discharging any function of the office; and that he
will not, while a member of the military forces on active duty, act
in his official capacity . . . or perform any of the duties thereof."[8]

While he was awaiting news of permission to run, he learned
that his desire to go overseas was to be granted. The First Army
Headquarters left for Great Britain on October 18, 1943. Shortly
after his arrival in Europe, Thurmond was able to confirm to
Westbrook that the Army had granted him permission to seek
reelection. In his November 23, 1943, letter to Westbrook, Strom
described the Cathedral at Wells, which he had visited on a
sightseeing trip, remarking that he was "so glad that the Germans
have not destroyed it through bombing." And he noted that he
would be attending school for several weeks in London, beginning
early in December, but that he had not yet visited London. He also
remarked on the rainy climate and noted, "We had several beautiful days last week, and it was a genuine delight to witness the
sunshine."[9] In that letter we see that J. Strom Thurmond has
become James S. Thurmond. The military services do not recognize middle names, and Strom, under military discipline, began
referring to himself as "James S.," even in private communications.

On January 21, 1944, Thurmond received word of his reelection
to the circuit judgeship by the state legislature. In his letter of
thanks, again to J. B. Westbrook, he briefly mentions his unit, the
First Army, and notes that "in the last war, it played a leading role,
and I feel it is destined to do the same in this conflict." Here,
perhaps, he was hinting about the intended role of the First Army
in the greatest military operation in the history of the world—
Operation Overlord, as it was called. He closed the letter with his
hope that "after the war is over and I get back home, I wish to have
the honor of having you come over and visit me sometime," which
showed both his hope of safe passage through the war and his
southern manners.[10]

On May 15, 1944, Thurmond was promoted to lieutenant colonel, so he was able to celebrate the successful culmination of two
campaigns that year. Perhaps the greatest challenge of his life lay
just ahead, however, as he prepare to participate in Operation
Overlord—better known today as D-Day.

Strom Goes Ashore

Despite being in England and closer to the action, Lieutenant
Colonel Thurmond was not happy. He wanted to see combat
action and his assignment in personnel was not likely to get him

there. Fortunately for Strom, the commanders of the Allied invasion of Europe were confident and that confidence provided the opportunity he sought.

D-Day plans included a need for Civil Affairs officers. Civil Affairs was charged with assisting local authorities to reestablish control after their territory had been liberated. So confident were the Allies that they planned to send Civil Affairs officers in on the first day of the invasion. Strom volunteered and was temporarily assigned to the 82nd Airborne Division. (Joining him in this duty were Major Bernard P. Deutsch and Captain John J. Knecht.)

On May 23, 1944, Thurmond left Bristol for Leicester, England, to join the 82nd at its staging area. For the next few days, Thurmond and the others studied maps, located towns and other population areas, and gathered as much information as they could on the sparsely settled agricultural region around Blosville, France, near the Allied landing area on Utah beach.

Prior to going ashore, the Civil Affairs officers were addressed by General Dwight D. Eisenhower, the D-Day commander. General Eisenhower reminded them that despite their political-type assignments, they were still soldiers, "just as modern as radar and just as important to the command." As if to emphasize this point, Thurmond and the others learned that they would cross the channel in gliders, towed by aircraft, and then be released to find the best landing they could in the darkened Normandy countryside— behind the German lines.[11]

The D-Day invasion of Adolph Hitler's Fortress Europe was planned for June 5, but bad weather forced a delay. Early on June 6, the decision was made to attack, and at 0630 hours (6:30 A.M.), the first elements of the Allied invasion began moving ashore.

Throughout the day, Thurmond and the rest of his companions did what they could to follow the action from Greenham's Common where they awaited their own H-hour. Finally, at almost 7:00 P.M., the glider contingent (containing about 150 of the motorless planes) moved out. Thurmond was in Glider 34, along with a ¼ ton truck and a trailer and other personnel. It took the glider column nearly an hour to form in the air, and only then could they begin their journey across the English Channel.

At 2100 hours (9:00 P.M.), the column crossed the coast of France over Utah beach. Almost immediately, the noise of the planes attracted the attention of German antiaircraft gunners. The column came under intense ground fire and the motorized towing planes had to cut the gliders loose and head back across the channel. The gliders began their descent, hoping for a soft landing.

Instead, most of the gliders were demolished as they ran into stone walls and other obstacles. Strom's glider crashed into a small field and his left knee was severely bruised and cut, along with cuts on both hands. As the men tried to unload the equipment another problem developed. The noise of the landings had attracted the attention of the German defenders, and the Americans were immediately targeted by artillery and small arms fire.

Despite his injuries, Lieutenant Colonel Thurmond gathered a small party from his glider and led a reconnaissance group in an effort to find a command post where a rendezvous could be established. Thurmond then borrowed a vehicle from an officer of the Fourth Infantry Division, made a reconnaissance of other nearby gliders, and helped the wounded reach the rendezvous site.

Thurmond had located a good site at a crossroads near Blosville, and he led his group from the first rendezvous to the new one— constantly under fire from the Germans. There they established a defensive position and spent the rest of the night. The next morning, their position was still surrounded and they decided they had to move to save the unit. They moved six times that day, each time seeking the protection of ditches, hedge, and foxholes. By 7:00 P.M. on June 7, Thurmond decided the only way to save the unit was to get to the division headquarters, no matter the cost. To get there, they had to fight their way through the enemy lines. Their efforts brought them near the Chef du Pont, which was the scene of heavy fighting, but by 9:00 P.M., the column had reached division headquarters, having twice crossed through enemy lines.

On the way, Thurmond had located the records of the German lieutenant general who commanded the 91st Division, and these records were reported to G-2 (Military Intelligence). For the most part, however, Thurmond's part in the military side of the invasion was over.

After joining up with division headquarters, Thurmond was able to begin his assignment. His activities in the first few days following the invasion were necessary but unspectacular. He procured local labor to dig graves, contacted the mayors of the local French communities, arranged to have dead farm animals buried, cleared grenades and bombs from the hospital at Ste.-Mere-Eglise, and assisted in locating the bodies of paratroopers killed in the vicinity of Ste.-Mere-Eglise for the quartermaster. When the town of Cretteville was taken by the 82nd on the morning of June 8, Thurmond and the division Civil Affairs officer immediately entered the town and conferred with the mayor. They saw to the feeding and care of refugees and held a ceremony at which the French Tricolor was raised.

On June 13, Thurmond again moved forward with a portion of division headquarters to an advance command post just west of Picauville. (This area was the "front," and under land and aerial fire from the Germans.) On June 14, he returned to headquarters.[12]

Thurmond had another adventure in late June as he set out for the French port at Cherbourg, which he thought had been captured. (It had not been captured, and as he neared the area, he realized he was in a combat zone.) On the way, he captured four German parachutists. He had two of the soldiers lie across the Jeep's hood and he put the other two on the back seat. All the while, he was guarding them with their own pistols.

For the balance of the war in the European theater, Strom saw little combat action, but his part in the D-Day invasion had been noted. On November 28, 1944, he was awarded the Bronze Star,

> For heroic achievement in action against the enemy from 6 June to 14 June 1944, in France. Lt. Col. Thurmond voluntarily accompanied glider elements of the 82nd Airborne Division on its first combat mission to the European continent. Heavy enemy fire forced the glider to a crash landing within the enemy lines. Although subjected to heavy fire and suffering from a painful injury incurred in the landing, Lt. Col. Thurmond assisted in unloading the glider. Then, without regard to enemy small arms and mortar fire, he repeatedly exposed himself as he went among other gliders that had landed in the vicinity, and courageously directed the regrouping and reorganization of the scattered units. The personal bravery displayed by Lt. Col. Thurmond reflects credit on himself and the military service.

Strom claimed no glory for his part in the invasion, but in a letter to J. F. Ouzts, Jr., he did comment that he "had so many narrow escapes that it is a miracle to me that any of us who landed by glider are still alive."[13]

As the Army moved deeper into France and later into Germany, Strom picked up a few souvenirs. One was a copy of Hitler's *Mein Kampf*, which he sent to J. B. Westbrook. Another more lasting souvenir was disgust and horror at the atrocities the Germans had committed on Jews and political dissenters. Thurmond was among the first into Buchenwald, a concentration camp where hundreds of thousands of people were put to death.

From the European theater, Thurmond went to the Asian theater and was stationed near Manila in the Philippines. There he had the opportunity to visit Corregidor, where he noted the vast maze of tunnels built by the Japanese for defense. He also saw the area on Luzon where the Japanese had hidden themselves in small caves and tunnels and continued to kill American soldiers.[14]

First Army headquarters personnel returned to the United States on June 3, 1945. An early assignment took Strom back to South Carolina with the First Army headquarters at Fort Jackson, near Columbia. Since he was close to home, it was natural that he would be asked to give speeches. At a Columbia Rotary club, he exhibited several captured knives and pistols and an iron cross. He told the audience that many of Germany's cities had been battered into ruins with many civilian deaths. But he wanted his audience to know the reason: the Germans had chosen to fight directly in their cities rather than in the surrounding countryside. At a Kiwanis luncheon in Augusta, Georgia, he warned that "the German people have no sense of war guilt and will undoubtedly start another war within twenty years unless we keep them disarmed and supervise everything they make and what they do with it."[15]

After three and a half years of service, Thurmond was released from active duty at Fort Bragg, near Fayetteville, North Carolina. In addition to the Bronze Star, Thurmond had received five battle stars and seventeen decorations, including the Legion of Merit with "V," Purple Heart, French Croix de Guerre, and the Belgian Order of the Crown.

And unlike many returning veterans who were filled with uncertainty about their future, Strom Thurmond had the option of returning to his prestigious position as a circuit court judge (his term would not expire until 1948.) If he chose to, he could return to horseback riding and tennis, to dispensing justice and reminiscing about the good old days. At age forty-four, Strom had earned the right to slow down. But it was not to be. If anything, his military service had made him impatient. His active life called for new challenges and within a short time, he sought them.

A book written about the kind of work done by Lieutenant Colonel Thurmond during the war was subtitled "Soldiers Become Governors." Prophetically enough, that is exactly what happened.

Chapter 6

A SOLDIER
BECOMES A GOVERNOR

A look at the history of our nation shows that after most military conflicts, we elect a military leader as our president. George Washington freed us from the British and served as our first president. Both Andrew Jackson and William Henry Harrison defended our early borders from Indians and served in the War of 1812. Zachary Taylor led the efforts in the Mexican War. Ulysses S. Grant saved the Republic during the Civil War. Even Theodore Roosevelt had his first brush with fame as the leader of the "Rough Riders" in their charge up San Juan Hill in the Spanish-American War. And after World War II, we once again elected a general, Dwight D. Eisenhower, as our president. In addition to these better-known examples, a host of governors and members of Congress have come from the ranks of the military. Even at the local level, returning veterans have often been honored with positions on city councils and as mayors and state legislators. With few exceptions, America honors its heroes.

This formula does not always work, though. William C. Westmoreland, military leader of the Vietnam War, sought the Republican nomination for governor in South Carolina and did not even win the primary. And former general Alexander Haig unsuccessfully sought the Republican nomination for the presidency. But for the most part, a military background is a solid asset in a political resume.

When Strom Thurmond returned from his three and a half years of service in World War II (with high rank and many medals), he had done nothing to harm his chances of being elected to high political office. And seeking political office was obviously his intention from the moment he left the service. Despite the two remaining years on his term on the circuit court, Strom had no intention of settling back into the quiet life of a judge.

Over the Christmas holidays of 1945, Strom spent his time making the rounds of various politicos, lining up as much support as he could in the manner he knew best. Although one of these trips would come back to haunt him, he found he was in pretty good shape politically, despite his absence.

When Thurmond began casting around for a theme for his campaign, his first impulse was to look within his experience as a judge. His dealings with crime and punishment stood him in a solid position to make crime an issue—which he did, at least initially. On January 22, 1946, he addressed the S.C. Sheriff's Association on the topic of crime. He put forward his own explanation for the upsurge in crime: "In periods of great national stress, we know that human nature reacts to the tempo of the times. The spirit of wartime abandon with its last fling philosophy was prevalent. This provided justification to weaker wills to violate the convention of society." He also used this opportunity to direct some bombastic oratory at another of his topics—young criminals. "It is not a pleasant picture . . . when a country like America must bow under the disgrace of . . . [the fact that] . . . one fifth of our most deadly outlaws and machine gunning desperadoes have not yet reached voting age."[1] (At that time, the voting age was twenty-one.) Apparently, crime was to be a central campaign theme—until Thurmond was handed a more powerful issue early in the campaign.

This speech was followed in quick succession by appearances in Conway, Darlington, Timmonsville, Dillon, Myrtle Beach, and Marion. Along the way, Strom also dropped by Fort Jackson to pick up his Legion of Merit Award, presented by Major General Clarence H. Martin. By May 3, Strom's frantic pace had been noticed by the newspapers in his part of the world. The Johnston Herald (in Edgefield County) ran an editorial urging Thurmond to run for governor. This was followed closely by the passage of a resolution at the Edgefield City Democrats convention urging him to make the race. On May 12, he was in Columbia at the Elk's Mothers' Day observance. There, he was assured of support from some of his friends in the state capital. Among his intimates, almost everyone was supportive of the effort with the exception of his mother, who advised Strom against entering the race.

By May 15, Thurmond had made up his mind—he was ready to announce. That morning, he sent letters to Governor Ransome J. Williams and Chief Justice Gordon Baker announcing his resignation as judge of the Eleventh Judicial Circuit.

His May 15 announcement touched on issues that were of greatest interest at that time. One hot topic before the legislature involved liquor. The repeal of prohibition at the national level had not settled the issue in South Carolina. The battle over alcohol raged on, and Thurmond, uncharacteristically skirted the issue. After reminding the people that he was a teetotaller (and therefore opposed to alcohol), he stated that he would "enforce to the best of my ability whatever law on this subject the duly elected representatives of the people [state legislature] may regard as expressing the wishes of the people" Given Strom's own stance, this statement was not strong. Instead, it sought to place him in the middle of the controversy: in short, he was not for it but would not oppose whatever view was expressed by the people. This was a rather wishy-washy sidestep on a major question, but part of the reason for it may lie in Strom's long-held belief in less government. Here, he demonstrated tolerance for views other than his own and upheld his conviction that government had little right to infringe on personal conduct.

On other issues, however, Strom took stronger positions in his May 15 announcement. He stated that, if elected, he would "not use the power of executive clemency to undo their [the courts] judgements." This was in direct response to the overuse of the pardon power by some recent governors. (While the pardon issue received only a passing mention, it was an issue that would not die. In a future contest with Olin D. Johnston, the pardon issue would take center stage.)

Thurmond went on record as being "strongly against the state police system." This was in reference to efforts to strengthen the state constabulary and possibly create a stronger state police force. He asserted that "law enforcement in general should be left to the counties and municipalities." This was in line with his constant goal of keeping government as close to the people as possible.

Thurmond took care to include returning veterans in his plans, making sure to remind the people of his own involvement and stating: "They should be given every opportunity to catch up on their education, and the state should do its full part, in cooperation with the Federal Government, to help them make up for what they lost while at war."

Strom also outlined his vision of the future: "We stand on the threshold of an opportunity which we shall never see again in our lifetime." He called for the state to develop all possible economic opportunities so "we can quickly modernize and expand our public schools and college facilities, guarantee to our teachers the compensation which they deserve . . . bring about the increase in the wages of our working people . . . broaden and expand our programs of public health, public welfare, and assistance to the aged, the blind, and our dependent children." Here was a call to FDR's New Deal liberalism—an approach that flies directly in the face of the prevailing view of Thurmond as a reactionary conservative. When he sought the governorship, he did so as a liberal, calling for "a progressive outlook, a progressive program and a progressive leadership." Strom intended to provide all three.[2]

The most interesting aspect of Strom's announcement for governor is not what it contained but what it did not contain. The speech did not have a single direct reference to the "Barnwell ring" (composed of Strom's old enemies, Sol Blatt and Edgar Brown), which was to become the central theme of his campaign. In fact, he made no mention of it until the campaign was officially underway.

In 1946 an especially large number of candidates sought the governorship—Thurmond was one of eleven candidates. The other ten were A. J. Beattie, Carl B. Epps, John D. Long, James McLeod, Dell O'Neal, Marcus A. Stone, John R. Taylor, Roger W. Scott, Governor Ransome J. Williams, and A. L. Wood. By and large these candidates were lightweights and virtual unknowns. Thurmond stood head and shoulders above the rest. The only other credible candidates were James McLeod (a Florence physician) and Governor Williams (who had been elected lieutenant governor and assumed the governorship when Olin D. Johnston was elected to the U.S. Senate.)

In those days, campaigning in South Carolina meant a series of joint campaign appearances all over the state. All the candidates for statewide office would normally travel this circuit, giving speeches to whoever might show up. Of course, as this was before the advent of a two-party system in South Carolina, the campaigning was within the framework of the S.C. Democratic party. In 1946, the campaign officially began on June 11 in Winnsboro and ended August 8 in Columbia, five days before the primary election.

While Thurmond may have intended to campaign on the basis of the liquor question, pardons, and an uplifted economy, he quickly changed his mind. At the first appearance in Winnsboro, one of the other candidates, Dr. Carl W. Epps (a Sumter physician was the first to charge that the state was run by a "ring" (referring to House Speaker Sol Blatt, Senate Leader Edgar A. Brown, and Senator R. M. Jefferies of Colleton.) Strom also attacked the "ring," noting: "It is a matter of common knowledge that the government of South Carolina is under domination of a small ring of cunning, conniving men." But in this first address, the ring was not his only focus; he also talked about industrial recruitment, declaring that he "did not want new industries on the strength that we have cheap labor." For the balance of the campaign, however, he would make the "ring" almost his sole issue.

A brief look at the positions of the other candidates will give some idea of the political landscape in South Carolina at that time. By June 11, their positions were becoming defined. The other two serious candidates, Dr. James McLeod and Governor Ransome Williams, staked out sound positions on two issues. Dr. McLeod campaigned for expanded medical facilities throughout the state: health was becoming an important issue throughout the South. Governor Williams was in favor of making liquor unprofitable in the state by operating state liquor stores.

The other candidates presented a mixture of ideas and seriousness. A. J. Beattie, a former comptroller general of the state, advocated elimination of property taxes through the adoption of "indirect" taxes. Dr. Carl B. Epps introduced the issue of "ring" rule and campaigned for expanded medical facilities in the state. John D. Long was a white supremacist who campaigned on the theme that "history and experience have proved the wisdom of white man government." Dell O'Neal was the real character of the group. His campaign could best be described as a "lark," as he campaigned for a "wet" ticket. His outspoken advocacy of liquor made for many humorous moments "on the stump." Roger W. Scott put forward no specific ideas, instead attacking his opponents as a "bunch of feather dusters." Marcus A. Stone was the capitalist candidate who campaigned for "less government in business and more business in government."[3] John R. Taylor favored methods to "effect the greatest possible" tax savings—without ever putting forward a specific plan to accomplish them. And A. L. Wood, the most outspoken "dry," was against liquor and was opposed to any plan to tax liquor for teacher's salaries. He felt that "drunkards could be cured by putting Christ in them."[4]

Thurmond, however, had seized on the most emotionally appealing issue of the campaign with his denunciation of the ring. He declared that South Carolina had government "of the ring, by the ring and for the ring."[5] By June 19, he was ready to name the foe that he faced. He formally attacked the "Barnwell ring," named after the county that Blatt and Brown represented. In a public statement, Strom said he had been informed the ring was raising money for his defeat. He said he "would gladly accept the challenge of opposition from that crowd," adding, "it will be interesting to see whom they lavish their money on in this race."[6]

From the beginning it was obvious that Thurmond was the front runner, and as such, he found himself under attack. Scott attacked him as being a tool of Senator Olin D. Johnston and charged that if Thurmond were elected governor, he would be seeking Burnet Maybank's U.S. Senate seat in 1948. Strom replied, "No group is running me for Governor and no group will run me if I'm elected."[7]

On June 25, Thurmond carried his attack on the "Barnwell ring" to Barnwell county. Before any of the candidates spoke, Senator Brown rose before the assembly and "cautioned the Barnwell County voters . . . that each candidate should be given a just hearing and a good hand, regardless of what he might say." Strom went ahead with his denunciation of the ring, to its "face," and was booed—as expected.[8]

The campaign took an interesting turn around the first of July, however. Thurmond had issued a challenge to the other candidates to debate the existence of a "ring." Marcus Stone had originally agreed to the debate but had then canceled at the request of Blatt and Brown. These letters were open letters, printed in various newspapers. Blatt tried to point out some hypocrisy by writing that Strom had asked him for his support by dropping into one of his parties during the Christmas holidays. (This was the visit that came back to haunt Thurmond.) Further, Blatt's letter charged that Thurmond had offered to provide a relative of Blatt's with a job in return for Blatt's support.

Thurmond denied both charges and intensified his attack against Blatt and Brown. In a speech to the voters of Spartanburg, he stated: "Their domination of the government even extends into the office of Governor but when Strom Thurmond is your Governor, their influence will cease and they will be forced to scurry back to their holes." He then outlined, in detail, the numerous powers held by these men and various incidents in which they had apparently used their power for their own gain.

One such incident involved Sol Blatt's domination of the house of representatives. As speaker, Blatt had the power to appoint legislators to the different committees. In one instance, despite

House Rule 17, which limited the size of all standing committees to twenty-one members, Blatt appointed some forty-two members to the powerful Ways and Means Committee, thereby aiding in his reelection as speaker and in the election of another Barnwell member as chairman of the committee.

Thurmond closed his attack with a forceful denunciation of their tactics and the plea that "I am doing all in my power to break that stranglehold. I ask for your help in this task—for it is not an easy job to wipe out the stench and stain with which they have smeared our government for these many years."[9] These were strong words and in them the old resentment of the Barnwell gang was apparent. In Strom's mind, they had conspired to prevent him from getting his judgeship, and they were at it again—conspiring to deny him the governorship.

Blatt and Brown struck back, with Brown labeling Thurmond's side of the story as "tissues of falsehood." But these men, while powerful within the small numbers of the legislature, were not popular with the people of the state outside Barnwell County. If Blatt and Brown had decided to support Thurmond's candidacy, they could not have done better than with the strategy they took. By responding to his barbs, they helped to perpetuate the image that Strom was the front-runner. And the feud drove almost all the other candidates out of the newspapers. Their argument consumed most of the press for the remainder of the campaign, and it ensured that Strom got more than his fair share of coverage. Thus the men from Barnwell inadvertently helped Thurmond in his campaign.

Only Dr. McLeod continued to gather support with his steady campaign style; he avoided the histrionics of the others. The primary issue before the people, however, remained the contest between a crusading Strom Thurmond and "ring" rule. And when it came down to deciding the issue of who was telling the truth—a popular judge turned decorated war hero or two politicians—the people sided with Thurmond. On August 13, the people went to the polls with the following results:

Thurmond	86,514	Epps	4,644
McLeod	73,603	Stone	3,923
Williams	30,839	Beattie	3,004
Taylor	20,952	Wood	2,469
Long	15,212	Scott	2,345
O'Neal	14,842		

The election laws required a majority to win, so a runoff between the top two vote getters, Thurmond and McLeod, was scheduled for September 3. Thurmond took advantage of the lag between the elections to stress the last important issue of the campaign—that if elected, he would serve a four-year term without seeking higher office. Two of the state's previous governors (Johnston and Maybank) had resigned in mid-term to move to the U.S. Senate. On August 23, Strom pledged, "I do not intend to use that high office as a springboard to the United States Senate. The condition of our state government is such that it will take me the full term to correct the evils."[10] The September 3 election gave the people of South Carolina a choice between the best two candidates, Thurmond and McLeod. The people chose Thurmond by a margin of 139,821 to 106,749.

It bears repeating that in the 1946 gubernatorial election, Thurmond was blessed with the right kind of enemies. The enmity of the men from Barnwell helped much more than it hurt. Strom was able to campaign as an outsider, even though he had worked with both men in the past. While this proved to be an effective strategy in the short-term, Thurmond would take it to even greater heights in the future.[11] With the title of governor-designate firmly in hand, Strom went to the Southern Radio and Music Conference in northern Georgia to do some swimming and to get a tan. With no opposition in the general election, he was ready to tackle the problems facing the state.

The Transition

After the country music retreat and a quick trip to the American Legion Convention in San Francisco, Thurmond returned to South Carolina to begin the transition phase and write his inaugural speech. On October 17, he opened an office in Columbia and was there every Thursday and Friday throughout the fall. Even before he was sworn in, he made his impact felt on the affairs of the state. He attended a meeting of the state Budget Commission and warned them not spend all the state's money because "we must have some for the teachers."[12] Shortly after Thanksgiving, he announced that he had formulated a plan to control liquor, but he did not give any clues as to what that new plan might be. He did say it would "promote temperance, cut liquor drinking and make more money for the state."[13]

Otherwise, Thurmond kept relatively quiet during the transition. He did make a point of contacting all heads of state executive departments for their thoughts prior to drafting his inaugural speech, however.

Elected executive officers such as governors and presidents may not exercise much power in any given situation, but they are judged (or should be) on the effectiveness of accomplishing the programs they outline in their inaugural addresses. These statements make interesting reading, especially if the record of the office holder is also available for comparison.

Strom Thurmond was sworn in as governor of South Carolina by S.C. Supreme Court Chief Justice Baker on January 21, 1947, before a crowd of about five thousand people. His total inaugural message was about fifteen thousand words, but the gathered listeners were spared from listening to all the details of his plan. He presented a summary, but even in its short form it described a comprehensive program addressing twenty-four broad areas.

If those assembled expected to hear more vituperative "anti-ring" oratory, they were disappointed. Thurmond mentioned the ring issue only briefly and stated that it was no longer an issue with him. "Let me say here and now that I have no feeling against any person or group of persons who may have differed with me last summer. I shall be the Governor of all the people and there shall be no favoritism in the discharge of my official duties." He could afford to be magnanimous at that point because he had already gained a modest amount of revenge. In the aftermath of Strom's election as governor, Sol Blatt had resigned as speaker of the house.

With the hand of friendship extended to the legislature, Thurmond launched into what he hoped would be the accomplishments of his administration. First and foremost was his call for a reorganization of state government. He noted that there were one hundred state agencies that "often overlap in their duties and frequently duplicate the efforts of each other." He called for the creation of a commission to make recommendations for agencies that could be eliminated and consolidated. To aid in this process, he also called for revisions to the S.C. Constitution, which had been adopted in 1895, and the creation of a state purchasing and personnel system.

Another topic was the elimination of dual office holding by state employees. Many people served on multiple committees and commissions, thereby having undue influence on the affairs of the state. Thurmond noted that the state constitution already contained provisions against this practice, but he called for a state law reiterating the legality of this provision. He cited his own dual office holding as a member of the state senate and a trustee of Winthrop College. But his reference was not entirely accurate— Strom said he had resigned the trusteeship "after serving for a time." In reality, he resigned his trusteeship, under pressure, almost two years after having been elected as a judge.

Another major portion of his inaugural was devoted to education. Thurmond advocated a greater partnership with the federal government with the understanding that "such aid should be without Federal control. The fear of Federal aid to education is without foundation, for we shall have more Federal control without it than with it, Because the effect of Federal court decisions requiring equalization as between the races will cost the State much more money and consequently lower the quality of the total school program unless aid is received from Federal sources." From this it can be seen that "separate but equal" schools were still the goal in the South. And as the days passed, Thurmond was forced to recant on his advocacy of greater federal funding.

He then outlined a sweeping plan that included establishment of kindergartens and nursery schools, creation of an educational radio network, stronger enforcement of compulsory attendance laws, and strong programs in vocational rehabilitation, adult education, and vocational education. These programs were exactly what would have been expected from a progressive, education-oriented governor—but Thurmond's role in their eventual creation is often overlooked.

Election reform was another topic high on Thurmond's agenda. At that time, South Carolina did not have a secret ballot, and Strom was determined that it should. In another surprise move, he advocated the elimination of poll taxes, which had been a vehicle to prevent blacks from participating in the political system of the state. Thurmond also used his inaugural to call for a host of "liberal" measures, including a state minimum wage law, a program to compensate workers suffering from "occupational diseases," more attention to "negro education," and equal pay for equal work for women, with the proposal that women be allowed to serve on juries.

He concluded his address with his promised liquor control plan, which called for a sharp reduction in the number of state-licensed liquor stores, a new graduated license tax on dealers, and a board for liquor-control administration.[14]

While these were the main issues Thurmond addressed in his speech, they were not the only ones. In addition, he touched on local government, agriculture, labor, health, safety, veterans, aviation, utilities, and industries. In short, every citizen of the state could find some solace in Thurmond's inaugural address. If this sounds like an ambitious program, it was. One news analyst noted that Thurmond's address contained "probably the most extensive and progressive program in South Carolina's history."[15]

Yet, comparison of the accomplishments of Thurmond's term in office to his stated goals in the inaugural address shows he was a successful governor. His success was especially surprising in light of his campaign against the legislative leaders of the state. Given the overwhelming influence of the legislature in South Carolina, it was remarkable that Thurmond was able to accomplish anything at all.

Strom Goes to Work

Immediately after delivering his inaugural address, Strom set about accomplishing the goals he had outlined. His first task was to hire an executive secretary, and he chose William L. Daniel, Jr., a former full colonel in the army and a Citadel graduate. In the absence of a wife, Strom's sister Gertrude served as the official hostess at the Governor's Mansion.

The South Carolina legislature does not meet all year; generally it conducts business between January and June and then legislators go home. For that reason, the governor must present his initiatives at the beginning of the year and continually push for their approval. With Strom's inaugural message to guide them, the legislators addressed and quickly adopted many measures urged by the governor. Among those enacted were the imposition of a graduated liquor tax, adoption of a liberal teacher salary schedule, creation of a state system of area trade schools, adoption of a permanent law for nine months of support for state schools, and the broadening of state welfare programs to include support for the aged, dependent children, and the physically and mentally handicapped. These measures were adopted in the legislative session of 1947, at Thurmond's urging.

Not everything went Strom's way during that session, however. In one instance, the general assembly passed a joint resolution calling for a referendum in 1948 that would permit the people of the state to express themselves on legalizing divorce in cases of adultery, physical cruelty, desertion, or habitual drunkenness. Thurmond did not sign this bill, citing as a reason the fact that two-thirds of the legislature had supported it, and it was therefore veto-proof. At that point, Strom's moral code was against divorce, period.

A second defeat came as a result of Thurmond's veto of a bill passed by the general assembly that would have suspended car inspections in the state. During the war, due to a lack of replacement parts, the legislature had suspended vehicle inspections. Strom felt that the increasing accident rate and the growing availability of replacement parts justified a return to vehicle inspection. Originally, the S.C. House members sustained his veto, but on May 7, they overrode his wishes by a margin of 80 to 31.

The only other major legislative incident from his first year came when Representative Tom Pope of Newberry charged the existence of a "Thurmond ring," in regard to the selection of a University of South Carolina trustee. Pope felt that Thurmond was attempting to usurp the legislature's power to appoint trustees by delaying an appointment until the legislature adjourned. (State law gave the governor the power to make interim appointments if the legislature was not in session.) Thurmond denied the charge, stating that the "election of trustees of state institutions is a matter for the legislature."[16]

While relatively busy with state business, Thurmond managed to indulge in some political activities that had implications outside the state. In April he had lunch with General Dwight D. Eisenhower. After their meeting, Strom incorrectly asserted that Ike was "uninterested in any political office."[17] A short time later, Thurmond took to the podium to assail Vice President Henry Wallace for his attacks on President Truman's aid to Greece and Turkey. Thurmond characterized Wallace as "a Republican all his life until he was appointed to the Cabinet." Time would prove Strom to have been wrong again, for if his assertion was that Wallace was a closet Republican, Wallace later disproved it with a vengeance in the 1948 presidential contest.[18]

For the most part, however, Thurmond tended to the business of governing. This is not to say that he kept himself out of trouble in his dealings with the outside world. Indeed, he was the center of controversy several times during his first year in office for issues that were not directly related to the discharge of his duties. One such incident involved a speech he had planned to make before a black group known as the Lincoln Emancipation Clubs of South Carolina. These groups were the vestiges of black Republicanism, and one of the sponsors, I. S. Leevy, had run for Congress in South Carolina as a Republican. On February 15, Strom canceled this speaking engagement, giving as his reason, "it now appears that a political organization of wide significance is sponsoring the meeting." The unnamed organization Thurmond suspected was the NAACP.

Indeed, the NAACP was active in the state at that time. In June of 1947, a black South Carolinian, John W. Wrighten, tried to enroll in the University of South Carolina's law school and was denied admittance. To press his case, Wrighten was provided an attorney in the employ of the NAACP. The attorney was Thurgood Marshall, who later became a U.S. Supreme Court justice.

Thurmond's refusal to address the Lincoln Emancipation Club meeting should not be extrapolated to the belief that he would not address any black group. On March 28 of that year, Strom spoke to the three thousand black teachers of the Palmetto State Teachers Association at their convention in Columbia.

One of the challenges faced by Strom very early in his service as governor involved a racial question of extreme import. His handling of this case drew praise from black South Carolinians and was noted by several northeastern newspapers. The incident in question was the lynching of a black man for the murder of a white cab driver in Greenville, South Carolina.

The Lynching of Willie Earl and Strom's Response

Thomas Watson Brown did not want to be a cab driver. He was a World War I veteran who had been wounded in the defense of his country. The wound made Brown unfit for any kind of work except cabbing, which allowed him to take time off when he was not feeling well.

Willie Earl was a young black man who had a job as a truck driver. Unfortunately, he was also epileptic, and despite efforts by his friends to hide the fact, his illness was discovered and he lost his job. His only recourse was to work as a construction laborer, a job at lower pay. His attitude began to suffer and as it did, he began to drink. After assaulting his boss on the construction crew, Earl spent a short time in jail.

On the night of February 15, 1947, Earl decided to visit his mother in nearby Pickens County. He called a cab—one driven by Tom Brown. Later that night, Brown was found, near death, and on February 16, Earl was arrested and put in a Pickens County jail. At 5:00 A.M. on February 17, Earl was abducted from his cell at gunpoint and killed by about thirty white men. This was the first mob murder of a black crime suspect in fourteen years in South Carolina, and Governor Thurmond was incensed (as he had been years earlier at the night-riding Klan activities in Greenville).

Thurmond ordered the chief constable of the state, Joel Townsend, to use "every facility at his disposal until this case has been completely solved." Thurmond went on record that he was determined "to do everything within my power to hold those involved responsible to the courts of this state. This crime is a disgrace to the state. Such offenses against decency, law and the democratic way of living will not be tolerated by the law abiding citizens of this state."[19]

In addition to the use of state constables, Thurmond requested that an outside prosecutor be brought in to ensure a vigorous prosecution of anyone apprehended and charged in the case—the first time ever that whites had been charged in a case of this nature. The arrest of such people may not seem shocking—today, we would expect it—but at that time, white men who lynched blacks were never brought to trial. Witnesses could never be found who could give accurate testimony.

This case came to trial on May 5 and the New York *Times* gave it detailed coverage, writing that "leading and responsible citizens point with pride to the incidents of high-minded courage that brought about the arrest and indictment of the defendants with such dispatch. A large share of the credit is given to the youthful new Governor, J. Strom Thurmond. . . . There seems little doubt that Governor Thurmond has earned the enmity of the purveyors of race hatred. . . . Negro leaders here [in South Carolina] assert that if their race had primary voting privileges they could easily cancel out any white 'resentment votes' as a Negro gesture of gratitude to Governor Thurmond."[20] And there were whites who resented his actions. Thurmond received hate mail, some of it unsigned. He maintained his position, however, asserting that justice must be done.

Despite their shock at being arrested, the defendants had enough sense to hire an outstanding attorney to handle their defense: Thomas Wofford of Greenville. (Wofford was a Thurmond acquaintance and the two would have occasions for cooperation in the future, but at the time they were on opposite sides of the fence.) For Thurmond and the law-abiding citizens of the state, the outcome of the trial was disappointing. An all-white male jury acquitted twenty-one of the defendants and another seven were freed through a directed verdict from the judge. With the exclusion of the time already spent in jail by the defendants, no time was served for the murder of Willie Earl. But the arrest and trial of the perpetrators had a sobering effect on racial violence. By his firm response, Thurmond had demonstrated that this type of incident would no longer be tolerated. This was the last recorded incident of lynching in South Carolina.

Back on the Warpath

By July the state legislature had gone home, but Governor Thurmond still had business to complete. One issue that came up early in the month was that of dual office holding. He had campaigned against it, and the state supreme court had reaffirmed its illegality. Strom had been putting pressure on those who held two public posts—privately and otherwise—to relinquish one of the posts. State Senator E. W. Cantrell was one of those serving in two positions. In addition to his state senate seat, Cantrell also served as a member of the Clark's Hill board (the previously mentioned power project on the Savannah River). Cantrell finally resigned his Clark's Hill position, claiming poor health as a reason. Thurmond's response was somewhat caustic: "I care not what reason they assign so long as they resign," he said. Thurmond then appointed his law partner, J. Fred Buzhardt, to the position while continuing to call for the resignation of state Senator Edgar A. Brown from the same board.[21]

Later in July Thurmond was handed another political fight as the S.C. Highway Commission dismissed Chief Highway Commissioner J. S. Williamson and replaced him with Claud R. McMillan. The press speculated that the move was part of a Thurmond-led reprisal against Williamson for the use of highway patrolmen in the campaign of James McLeod, Strom's strongest opponent in the gubernatorial race.

Thurmond's summer plans called for him to attend the national governor's meeting in Salt Lake City. The air of politics hung heavily over that meeting, as its attendees included Thomas E. Dewey of New York (the eventual Republican presidential nominee in 1948) and Earl Warren of California (Dewey's running mate and later chief justice of the U.S. Supreme Court). Somewhat closer to home, Strom had the chance to get to know Fielding Wright of Mississippi—and this tandem would make their own election history in 1948. Strom was one of the speakers at the conference, and his topic—somewhat out of place for a governor—was mobilization. He asserted that "our first concern must be the taking of effective measures to safeguard our own freedom." Strom advised that the nation would be prepared for total mobilization if the need arose to confront the communist menace.[22]

As the summer wore on, Thurmond became involved in a controversial appointment, this one involving his selection of

James J. Reid as chairman of the Industrial Commission. On August 29, S.C. Attorney General John M. Daniel had issued an opinion that this appointment was "invalid." One state newspaper, the Anderson *Independent*, called this a "terrific setback" for Governor Thurmond.

Thurmond's response was to insist that the attorney general's opinion was merely that, an opinion, and that Reid was still a member of the commission. On September 6, four other members of the Industrial Commission called on Reid to resign, and he obliged them on September 9 of that year. As in many other conflicts, Thurmond had the last word. He reappointed Reid, who received Senate confirmation when the 1948 legislative session began and resumed his seat on January 14, 1948.

On September 16, 1947, Strom addressed the South Carolina Realtors' meeting in Myrtle Beach, and perhaps still rankled at the Industrial Commission situation, Thurmond took that opportunity to attack the housing situation—particularly with regard to rental rates in the state. Declaring that he was outraged, he assured the Realtors that he would "do everything in my power to help keep rent controls until some degree of sanity returns to profiteering real estate owners." The assembled real estate professionals were furious that Thurmond would attack their practices at their own convention. One of Strom's colleagues, Governor Jim "Kissin' Jim" Folsom of Alabama, sent Strom a telegram congratulating him on his stand, however.

The Realtors did not take the attack lying down. On October 14, William M. Means of Charleston attacked the governor's own profiteering in his sale of the Edgefield Hotel. Means noted that Strom had bought it from the receivers of the People's State Bank in 1937 for $14,000 and sold it for $60,000 in 1947.[23] Strom's response was that he had spent "between $30–40,000 in new furniture and for remodeling. I sold the hotel for a very reasonable profit."[24]

While Thurmond was not making any points with Realtors, he was making a pitch for the support of South Carolina's women. In a September 30 speech to the Georgetown Lion's Club (on Ladies' Night), he said, "There is no reason why we shouldn't have women in executive and elective offices." He reiterated his inaugural message when he added that women should receive equal pay for equal work and should be allowed to serve on juries. Later, he prepared an article for the November issue of the *South Carolina Club Woman* magazine, in which he noted that "I have appointed and will appoint women to various positions. But I will not appoint them simply because they are women—in order to give women some representation. I will appoint them because they are public spirited citizens."[25]

Thurmond made good on this promise, and he took the additional step of appointing several women to serve as "full colonels" on his honorary military staff. (In those days, governors often awarded the honorary title of "colonel" to citizens in the state. When women were appointed, they had traditionally been given the rank of lieutenant colonel. Strom opposed this practice and noted, "I do not believe in halfway measures."

For the balance of the year, Thurmond's public attention was devoted to three issues: politics, his future, and the burgeoning issue of race relations in the South. On the political front, a story broke in October that he had assembled an "enemies list" containing the names of seven state officials he wanted removed from office. Thurmond called the charges "just so much poppycock" and stated that the story was an effort to put him on the spot because of the upcoming fight in the legislature regarding his efforts to reorganize state government. One humorous sidelight to this incident was Senator Edgar Brown's pretended dismay about not being included on the list.

Thurmond also began some serious thinking about his own political future. The next logical step for South Carolina governors had been the U.S. Senate. Senator Burnet R. Maybank was up for reelection in 1948. While Maybank was perceived as potentially weak, two problems confronted Strom. First, he had promised to serve his entire four-year term as governor, which would not expire until 1950; and second, Maybank was a friend. However, Senator Olin D. Johnston's term expired in 1950, and there was no love lost between Johnston and Thurmond. The obvious choice, then was to oppose Johnston in 1950. Another obvious point was that work must be started early to defeat an incumbent.

Despite rumors that were circulating as early as October 10 that Thurmond would be a candidate for Maybank's Senate seat, he had probably already decided to oppose Johnston. That same month, Thurmond released to the press the names of forty-nine convicts who were paroled without state supervision when Johnston was governor. (Ostensibly, the purpose of this publicity was to dramatize Strom's call for acts limiting the pardoning and parole power of the governor. The recurrence of this issue in the 1950 senatorial campaign supports the theory that it was also an early salvo in a long battle.)

The final major public issue of Thurmond's first year as governor involved the increasing impetus toward racial equality in the South. The first major blow to the segregated nature of the state's political system was struck on July 12 when U.S. District Judge J. Waites Waring ruled that blacks were entitled to be enrolled to vote in the Democratic primaries in South Carolina. The ruling was the result of a case filed by George Elmore against the Richland County Democratic Executive Committee and Democratic Club.

Some explanation of the political situation is necessary to clarify this case. As has been mentioned previously, the only real political party in South Carolina from the mid-1870s until the 1960s was the Democratic party. State laws limiting participation in the Democratic party to whites were on the books until 1944. At that time, fearing that legislation would enable the courts to rule on the legality of all-white primaries, the state repealed all laws regulating primary elections. The state Democratic party operated as a private club with the hope that its private nature would prohibit judicial interference. This hope proved to be forlorn, as Judge Waring's ruling illustrated.

On October 10, another battle was enjoined when state NAACP President J. M. Hinton said that the group would sue for admittance of blacks in "all of the facilities of tax supported institutions." This was one of the first times that a black leader had publicly attacked the principle of "separate but equal." Until then, the quest had been for equality in the funding of separate institutions.

The state's white leadership did not have much time to ponder this new approach, for they were busy dealing with the more direct attack on their power—Judge Waring's ruling. The state's Democratic party appealed the ruling to the Fourth U.S. Circuit Court of Appeals, and on December 30, Judge John J. Parker, writing for the majority, upheld Judge Waring's ruling. The opinion affirmed that "no election machinery can be upheld if its purpose or effect is to deny the Negro, on account of his race or color, an effective voice in the government."[26]

Thurmond played almost no public part in the efforts to appeal the decision. One thing that should be established at this point is his reverence for the law. He forced himself to look at laws as they were intended—even if he personally disagreed with the intent (as perhaps was the case in regard to Thurmond's previously noted support of check-off provisions for union dues). This was purely a judicial matter, and Strom left it to the courts, but it certainly contributed to the climate that existed during his first year as governor.

These items—politics, personal ambition, and racial questions—all set the stage for the events of 1948. Before that however, Thurmond took a brief respite from being a "public man." Somewhere in the frantic pace of returning from the war, resuming his career as judge, running for governor, being elected, and beginning his service, Strom had decided to marry.

Chapter 7

THURMOND AND HIS BRIDE

I nsight into a public person is often obtained through inspection of their private lives and families—their parents, the
people they marry, and their children. In the case of
Strom Thurmond, his close relationship with his father (and its
impact on his life) was clearly recognizable. And throughout the
years, Strom also kept in close contact with his mother. His interactions with his brothers and sisters were as frequent as the
schedule of a busy person permitted. And he always exhibited an
understanding of "family" responsibilities, including the practice
of hiring relatives when they were qualified for employment.

Thurmond's relationships with women, however, were desul-
tory and difficult to fathom. As a young man, he exhibited an
interest in women—he dated frequently. But he never took these
relationships seriously. Indeed, he was known for showing up late
for dates or even canceling them if something more important or
more interesting came up. Generally, the more "important" thing
was work-related. It is safe to say that as a young man, Strom was
married to his career. He pursued his life's ambitions to the
exclusion of some aspects of personal happiness that many feel are
important—such as marriage and family.

If Strom suffered from the vacant aspects of his life, there was
no overt show of it. Indeed, his single status was of real value to
him as he climbed the ladder to a successful career in public
service.

First, as a young man, Thurmond was a hard worker—workaholic
may not even be too extreme a description. Remember that he had
a full-time position as superintendent of education when he studied law. Thereafter, he continued to serve as superintendent while
also practicing as an attorney. As a member of the state senate, he
maintained a vigorous law practice and still had time for a state

leadership role in the Junior Order. In addition, he was constantly looking for and accepting speech-making opportunities. A politician with ambition spoke wherever and whenever there was a chance. Strom has been constantly making speeches since the mid-1920s.

Of course, many individuals seeking public life have done these things while being married and raising a family. But Thurmond's refusal to do so enabled him to devote his time single-mindedly to achieving his goals. Yet another aspect of being single that might have served him well was in the area of his personal courage. How likely was it that a married judge would have decided to walk, unarmed, into the middle of a bloodbath as Strom did in the Logue incident?

Further, how many married middle-aged judges (with legitimate deferments) would have volunteered for military service and requested active duty assignments for themselves on D-Day? This is not to suggest that married men do not have courage—certainly married men have served in all our country's military conflicts and many have exhibited outstanding bravery—but it would have been a mitigating factor. For whatever reason, Strom had complete freedom of action in all his decisions—he was responsible for no one but himself—and this served him well.

This changed abruptly when he returned from his military service and was elected governor. Of course, Strom was in no position for courtship while he was running for governor, but immediately after realizing his stated childhood ambition—becoming governor—he set out to find a wife. His choice astounded everyone: he selected a young lady twenty-three years his junior.

Jean Crouch

Born to Horace and Inez Brezeale Crouch on July 14, 1926, Jean Crouch was the youngest of four children. The family lived in Elko, a small farm village in Barnwell County where her father served as the county superintendent of education. As a child, Jean was active in outdoor activities as well as being musically talented: she played the piano, violin, and saxophone. At Williston-Elko High School, Jean was a member of the girls' basketball team. She also racked up a fair number of school honors, such as being a member of the Beta Club (scholastic achievement), valedictorian, winner of the Daughters of the American Revolution Medal for Good Citizenship, and, ironically, the Solomon Blatt Medal for Expression.[1]

After graduating from high school in 1943, Jean entered Winthrop College in Rock Hill, where she majored in commerce with the intention of teaching secretarial studies. While a student at Winthrop, Jean was active in dramatics and the Baptist Student Union. Whatever Jean's career plans may have been, her world was changed dramatically when Strom Thurmond decided she was the woman for him.[2]

The Courtship

The historical record of the relationship between Strom and Jean is preserved in letters between them and in the news articles of the day. As Strom was a public man, his relationship was also public. Strom had apparently first noticed Jean when she was fifteen years old. The incident occurred in the fall of 1941 when Jean's high school class came to observe a session of the court presided over by Judge Thurmond in Barnwell County. Her father, Barnwell County Superintendent of Education Horace Crouch, called his daughter up to meet Thurmond. At that first meeting, Strom told the young lady she had pretty eyes, and she never forgot the compliment.[3]

In the spring of 1946, during a visit to Winthrop, Strom saw her briefly. Later that year, as governor-elect, ostensibly on a fact-finding tour regarding education, Strom visited Horace Crouch and inquired about his daughter. Upon learning that the young lady would be attending a S.C. Education Association meeting in November, Strom decided to place himself on the program.[4]

Strom then arranged with Winthrop President Henry Sims for a group of the student leaders to attend his inauguration, and among them was Jean Crouch, senior class president.[5] On another occasion when a Winthrop contingent visited the state capital, Strom invited Jean to have lunch with him and his sister at the Governor's Mansion. Shortly after that, their relationship began—and it was very formal and supervised from the beginning.[6]

In March Strom invited Jean to attend the American Legion horse races held in Columbia, carefully suggesting that she bring along a girlfriend. During spring break that year, Strom had Jean visit the Governor's Mansion again, (chaperoned) and at the end of the visit gave her some gifts including perfume. Jean no doubt suspected that Strom's interest was more than that of a public official interested in bright students in his state, but at first, she took pains to keep the relationship on a formal basis. Her "thank-you" note was addressed "Dear Governor Thurmond" and was closed with "Always." Strom, however, had no intention of letting the situation remain constant, and on April 19, he appointed Jean as "Miss South Carolina" of the Azalea Festival that was held annually in Charleston.[7]

After Jean's trip to Charleston, she changed the tone of her communications somewhat. In her salutations, she called him "Governor" and closed her letters with "Love." She was even so bold as to suggest to Strom that he had better "not leave Rock Hill without at least calling me."[8] For his part, Strom did everything he could to let her know he was personally interested. He gave her gifts and by May of that year, had decided to offer Jean a job in Columbia so that she would be close by.[9] He made his offer with the understanding that if she went to work directly in his office they would not be able to have any further personal contact but intimated that if she worked in another state agency their personal time could be expanded. When Jean chose to work directly in Strom's office, the relationship cooled considerably—at least for the short term. Jean turned down an invitation to visit, and she returned to using the salutation "Governor Thurmond" and closed her letters again with "Always."[10]

To Strom, given his personal interest, Jean's decision to work directly in his office was a real blow. Of course, he had really thought she would be an asset to the state or he would not have offered the position, and he made it clear he was willing to accept her decision. (Later, though, after things heated up between them, he asked her why she had chosen to work in his office when he told her a personal relationship would then be virtually out of the question. Jean replied that she intended to be in his presence constantly so he could not forget her.)[11] This little interchange demonstrates the kind of relationship they had: the kind of innocent love you might expect between two starry-eyed adolescents.

After graduation, Jean took a short trip and reported to the governor, by letter, that her intentions were to report to work on June 30.[12] The situation between them was still somewhat frosty due to Strom's acknowledgement of the impropriety of having someone of personal interest on his staff. This interest did not prevent him from inviting Jean (and another stenographer) to attend the national governor's conference in Salt Lake City that year. On this trip, the governor studiously ignored Jean until she made a point of it, and from that point on the relationship blossomed.[13]

Just how far the relationship progressed was demonstrated in a letter Jean wrote to Strom in August: she called him "Sweetheart," told him she missed him, and alluded to a "city" woman Strom would be seeing on a trip to New York. She wrote, "Have you seen her yet? I really want you to be with her, so you can be sure of yourself when you return to South Carolina. Have a grand time, but please miss your little country girl—no talents, political influence, or money—but who loves you with all her heart."[14]

Strom called her the next day, and she wrote another letter that she assured him was not written on "State time." But it, too, had the urgent tone of adolescent love: "Don't forget that I'm thinking of you constantly and sending you, My love always."[15] And by the end of the week, she had told Strom, for the first time in writing, "I love you."[16]

Lest it seem that this was all one-sided, remember that Strom continued to play an active role in leading the relationship toward his desired goal—marriage. By September 9, their relationship had reached the point that Jean suspected a marriage proposal was imminent. On that day, she wrote her parents seeking approval—in case a proposal was forthcoming.

Strom's method of proposing was notable. He called Jean into his office of September 13 and dictated his proposal to her. "You have proved to be a most efficient and capable secretary. It is with a deep sense of regret that I will have to inform you that your services will be discontinued as of the last day of this month. Your qualities have been appreciated by all of us here in the office, and I know that you will be greatly missed, however, I must confess that I love you dearly and want you for my own." Strom closed his dictated proposal with "anticipating an early reply and hope that it shall be forthcoming as quickly as possible, as upon your answer will depend my future happiness. Yours in love."[17] When she brought it back for him to sign, he corrected two typographical errors and sent it back to be retyped. Jean's one word answer, also typed, was "Yes!" and she waited until the end of the business day to deliver it.[18]

After Strom had her acceptance, the excited couple traveled to Elko so Strom could formally request the honor of her hand—from her parents. Getting the approval was not easy, as Mr. Crouch seemed unable to deal with the problem at hand; he kept talking instead about one of his mules. With some exasperation, Strom turned to Mrs. Crouch, who also had reservations concerning the marriage.[19] Strom, however, was not to be denied. At the end of the conversation he said, "Well, as long as you haven't voiced any objections, I'll conclude that at least you don't object." This bit of lawyer's logic put a good face on a less than perfect situation. Indeed, Jean's parents were not very happy at the thought of the impending marriage; they were concerned for the future happiness of their daughter.[20]

How different the times were then—that the governor of South Carolina should actually seek permission to marry someone of legal age in 1947 seems remarkable. His desire to get this permission can be attributed to his upbringing and also, perhaps, to his desire for some concrete sign of approval from Jean's parents— which was not forthcoming.

Even in the absence of an objection (and with the willing consent of his bride-to-be), Strom was hesitant to make a formal announcement. The stories of other amorous governors, such as "Kissin' Jim" Folsom of Alabama (the recipient of a paternity suit) were circulating, so the timing had to be just right. The perceptive office staff was already speculating about the relationship between Strom and Jean by late August,[21] and by October 2, the press began speculating that there might be a wife for the governor.[22]

On October 12, Strom and Jean attended a football game between Furman and the University of South Carolina, and that same day, the engagement was announced to the state. For his part, Strom reacted to his impending nuptials as any young man would—he was excited. In his excitement, the day before the wedding, Strom impetuously stood on his head to demonstrate his fitness for a Life magazine photographer. The full-page photo was accompanied by a derisive caption that began, "Virile governor demonstrates his prowess." (This incident would haunt Thurmond politically for years.)

After the announcement, Thurmond the politician must have been completely dominated by Thurmond the man. This seasoned war hero had faced German fire with composure, but his excitement about marrying the girl of his dreams made him act uncharacteristically.

Women, then, may be Strom's blind spot. This is not to suggest that Strom was, is, or has ever been a "womanizer." Indeed, his strict moral code forbade it. But his southern attitudes concerning women (sainthood for mothers and pedestals for others) certainly came into play in this first marriage. Indeed this relationship is so innocent one feels abashed to read their correspondence. Although everything about a public person's life is theoretically public, a good case could be made to leave out this part of Strom's story—it was so obviously not part of his politics that it seems out of place.

Yet this story, perhaps above all others, may reveal the most human part of Thurmond's life. Here, in the middle of a life dominated by a machine-like ambition, is an island of affection and warmth that broke down all of his previously erected defenses. When Strom stood on his head, it was an utterly uncalculated gesture, a truly spontaneous action motivated by genuine emotion. And as will be shown, Strom's devotion to Jean remained constant and fervent throughout her lifetime.

As the year 1947 headed to a close, the staff at the Governor's Mansion prepared for a wedding. On Friday, November 7, less than thirty days after making their public announcement, and under a sky that threatened rain, Jean Crouch and Strom Thurmond were married at noon in a small ceremony that included only family and a few close friends. After a two-week honeymoon trip to Miami and Havana, the Thurmonds settled down to what passes for domestic tranquility at the Governor's Mansion.

A New First Lady

With her marriage to Strom, Jean became the state's youngest first lady since 1789 when Governor Charles Pinckney brought his eighteen-year-old bride, Mary Eleanor Laurens, to the capital. The initial announcement and rapid marriage of Jean Crouch to Strom Thurmond produced varying degrees of shock across the state. No one questioned the right of the governor to marry. The controversy was the direct result of Jean's age and her position in state government as a secretary in the governor's office. (There were no charges of misappropriation of government funds; the office romance aspect merely added heightened interest.)

The avid interest of the people in the state is evidenced by the turnout at a November 30 reception hosted by the governor to introduce his new bride. Over five thousand people showed up at the Governor's Mansion to meet her (more than attended Strom's inaugural as governor). And as time passed, the people of the state came to embrace the first lady with a devotion and affection that is reminiscent of America's fascination with Jacqueline Kennedy Onassis. The women of the state were particularly fond of the impression made by the state's new first lady.

Jean Thurmond was the image of a model wife of the day: she was publicly devoted to her husband and to the good he could do for the state. This is not to suggest that she was a wallflower; on occasion, she was moved to speak up, as in her first interview with the Columbia Record. In it, Jean suggested that the state should "tax the wealth where it is and educate the children where they are."[23] (Under the tutelage of the governor, Jean later came to recant this "share the wealth" approach.) But for the most part, she played the more traditional role of First Lady.

Indeed, a close examination of Strom's actions while they were married shows little evidence that Jean held any advisorial role except the role that spouses normally play in the lives of their mates. While she critiqued speeches and commented beforehand on some of his intended actions, Jean's opinion was not necessarily sought nor followed on important issues. For instance, Strom made a variety of decisions without even consulting Jean, including his decision to accept the presidential nomination of the States' Rights party in 1948.

That instance did not appear to have been an unfeeling act, merely an unthinking one. Thurmond had been making decisions based purely on his own needs for so long that he did not realize he should now consult someone else before he made decisions. But he showed no inclination to change the pattern much.

Jean's attitude on this (and other things) is reminiscent of that archetypal southern belle, Scarlett O'Hara of *Gone with the Wind* fame. Indeed, one of Jean's favorite expressions was "I'm sure everything will turn out all right in the end. I'm not going to think about it any more right now."[24]

For the balance of Thurmond's term as governor, his candidacy for president in 1948, and throughout his two tumultuous campaigns for the U.S. Senate in 1950 and 1954, Jean Thurmond stood by and supported her husband—right or wrong. Her face became increasingly familiar to the people of South Carolina, who developed a strong loyalty to her. Her untimely death only served to further endear her to those in her state.

All of that was still ahead of the happy couple, however, as they approached the year 1948. For Strom, the world was a great place. He had accomplished his lifetime ambition and had married a beautiful young woman in the span of a year. But, as had happened before in his career, events soon transpired that would alter his focus and put him on a path he did not appear to choose for himself.

The catalyst was a report issued by President Harry Truman's Civil Rights Committee, "To Secure These Rights," and the president's decision to push the recommendations spelled out in the report. As a part of the South's organized response, Thurmond would be drafted as a presidential candidate for the States' Rights party. If he had ever nursed any serious ambition about the highest office in the land, he kept it to himself. And when the opportunity presented itself, it was not the situation he would have hoped for—yet once again, Strom astounded the political insiders, if not himself, by accepting the challenge.

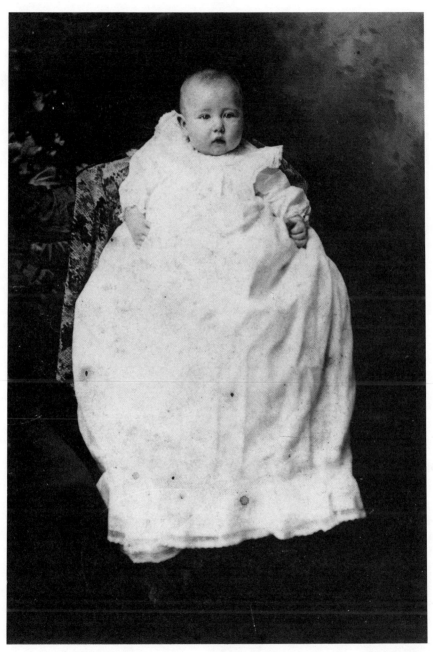

Baby photograph of Strom Thurmond

John William Thurmond, father of Strom, circa 1910

Strom with his mother, Gertrude Strom Thurmond, at home in Edgefield,
December 1946

John William Thurmond with gubernatorial candidate Ira B. Jones, circa 1912; it was at this meeting when ten year old Strom decided that he would be governor of S.C. one day.

Ninth grade at Edgefield High School (1917–18);
Strom is second from the right on the first row

With the 1923 track team at Clemson College;
Strom is second from the right on the first row

While teaching in Edgefield, Strom spent his summers at the Summer School for Farm Boys at Erskine College (1925)

With Governor Maybank in 1939
(Strom was serving as a judge at that point)

Driving a captured German vehicle near St. Mere-Eglise (1944)

Campaigning for Governor in 1946 in Spartanburg with John Long, Del O'Neal, and Dr. James McLeod

Chapter 8

THURMOND

FOR PRESIDENT

E lection eve, November 1, 1948, saw four principal contenders for the office of president of the United States. The
universally acknowledged front-runner was the Republican nominee, Governor Thomas E. Dewey of New York. Dewey
had run a good race against Franklin Delano Roosevelt in 1944 and
was considered a shoe-in in the 1948 race. Nipping at his heels was
President Truman, who had succeeded to the presidency upon the
death of FDR. While Truman had been counted out, his aggressive
whistlestop campaigning and his faith in the "little people" had
buoyed the spirits of the nation.

The third contender was Henry A. Wallace. Wallace had been
FDR's third-term vice president but had left the Democratic party
to run for president on the Progressive ticket. Wallace's positions
were so liberal that even the left-oriented Americans for Democratic Action (ADA) had publicly charged that Wallace's third-
party effort was a tool of the Communists.[1]

The other contender was the candidate of the States' Rights
Democratic party. While the other candidates hoped to win outright, that is, by collecting enough electoral votes to be elected, the
States' Rights candidate was really running to lose. If he could
garner enough electoral votes to prevent a win by Dewey or
Truman, the Congress would have to decide who would be president. The goal of the States' Rights party was preserving segregation in the South—and if the election went to Congress, they would
have some bargaining chips.

On election eve, while the other candidates were surrounded by
their aides and newsmen, the States' Rights candidate, Governor
Strom Thurmond, ate a quiet dinner with his wife at the Governor's
Mansion in Columbia, and calmly awaited news of the election.

Despite late predictions of a Dewey victory, the outcome was still in doubt. Now, as the votes began to roll in, each candidate had the opportunity to reflect on the chain of circumstances that had created this unique situation in American politics. No one had more to reflect on than Strom Thurmond.

Civil Rights and President Truman

Most candidates for public office have an issue. Many times these issues are positive statements about programs they would like to see enacted. The campaign of the States' Rights Democrats was largely a negative campaign. Not advocating any programs, instead they preached the politics of reaction. President Truman had given them plenty of ammunition with his efforts on behalf of civil rights.

Early in his administration, President Truman had authorized a commission to study the question of racial discrimination, predominantly in federal programs. In October of 1947, this commission had issued a far-ranging report titled "To Secure These Rights." This report recommended enactment of federal legislation to make lynching and poll taxes illegal. These goals were aimed at practices in many southern states that either did not protect the rights of black citizens or sought to prevent them from participating in the electoral process. Another proposal was the implementation of a Fair Employment Practices Commission (FEPC). This commission was to guarantee equal employment opportunities for members of both races.

On February 2, 1948, President Truman went before Congress to ask that legislation be enacted to implement these proposals. By doing so, he touched off a southern storm, the sole goal of which was to blow him out of office. Immediately after Truman sent his proposal to Congress, charges arose among white southern politicians that Truman sought to buy black northern votes with his stand on civil rights. Southern leaders were incensed that he would attack the traditions the South held dear. Governor William M. Tuck of Virginia had suggested that the South (which had almost unanimously supported Democratic presidential candidates since the late 1870s) could deny Truman over a hundred electoral votes. He went even further and suggested that the Virginia delegates be allowed to attend the national Democratic convention without any instructions so they could vote for whomever they chose.

In South Carolina Governor Thurmond held a little ceremony to celebrate his break with Truman's policies. He invited newsmen into his office and pointed to a blank place on the wall that had held Truman's personally autographed picture. After predicting that Truman would be defeated, Strom then promised the southern press that "we definitely do not intend to take this thing lying down. We are going to fight it to the end."[2]

Other South Carolina politicians agreed wholeheartedly. Senator Olin Johnston suggested holding two state Democratic conventions—one before the national convention and one after to "survey the situation." The Jasper city Democratic party seceded from the national party at a meeting attended by twenty-five hundred people.[3] On March 1, the S.C. Democratic Executive Committee unanimously adopted a resolution opposing the nomination and election of Truman and proposed a conference of southern Democrats to develop a way to "make the weight and principles of the South felt in national party councils."[4] As has often been the case in the history of South Carolina, the state hurried out on a limb and brought a saw.

Almost immediately, U.S. Senator Howard J. McGrath, chairman of the Democratic party, sent out feelers to various southern leaders to gauge the sentiment. The word came back quickly—dump Truman. A survey of southern delegates to the national convention presented even stronger evidence; they were prepared to bolt the national convention (and possibly the party) if strong civil rights planks were put into the platform of the Democratic party and if Truman was the party's nominee.[5]

McGrath held a meeting in Washington with various southern leaders on February 23. They told McGrath they wanted reinstatement of the two-thirds rule at the National Democratic Convention. By requiring a two-thirds majority to nominate a presidential candidate, the South had been able to exercise a sort of veto power over the party's presidential nominees. This provision had been abandoned at the request of FDR, but the southerners wanted it back. McGrath's answer did nothing to bring the South back into the party—his answer was no.

With negotiations at a standstill, southern leaders met again to talk strategy. On March 13, seven southern governors met in Washington to talk about the upcoming presidential election. They were James E. Folsom of Alabama, Beauford Jester of Texas, Preston Lane of Maryland, Ben Laney of Arkansas, M. E. Thompson of Georgia, Strom Thurmond of South Carolina, and Fielding

Wright of Mississippi. (Senator Harry F. Byrd was also present representing Governor William M. Tuck of Virginia).

Six of the governors (all but Lane of Maryland) voted to "fight to the last ditch" against anyone advocating passage of a civil rights program, but at Thurmond's urging, they took no precipitate actions, instead agreed to a "cooling off" period and made a decision to meet again.[6]

With the rising storm against Truman, even some northern politicians began to get skittish about him. Veteran Boston politician James M. Curley suggested that the Democratic party begin looking for someone else; in his opinion, Truman could not be elected. This pronouncement followed on the heels of a move by many national Democrats to draft General Dwight D. Eisenhower as their nominee.

To put this anti-civil rights movement into some perspective, the southern states were involved in a struggle to preserve their segregated society. Even as they fought efforts in the political arena, the court system was tearing down one segregationist institution after another. One of these decisions came right in the middle of the pre-campaign rhetoric. On April 19, the U.S. Supreme Court upheld a lower court's ruling that blacks had the right to vote in the South Carolina Democratic primaries. (All the state's laws dealing with primaries had been repealed in 1944 at the urging of Governor Olin Johnston so that the Democratic party in South Carolina could assert the claim that it was a private club. With its decision, the Supreme Court affirmed that no action was acceptable that denied blacks the right to participate in the political system.)

With the Supreme Court ruling going against them, the southern leaders were thrown into the unenviable position of campaigning against rights for people who could now vote them out of office. Following the Supreme Court decision, state Democratic Chairman William P. Baskin ordered that seven hundred blacks who had registered for the Columbia city primary should be allowed to vote. Upon hearing the Supreme Court decision, Governor Thurmond stated that "every American had lost a part of his fundamental rights."[7] He was quickly called to task by J. M. Hinton, president of the NAACP, who wrote Thurmond that his response was "below the expectancy and dignity of the office held by you."[8]

The Democrats in Jackson, Mississippi, dropped a bombshell of their own when their Democratic Executive Committee met on April 23 and chose as their presidential candidate Strom Thurmond of South Carolina. Unless he was nominated at the national convention, Mississippi urged all the southern states to bolt the party. Normally, Thurmond was not at a loss for words about anything, but this caught him off guard. His statement to the press was simply, "I was surprised."

The states with the largest black populations were the ones most concerned with the loss of legal segregation. As two of the southern states with the largest numbers of black residents (the others being Alabama and Louisiana), the actions of Mississippi and South Carolina were almost predictable.

The next step was also predictable. A meeting of southern Democrats was called for May 10 in Jackson, Mississippi. On the eve of the meeting, Governor Wright of Mississippi took to the radio to lecture his black citizens on the effect of civil rights activities. In a speech reminiscent of King John: "Villains ye are, villains ye shall remain;" Wright told his constituents. "I must tell you that regardless of any recommendation of President Truman, despite any law passed by Congress, and no matter what is said to you. . . . There will continue to be segregation between the races in Mississippi."[9]

At the May 10 meeting, twelve hundred representatives from twelve southern states gathered to hear the plan of attack for dealing with Truman. (The only southern state not represented was Georgia.) Three state governors were present: Ben Laney of Arkansas, Thurmond, and Fielding Wright of Mississippi. When his turn came to speak, Thurmond attacked Truman: "Never did we dream that a Democratic president would stab us in the back and in one fell swoop seek to impose federal laws more detrimental to the south and the nation than those proposed in the Reconstruction period by the Republican Party."[10] This issue, in part, goes a long way toward explaining the vehemence with which many white southerners opposed these moves. During Reconstruction, the radical Republicans had stripped all white southerners of political power and replaced them with blacks and northern carpetbaggers. In effect, the South was occupied territory for some fifteen years after the war ended. This memory remained strong in the hearts and minds of southerners. Truman's actions were akin to pouring gasoline on an open flame—and the fire blazed.

The upshot of this meeting, however, was that the southern Democrats would meet again on July 17 in Birmingham, Alabama, if the national party adopted a program inconsistent with states' rights. What that really meant was that the group would meet

again if the national Democratic party failed to support segregation. (One result of this May 10 meeting was a nickname for the
group. The name, Dixiecrats, was coined by Pete McKnight, the
managing editor of the Charlotte *News*. He was looking for a way
to lump the various elements together and suggested they "ought
to adopt it." The official name, however, was States' Rights Democrats, and they often corrected those who referred to them otherwise.)

In the last major offensive before the national democratic convention, the South Carolina Democrats held their state convention
on May 19 in Columbia. The convention was supposed to be a test
of wills, not only between regular Democrats and States' Rights
Democrats but also between Strom Thurmond and U.S. Senator
Olin Johnston. The first battle was expected to be over the keynote
speaker, but no battle developed. Supposedly, Johnston forces
would nominate someone other than Thurmond's choice, and the
election would be a contest of strength between Johnston and
Thurmond. Thurmond nominated Senator George Warren of
Hampton (who also carried the banner for the anti-civil rights
group), and he was elected without opposition. Speaking to a
cheering crowd, Warren told the national Democratic party, "We
owe you no allegiance. . . . They agitate for a social concept
[integration], the inevitable result of which is amalgamation of
races, and they would force this upon us knowing that such is
repulsive to us and repugnant to our ideals and traditions."

The expected intra-party squabble among Democrats did not
shape up either, since the convention voted to withhold all eight
electoral votes from the national party if Truman were the party's
nominee. The convention also nominated Thurmond for president
as a "favorite son," with the understanding that the delegates
were really elected as "anti-Truman" votes.

By that time, Truman had few friends in the South. In October
of 1947 his popularity in the South had been 59 percent; now in
May of 1948, a scant eight months later, it had dropped to 30
percent. Into this situation, the South prepared to send its delegates to the 1948 Democratic National Convention in Philadelphia—and the major battle that was sure to come.

National Politics

As the national showdown over civil rights moved closer, the
national Democratic party appeared ready to disintegrate. On the
left, Henry Wallace's candidacy seemed to be pulling away the

hard-core liberal vote generally guaranteed to support the Democratic nominee. On the right, the conservative southerners were on the warpath against Harry Truman. Other states were adding their voices to South Carolina's anti-Truman stance. Most alarming to the national Democrats was the attempt to draft General Eisenhower to run for president. To oust an incumbent president (even one who was elevated to the job by the death of a president) was almost unthinkable. Yet, two states, Virginia and New Jersey, had already instructed their delegate to vote for Ike if they had the opportunity. (In South Carolina, Thurmond agreed to free "his" delegates in the event that Ike was a candidate.)[11]

Shortly afterward, on July 9, Thurmond formally appealed to Truman to withdraw his candidacy. "The liberal-minded people of America, those who believe in progressive social and economic development of our country do not want a Republican administration."[12] Thurmond's statement sought to paint Truman's candidacy as aiding the Republicans. In this effort, he was not alone. Most of the national press was already naming Dewey as the president-elect. Only Truman, himself, seemed to be optimistic at this point.

The next day, July 10, the various state delegations began their presentations to the credentials committee of the national Democratic party in Philadelphia. A challenge had developed to South Carolina's all-white delegation from the S.C. Progressive (black) Democratic party. This group had presented an alternative slate of delegates to the credentials committee in hopes of unseating at least some of the delegates. The white South Carolina delegation was aided by Senator Johnston's seat on the credentials committee, and the challenge from the black slate was rejected.

Since most of the delegates were in Philadelphia, a caucus of southern delegates was called in the Crystal Ballroom of the Ben Franklin Hotel. The goal of the caucus was to organize a response to the intended civil rights planks and Truman's nomination. At that meeting, the attending delegates (only 125 out of a possible 600) heard Thurmond declare again that the South had been "stabbed in the back." Even at this late date, however, there was no real southern alternative. No leading southern politician had agreed to lead the movement and no counteroffensive had been framed.

When the national convention opened on July 12, there was no real opposition to Truman's nomination. There was no one to rally the southern delegates, so their strategy became one of mere

opposition. The first issue was the adoption of the Party's platform. While these platforms usually seem to have little relevance
to party actions (for both major political parties), this one had
major significance.

The southern delegates were insistent that no major planks be
added that showed support for civil rights. They threatened to
walk out of the convention if any such planks were adopted. (The
NAACP responded to these threats with a series of ads that ran in
Philadelphia newspapers, headed "Let 'em walk.") At this point,
the northern delegates were not in any mood to compromise. They
saw the splintering of the Democratic party and blamed it on the
southerners.

A rising star of the Democratic party, Minneapolis Mayor Hubert
H. Humphrey, led the tumultuous floor fight to approve planks
that basically supported President Truman's initiative. When the
smoke had cleared, the planks had been adopted by the narrow
margin of 651.5 to 582.5—and the entire Mississippi delegation
and half of Alabama's delegates had left the convention floor to
the boos of the delegates from the rest of the nation. The remaining
southern delegates then shifted their strategy to do what they
could to defeat Truman. Governor Laney of Arkansas was the
initial choice of the South to oppose Truman. Thurmond had
released South Carolina's delegates to support him, but Laney
disappointed them when he declined to be a candidate. After some
scrambling, the South closed ranks behind much-respected Senator Richard B. Russell of Georgia. Governor Thurmond was chosen
to give one of the seconding speeches. In it, he did his best to
present the South's actions as being predicated on the principles of
states' rights. To a chorus of boos, he went so far as to assert that
the rights of the states to govern their internal activities "cannot be
bartered away and will not be bartered away."[13]

All this was much too little, too late, Russell's nomination
received only token southern support, and Truman was easily
renominated. In a move to placate the South, Alben Barkley of
Kentucky was selected as the vice presidential nominee. This
action did little to soothe ruffled southern feelings, however. The
Mississippi delegation, led by their governor, Fielding Wright,
had formally called for a meeting of southern Democrats in Birmingham, and they were already there (along with a major portion
of the Alabama delegation) waiting on whichever southern states
might want to send representation.

Thurmond and the South Carolina delegation had returned to
their state after the convention with a wait-and-see attitude. When

the call came for the Birmingham meeting, Thurmond was some-what aloof. He had already committed to attend an inspection of a S.C. National Guard unit in training at Camp Stewart, Georgia. But other southern leaders began to pressure him to attend. Strom recalled, "Governor Wright, Governor Laney, and other southern leaders contacted me upon my return to Columbia . . . They said it was important for me to be at the Birmingham meeting . . . I informed them of my engagement at Camp Stewart but promised to go on to Birmingham from there. A change in time from Camp Stewart to Birmingham was helpful, and I went on to Alabama after completing my engagement at Camp Stewart."[14]

Leaving his wife in South Carolina, Thurmond traveled to Birmingham. Once there, events moved fast and Thurmond's political instincts trailed behind his desire to "do something." He was to be confronted with one of the most important decisions of his life.

Destiny in Birmingham

To call the meeting in Birmingham a convention representing the beliefs of the southern people is a stretch. Many of those there had been elected as delegates to the national Democratic convention, but their charter to represent ended when that convention was over (or when they left the convention). The meeting did resemble a convention on the surface, however. There were speakers and a platform and various groups representing (or purporting to represent) numerous southern states.

The meeting began on July 17 when Gessner T. McCorvey of Alabama called it order. Walter Sillers, the speaker of the Mississippi House of Representatives, was elected as the permanent chairman of the gathering, and the proceedings began. The first item of business was a statement of principles prepared by the Resolutions Committee. This statement served as a "platform" of the States' Rights Democratic party. The key elements of the statement were that, "We oppose all efforts to invade or destroy individual rights; we stand for segregation of the races and the racial integrity of each race; the constitutional right to choose one's associates; to accept private employment without government interference. . . . We oppose and condemn a civil rights program calling for the elimination of segregation, social equality by Federal fiat." They also took this occasion to again label the civil rights issue as an attempt by President Truman to secure black northern votes.

With their principles expressed, the "convention" was still casting around for a leader to rally behind. Prior to the convention, the enigmatic Ben Laney was rumored to be the "party's" nominee. Another aspiring candidate was Brigadier General Herbert C. Holdridge.

One odd thing about this convention, however, was that its delegates never really had an opportunity to vote on opposing candidates. When Thurmond arrived in Birmingham, he was met by a group of delegates from Louisiana, Mississippi, and Alabama and offered the presidential nomination. Along with this offer came a time limit; he had about an hour to decide whether to accept it or not.

Thurmond's decision was made without consulting advisors or even calling his wife. As he recalled, "I knew that accepting the nomination would have future political repercussions, but I had little time to make up my mind, and I thought somebody ought to do something, so I finally decided to take the plunge. I didn't know then even if my own State would support me."[15]

Fielding Wright had agreed to accept the vice presidential nomination, and at 5:30 that afternoon, the two men were presented to the meeting as candidates. Senator James Eastland of Mississippi seconded the nominations, and to the tune of Dixie, the flag-waving crowd of about seven thousand cheered their nominees.

While there was general exuberance and exultation among the delegates, there was some resistance to getting on the State's Rights railroad. Governor Laney, smarting from not even being asked to serve as the nominee, suddenly suggested that "whatever is done must be done through and by the official Democratic organization in each respective state. The spirit of obstinacy and revenge is not the spirit of the Southland." Perhaps Laney had realized that this group really had no authority to nominate anyone for anything.[16]

Also unhappy was General Holdridge. When he rose to protest Thurmond's nomination, he was attacked by a mob and had to be rescued by the local police. So the Thurmond-Wright ticket did not exactly start off the campaign with a united constituency.

The convention in Birmingham is also noteworthy both for the people who were there and the people who were absent. With the exception of Senator Eastland, no major political figures were present. Conspicuous by their absence were Edward H. "Boss" Crump, the machine leader in Tennessee; Harry F. Byrd of Virginia; Herman Talmadge of Georgia; and Governor Earl K. Long (brother of Huey Long) of Louisiana. Their lack of interest spoke volumes concerning the support (or lack of support) that the pair could expect from other southern political leaders.

Notable among those who did show up was Police Commissioner Eugene "Bull" Conner of Birmingham. Conner would later earn the undying enmity of people everywhere for his police dog attacks on civil rights demonstrators. Another interested participant was Gerald L. K. Smith, the head of the neo-Nazi Christian Nationalist Crusade. Smith's group was anti-black and anti-Jewish and espoused race hatred as a way of life. When Thurmond was informed that Smith (who had not used his real name) had been there, he quickly denounced him. "We do not invite and we do not need the support of Gerald L. K. Smith or any other rabble-rousers who use race prejudice and class hatred to inflame the emotions of the people."[17] Here, at least, Thurmond had attempted to distance himself from the worst elements of the anti-civil rights movement.

Thurmond's quick response brought some praise from an unexpected source—Senator McGrath, Democratic party chairman. When he was told of Thurmond's stand, he remarked that Thurmond "took a lot of sting out of the revolt" by sidetracking the idea of white supremacy. He concluded that "Thurmond would be welcome at the White House" to see if there was not still some way to iron out the differences. This would be the last time for a long time that Thurmond was welcome at the White House.

He had gone a long way in a few short months toward severing his ties with the Democratic party. Over the next few months, during the campaign, he would set in motion events that would seal his fate within the party. Now, the die was about to be cast. Thurmond was ready to hit the campaign trail.

On the Road with Thurmond

The campaign strategy of the States' Rights Democrats actually had two distinct parts The first was to get their nominees (Thurmond and Wright) on the ballot. Differing election laws in different states made this process difficult. The second was to take the message of the group to the people—specifically, to the white people of the South.

Different states had different responses to the Thurmond candidacy. Previously, four states were mentioned as those that had the highest black population: Alabama, Louisiana, Mississippi, and South Carolina. In these four states, Democratic party leaders were also the leaders of the States' Rights Democratic Party. In all four of these states, the Thurmond-Wright ticket was listed as the Democratic ticket (replacing Truman). By July 30 of that year, the Alabama state party had gone so far as to pledge their electoral college votes to Thurmond. (In other words, the state party that had elected the electors had instructed them to vote for Thurmond regardless of how the vote went in their state.)

Other southern states were not so anxious to follow Alabama's lead, however. Soon after Thurmond's nomination, Senator Clyde R. Hoey of North Carolina predicted that if both Thurmond and Wallace were on the ballot, Dewey, the Republican, would win the electoral votes of the state. This tactic was used again and again against Thurmond's candidacy as Truman Democrats in other states used the spectre of a Republican victory to try to hold their states in line for the president.

Thurmond's fiery first campaign speech, on July 31 in Cherryville, North Carolina, did not dwell directly on the issue of segregation. It was couched in the language of states' rights, federalism, and the Tenth Amendment to the Constitution (which he read verbatim). After establishing the theme of the campaign, which was generally based on federalism, Thurmond then launched his attack on machine politics. He declared, "They think of us [the South] as always in the bag. They think of us as forever prostrate before them—as miserable camp followers of the big city politicians." Next, Thurmond turned his invective on the FEPC, labeling it the "nearest thing to communism this nation has ever seen. . . . If this proposal becomes law, the words 'private business' will be a thing of the past."

After attacking the twin evils of machine politics and communism, Thurmond then declared, "I did not risk my life on the beaches of Normandy to come back to this country, and sit idly by, while a bunch of hack politicians whittles away your heritage and mine. As for me, I intend to fight." In all fairness to Thurmond, he did not give a white supremacy speech at any time in his campaign. He stuck to the theme of the evils of usurpation of power by the federal government—and as such, he did not generate the mindless enthusiasm that a hard-core racial campaign might have provided.

Even so, the message was well received by this first audience in North Carolina—so well received, in fact, that by August 4, there were seventeen thousand signatures on a petition to have Thurmond's name added to the ballot. NC Election Commission

Chairman Hubert E. Olive had different ideas. Citing his inability to verify many of the signatures, he said, "I think it is clear that the petition . . . doesn't comply with the rules and regulations of the Board." Strom had lost round one in North Carolina.

The next major speaking event of the campaign was to be held in Houston at the Sam Houston Coliseum on August 11. This was to be the official acceptance speech of the candidates, and it was held in Texas to secure the support of this large block of crucial southern votes. This time, there were some ten thousand people present, with the same general atmosphere. Some people were there as nominal representatives of the party; some were there just because they wanted to be. Thurmond was especially optimistic about his chances as he predicted that he would receive over one hundred electoral votes, and that possible he would receive more votes than Truman would get in total. (At the time, the national press was suggesting that only a few states were secure for the president.)

Thurmond was successful in one respect on his Texas trip: in securing the support of some wealthy oilmen. The proposals calling for less federal control were just what the oilmen wanted to hear, and they began contributing to Thurmond's candidacy. Texas oilman H. R. Cullen even loaned his plane to bring Strom to the Houston meeting.

Money was an issue of sorts throughout the campaign. Naturally, money was hard to come by with no established party organization to raise it. By the end of the campaign, the States' Rights Democrats had raised and spent a little over $100,000 (items such as donated plane trips were not counted in this total). Late in the campaign, muck raking columnist Drew Pearson charged that some of the States' Rights funds were being used to support Republican Senator Joe Ball, who was fighting desperately to hold on to his Minnesota Senate seat under a fierce attack from civil rights advocate Hubert Humphrey.

The lack of adequate funding kept the campaign functioning at a relatively low level. After the Houston speech, it was almost two weeks before Thurmond did any more serious campaigning. Even then, his campaign trip was not exactly extensive, as it lasted only two days and covered only parts of Arkansas and Tennessee.

Remember, too, that at that time campaigns were generally shorter than they are today. Campaigning did not officially kick off until Labor Day. President Truman used his Labor Day address to say he was counting on the "little people" to elect him. Thurmond was relatively quiet during this time.

Thurmond was campaigning primarily against President Truman; he rarely mentioned Dewey. Thurmond repeatedly challenged Truman to respond to his charges on issues such as the FEPC and civil rights. For his part, Truman generally ignored Thurmond's candidacy. Thurmond was particularly agitated about Truman's desire to integrate the armed forces, labeling this move as both "unAmerican and dangerous."[18]

In a speech covered by the Washington *Post*, Thurmond advocated a "two-fisted foreign policy" in relations with the Soviet Union, and he sought to explain the South's views on the racial question. "All thinking southerners know that the solution to the south's economic problems . . . depend to a large degree on the educational and economic gains by our Negro population. Our progress as a section must be brought about by both races working together and living in harmony side by side as good neighbors. We believe in racial integrity and are opposed to racial integration. The former is for the best interest of each race, the latter is good for neither."[19]

Interestingly enough, Thurmond's position found support from some blacks. One was a black newspaper publisher in Newark named Davis Lee. He wrote an article for his paper, *The Telegram*, after touring the South. Discussing the prevailing white attitude he encountered, he said, "It is not one of hatred for the Negro. The South just doesn't believe that the negro has grown up. No section of the country has made more progress in finding a workable solution to the Negro problem than the South. Naturally, southerners are resentful when the North attempts to ram a civil rights program down their throats." This article naturally received significant play in the southern press.[20]

As the days progressed, States' Rights party efforts continued to be divided between being placed on state ballots and spreading the message. By September 18, Thurmond was on the ballots of twelve states: Alabama, Arkansas, Florida, Kentucky, Louisiana, Mississippi, North Carolina, North Dakota, South Carolina, Tennessee, Texas, and Virginia. He had lost other ballot fights, such as the one in Indiana, where Circuit Judge Lloyd E. Claycombe ruled that the petitions were "highly irregular." Within a few days, he was to be kept off the ballots of the states of Maryland and Oklahoma as well.

At the end of the first month of campaigning, a national Gallup poll had discouraging news for the Democrats and for the States' Rights Democrats. The poll showed that 46.5 percent of all Americans favored Dewey; 39 percent favored Truman; 3.5 percent favored Wallace; and 2 percent favored Thurmond. (Another 9 percent were undecided.) Not only the national news was discouraging; Thurmond was also getting some heat from South Carolina. Even in his own state, some were not ready to march off the cliff. The popular liberal governor was making some enemies back home.

Trouble in Carolina

When he accepted the presidential nomination, Thurmond had not even checked with his friends in the state Democratic party to see if they would support him. While many in the state were very supportive, some were not. The Walterboro newspaper immediately called for his resignation as governor upon his acceptance of the presidential nomination, suggesting that he could not be a presidential candidate and governor at the same time. Thurmond, of course, declined to resign, citing Governor Dewey's continued service as governor of New York. The call for his resignation had no real validity, but it was a sure sign to Strom that his new campaign did not have the support of all South Carolinians.

Thurmond also received an early warning from other governors that his stance in national politics would have an impact on his duties as governor. New Jersey Governor Alfred E. Driscoll refused to return an escaped black prisoner to South Carolina who had been sentenced to nineteen months imprisonment for stealing five dollars. Governor Driscoll refused extradition on the grounds that the man had already served enough time.

Meanwhile, a counter group of "real" Democrats was being organized in South Carolina. The Truman Democrats had a slate of presidential electors, and former state Senator Ashley H. Williams was their leader. Williams challenged Thurmond on his belief in states' rights, suggesting that it was a new issue with Strom. (This allegation was obviously false, as Thurmond had been an advocate of states' rights for the better part of his public life.) Williams also charged that Thurmond was really running for some other office (U.S. Senate), and for the first time—but certainly not the last—Strom's head-standing photo became an issue.

The gist of their attack was that "real Democrats" would vote for Truman. As the campaign entered its last days, this group sought to discredit Thurmond in the state by attacking his commitment to segregation. They cited a letter he had written to the appointed governor of the Virgin Islands, William H. Hastie. At a previous meeting of governors, Thurmond had invited all the assembled governors to visit the Governor's Mansion, including Governor Hastie, who was black. Hastie had declined, and Thurmond claimed he had not known Hastie was black. When the charges were raised concerning this invitation, Thurmond felt compelled to respond. "Governor Hastie knows that neither he nor any other negro will ever be a guest at the Governor's House in Columbia as long as I am Governor or as long as the Democratic Party of South Carolina continues to elect Governors of my state," he said.[21]

Governor Thurmond's sudden urge to relocate to 1600 Pennsylvania Avenue had caused some people in South Carolina to look for reasons to attack him. Once raised, these issues would not die easily. Thurmond would see them again in later campaigns.

Another item that would have political repercussions later involved Senator Edgar A. Brown, Thurmond's old nemesis. In mid-October Brown wrote a letter to national Democratic party Treasurer Joe L. Blythe, outlining why he thought the national Democratic party was disintegrating. This letter was printed in South Carolina newspapers, and those reading it got the impression Brown had deserted the national party and was voting for Thurmond.[22] (This would become a campaign issue when Brown and Thurmond faced each other in the 1954 U.S. Senate campaign.)

A final prelude to the future involved U.S. Senator Olin Johnston. On election night, when he thought he knew who would win the presidential election, Olin issued a statement that he had "stood with the Democratic party." By this nebulous statement, he was implying that he had voted for Truman. (Later events disclosed that he had not voted at all.) This sequence of events, however, was also to play an important part in Thurmond's future, as he and Johnston would be facing each other within two years.

Despite these rumblings, South Carolina as a whole stood for Thurmond. All the state's Democratic electors were pledged to Thurmond, and the Thurmond-Wright ballot was listed as the regular Democratic party in the state. (The people did have the chance to vote for Truman, but his name was not listed as the Democratic candidate.) With South Carolina nominally under control, Thurmond could concentrate his efforts on the final leg of his remarkable campaign journey.

The Stretch Drive

As the campaign continued into October, there was a general feeling that it was losing steam. In addition to the ballot setbacks in border states and other areas, the South itself seemed to be turning its back on his effort. In Texas Thurmond electors had been ejected by the Democratic party organization (and Lyndon Baines Johnson had been certified as a Senate candidate by eighty-seven votes over Coke Stevensons). In Tennessee the state Executive Democratic Committee had removed three anti-Truman electors from its electoral slate. In Georgia the Democratic party had selected twelve electors, all pledged to Truman, even though Thurmond's cousin Herman Talmadge was the governor-nominee of the state. By October 20, the States' Rights party had been able to get Thurmond on one more ballot (in Georgia) but the momentum was slowing.

All around him, there was evidence that the support Thurmond had hoped to get from southern states was just not there. An interesting sidelight came from some surviving Confederate veterans of the Civil War who were meeting in Montgomery, Alabama. Three were asked who they would vote for in the upcoming election. All three were opposed to Truman, but none was really in favor of Thurmond. Indeed, this seemed to be the case all over the South. A mid-October Gallup poll suggested that Dewey would win twenty states, Truman ten, and Thurmond four, with fourteen up for grabs between Dewey and Truman. Thurmond's four predicted states were Alabama, Louisiana, Mississippi, and South Carolina. The pollsters could not find any significant support for him in the rest of the South.

While Thurmond's support seemed to be static, Republican politicians were attempting to take advantage of the anti-Truman southern sympathies. Senator Robert Taft of Ohio ventured down to Nashville and hinted that the civil rights program of the Republicans would be easier to swallow than that of the Democrats and urged southern Democrats to support Dewey. In his speech, he asserted that there was a "basic agreement" between southern Democrats and the Republican party.

With this as a backdrop, on October 6 Thurmond ventured out of the South to make a campaign appearance. The place was New York City—in a state where he was not even on the ballot. Speaking at the Overseas Press Club, Thurmond attacked the de facto segregation practiced by New Yorkers. The undertone of his message was that they had no right to judge the South when their own hands were not clean. Thurmond also asserted that his party was not "motivated by racial prejudice." Later in the month on October 29, Truman made his own appearance in New York City— in Harlem, where he pledged to continue the fight for civil rights. The Gallup poll for the same day showed that Dewey's support had slipped to a solid thirteen states, while Truman's had remained the same at ten, and sixteen states were up for grabs. Thurmond was to win only three states by that prediction.

Thurmond's own later prediction was more optimistic. In his last major vote estimate, he suggested that he had a chance to win 142 electoral votes, and if he could do that, he said, he had a chance to win in the U.S. House of Representatives. Now, though, there was little anyone could do. The polls had shown that Dewey was losing momentum, with Truman gaining some and Thurmond remaining about the same. (Wallace was completely out of the picture.)

On election morning Strom and his wife went to the polls in Edgefield to cast their votes, then went back to Columbia to await the results.

A Decision Is Rendered

On November 2, 1948, the people of the United States reasserted their independence . . . this time from pollsters. Despite late predictions of a Dewey win, Harry Truman captured a majority of the electoral votes in the surprise election of the century. The "little people" had spoken, and they had their man. But what of Strom Thurmond and the States' Rights effort?

Thurmond won four states as predicted: Alabama, Louisiana, Mississippi, and South Carolina, for a total electoral vote count of thirty-eight. When the Electoral College cast its vote, Thurmond received his thirty-ninth vote from an independent-minded Tennessee elector. In the four states that he won, his name was listed under the regular Democratic party slate. In the rest of the southern states, the Thurmond-Wright ticket was listed under the States' Rights banner and therefore received few votes and was barely a factor. A comparison between the votes from South Carolina and North Carolina shows the differing impact of the Thurmond campaign:

	South Carolina	*North Carolina*
Thurmond	89,440	63,224
Truman	30,498	527,548
Dewey	5,101	220,693

Thurmond's total national vote was 1,169,312 or about 2.4 percent of the total. Interestingly enough, though, his candidacy might have made a significant difference. The states of Ohio and Illinois had both been predicted for Dewey, but Truman won by very close margins. Given Thurmond's electoral votes, a switch of 21,000 votes from Truman to Dewey in Ohio and Illinois would have prevented an outright Truman victory, throwing the election into the House of Representatives. As it was, Thurmond's candidacy was merely a footnote in an already-interesting campaign.

At the outset, though, the States' Righters never had any real hopes of winning the presidency. Their goal was to draw enough support away from Truman to throw the contest into the Congress—there, in the deal-making session that was certain to occur, the southerners hoped to trade their votes to a candidate who would support their right to continued segregation, at least at some level. In reality, the lack of even unanimous southern support showed that white southerners accepted the inevitability, if not the desirability, of changing race relationships. In the referendum, most of the South voted to support an end to segregation, even if that issue was not directly on the ballot.

From a political viewpoint, though, this campaign did serve to open the rift between the national Democratic party and the South. In the four southern states that voted for Thurmond, the people noticed that the sky did not fall. It was all right to vote for someone other than the Democratic nominee for president if the other candidate shared some of your beliefs. This lesson, once learned, served to change the face of American politics. The "solid South" was a thing of the past, at least as far as the Democrats were concerned.

Immediately after the election, Thurmond urged all Americans to "close ranks and work together behind President Truman," and he said, "I consider myself a member of the Democratic Party. I voted the ticket of the Democratic Party in South Carolina."[23] Strom hoped this message would signal an end to the intra-party divisiveness, at least in South Carolina. There was some talk of Thurmond and Wright allowing their electors to vote for Truman, but Thurmond was adamant that they should not.[24] And President Truman continued to show an unexpected streak of poor sportsmanship.

A fixture at presidential inaugurations is the inaugural parade. Each state sends a float (and generally its governor) to ride in the parade honoring the president. In January, when Governor Thurmond and his wife passed by the reviewing stand and waved at the president, Truman ignored Thurmond and his wife and grabbed the arm of Vice President Barkley to prevent him from returning the Thurmond's greeting. This mean spiritedness continued throughout Truman's term, at least where Thurmond was concerned. (And Truman went out of his way to cast barbs at Thurmond even after he left office.)

While Thurmond had campaigned on a platform of continued segregation, he did what he could to make sure he had not burned all his bridges to the rising number of voting blacks in the state. On the recommendation of the S.C. Probation, Parole and Pardon Board, the governor freed a black man who had been convicted of manslaughter. And shortly after the election, Thurmond became the spokesman for efforts to raise private money for the all-black Benedict College. He urged the white people of the state to give money because by doing so they would "have a real opportunity to help the negroes."[25] Certainly, such actions had political overtones. Great political savvy was not required to understand that he was extremely weak among what would surely become a large group of registered voters—South Carolina blacks. But political considerations notwithstanding, these actions were not in any way inconsistent with his previous actions toward blacks. Indeed, the presidential campaign with its blatant defense of segregation (softened somewhat by his efforts to base the campaign on federalism issues) is the real inconsistency. Until then, Thurmond had been active in promoting the interests of blacks—in education, as a state senator, as a lawyer, as a judge, and to a certain extent, even as governor—as in his inaugural address when he advocated better education and expanded economic opportunities for South Carolina's black citizens.

During the remainder of his term as governor, Thurmond continued to extend overtures toward South Carolina's black citizens. Most notably, he was the first governor since Reconstruction to appoint a black to a state board. All of it ended up meaning very little, however. South Carolina's black citizens did not forget, and Thurmond would feel their emerging weight in a future political battle.

In addition to the black population, Thurmond realized he had problems with whites, as well. His ambition and desire to "do something" had always had the blessing of his constituents. But his presidential campaign had aroused real resentment, and not just from a small group of statehouse politicos. People from all over the state had expressed their dissatisfaction, which could mean real trouble for a man who hoped to move up to the next level of service.

Without taking any time off after the election, Thurmond returned to the job to which he had been elected—governor of South Carolina. He was determined to rebuild the alliances that had been weakened by his surprise run for the presidency. He had his sights set of higher office—a try for the U.S. Senate. The path was not an easy one, however. He would have to beat an incumbent in the state Democratic primary. The incumbent was Olin D. Johnston, and for the first time in his political career, Strom would face a master campaigner.

Chapter 9

GOVERNOR AGAIN

T he pale winter sunlight in January 1949 shone on an unpleasant situation for Governor Strom Thurmond. His desire to "do something" had transported him from relative obscurity to something of a political oddity, on the national scene at least. Closer to home, South Carolina voters, who had been inclined to look on their war veteran as a hero of sorts, had been hit by a series of shocks. A surprise marriage, followed by an even more surprising presidential run, made the people of South Carolina reevaluate their feelings for their governor. Then, there was Thurmond's ambition to become a U.S. senator. Many expected a race in 1948, and when it did not materialize, they were certain of one in 1950. This likely race against Olin D. Johnston gave another group of people a reason to be more restrained about their governor—if not openly hostile.

Another factor was South Carolina's black population, which was on the verge of political freedom for the first time since Reconstruction ended. Thurmond had campaigned against more rights for them, at the federal level, at least. Now, in increasing numbers, they would be able to vote. He had to suspect that they would not be inclined to vote for him.

Finally, there was the need to continue to govern the state of South Carolina. Thurmond had virtually taken a year off from governing in 1948. While he was fighting the evils of federal intervention, he had not been able to push for the passage of programs that the state desperately needed if it was to move forward. Among those programs still languishing were several of his state government reorganization measures that Strom felt were vitally important.

Of course, the situation was not hopeless. He still had two years of his term to serve, and if everything went his way, he could accomplish other important portions of his program, reestablish his progressive image, rebuild his bridges with South Carolina's blacks (which had been in good shape in 1947), and make inroads on Olin D. Johnston's popularity. The operative word was "if," and in 1949, Strom's best-laid plans did not come to fruition.

The culprit was the anticipated battle between Strom and Olin in 1950. For the balance of his term as governor, he would have to deal with Johnston-instigated sniping. The new year brought immediate battles. As soon as the legislature convened, Thurmond saw the realities of the new political climate he had helped to create.

The first salvo in this barrage started innocuously enough with the annual message the governor delivers to the state legislature. In this message, the governor outlines his program for the upcoming session of the General Assembly. Normally, this speech was presented to the legislature during the day. In 1949, however, Thurmond requested that the speech be given at night. This would allow him to make his speech via a state radio hookup to the voters in "prime time." Senator Wilbur G. Grant of Chester immediately opposed the time change. (Grant, a well-known Johnston man, wanted to deny Strom any more publicity than was absolutely necessary.)

Thurmond's support in the legislature was still very strong, and he had his way. When he delivered his speech on the night of January 12, 1949, twenty-nine radio stations carried his message to the people. As expected, Strom used the opportunity to recall the previous successes of his administration, but he did other things, as well.

He reminded the people of South Carolina that he had run his presidential race on behalf of states' rights and warned them that "concentration of governmental power on the banks of the Potomac is fundamentally as dangerous to human liberty as it was on the banks of the Tiber in Italy, or on the banks of the Rhine in Germany or as it is on the banks of the Volga in Russia." By equating national power with the recently vanquished enemies of our nation (and the rising threat of the Soviet Union), Thurmond reminded everyone of his own war record and also tried to strike an emotional chord with his listeners. (This was also a reiteration of his often-repeated position that he did not attempt the presidential race to maintain white supremacy but to fight increasing federal intervention.)

After having made the point that his campaign was not anti-black, Thurmond then continued his efforts to rebuild some bridges with the black citizens of the state. "Our economic development is inevitably dependent upon equipping our people, both white and colored, to become productive citizens. The productive potential of our colored people is perhaps our largest undeveloped economic resource as a state," he said. Here, Strom reiterated his previous appeals to provide better educational opportunities (and thus better job opportunities) for the blacks in the state.

A second phase of his speech proposed several additional ambitious programs he hoped to see enacted during the legislative session. Thurmond knew that Johnston's strongest support came from organized labor in some of the upstate counties. To make inroads in that support, Strom asked the legislature for several laws that would benefit factory workers. (For the most part, these were not mentioned in his inaugural address but were presented for the first time in 1949.) For labor, he requested a state wage and hour law, compulsory air-conditioning for manufacturing plants, increased workers' compensation benefits with lower rates, and extension of the Industrial Commission's safety program.

For the environment, Thurmond called for laws that provided greater protection against forest fires, more reforestation programs, and a state fish-and-game commission law. He also reiterated the need for enactment of his reorganization proposals. By presenting this array of programs, he hoped to make sure the people of the state knew he was still working for them. His speech also served notice on the legislature that he did not intend to be a lame duck. There was still work to be done and Strom was going to be a firm taskmaster.

Despite his back-to-business stance, it was evident that other things would come to occupy increasingly larger parts of his time. In February Thurmond volunteered to go to Washington to testify "against Mr. Truman's so-called civil rights legislation." At the same time, he tried to make certain his efforts could not be equated with those of radical whites by issuing a warning to the Ku Klux Klan. In a speech to the state American Legion Convention, he warned, "No individual or organization can ever be permitted to take the law into its own hands and by force or intimidation, mistreat citizens of the state. In order that there be no misunderstanding on the part of anyone, I would like our citizens to know that I intend to see that this state law [S.C. Code 1131, which outlawed Klan activity] is enforced."

Thurmond had come to an important decision during the winter: he would not be part of any political organization outside of South Carolina. When the leaders of the states' rights movement called meetings, Strom was conspicuously absent. He missed a meeting in Jackson, Mississippi, in early February, and another meeting in late February in Birmingham. He had severed his ties with the group. And if anyone still thought Strom had ties with any white supremacy group, he did his best to dispel that idea by proclaiming April 5 as Booker T. Washington day in South Carolina, honoring the black scientist for his achievements.

If honoring blacks was a new twist, Thurmond surprised the state even more by publicly consorting with a Republican. On March 19, he participated in an interesting press conference with U.S. Senator Margaret Chase Smith, a Maine Republican who was a featured speaker at the state teachers' meeting. Senator Smith had voted to uphold a southern Democratic filibuster that was delaying a vote on parts of President Truman's civil rights program. Senator Smith explained that while Republicans had supported the filibuster, some of Truman's legislation might be "good legislation." At that, she was treated to a mini-lecture from Governor Thurmond on the evils of federal involvement in local issues. Taking advantage of the opportunity, Thurmond pointed out the dangers of centralized power. Senator Smith refused to "debate" with Thurmond, but it was an interesting exchange at any rate.

After the 1948 election, Republican leaders began visiting the South in larger numbers than at any time since the beginning of Reconstruction. They recognized the opportunity to build the coalition that took its first fledgling steps in that election. Along with the public appearances, the Republicans were demonstrating their support for some southern causes, as in the filibuster support. These efforts were not organized, but they began to have an impact on white southern Democrats. (As an aside, Drew Pearson used one of his columns in April of that year to suggest that the States' Rights Democrats would absorb the southern Republicans. Pearson was wrong, of course. The States' Rights party died but the Republican party had a rebirth, sparked by southern voters.)

These kinds of political considerations were a long way from the minds of most South Carolinians during the late 1940s, however. The chief issue was still one of intra-party squabbles, and a major battle appeared to be shaping up early in 1949. John Bolt Culbertson, now a Greenville County representative (and still anti-Thurmond, as he had demonstrated when Thurmond sought the judgeship), took an occasion on March 29 to tell his house colleagues what they already knew—that Strom was already running against Senator Johnston. By proclaiming a Thurmond candidacy, Culbertson hoped to bring Thurmond's intentions out in the open.

Unfortunately, many issues during this two-year period were to be tossed back and forth between pro-Thurmond and pro-Johnston forces in the legislature. The first issue to come up involved Thurmond's decision to appoint a woman to the S.C. Industrial Commission. Rumors had been circulating for several weeks that Thurmond would back up his previous speeches about wanting more women in government by appointing one to a high post. On April 27, Strom appointed Faith Clayton, of Central, South Carolina, to replace Isaac L. Hyatt. The first storm came from some labor leaders who said that Hyatt's removal would mean a loss of labor's voice on the commission. This argument did not address the fact that Miss Clayton, a S.C. Employment Service manager, was a member of Local 838 of the American Federation of Labor. (Of course, labor opposition was not unexpected—they were, after all, mostly Johnston men.)

The second source of opposition came from Johnston men in the legislature. Seeing an opportunity to embarrass Thurmond, they instituted a filibuster that sought to prevent Miss Clayton's appointment. The two-week filibuster ended on May 25 when the Senate agreed to postpone a decision on the Clayton appointment until January 11, 1950. In the meantime, Hyatt was allowed to serve.

Immediately upon the heels of this setback, Culbertson and Matthew Poliakoff (another Johnston supporter in Spartanburg County) requested that Governor Thurmond release the names of his "Colonels." (The most famous Colonels are those appointed by the governor of Kentucky, but South Carolina's governor also had the authority to name individuals to this completely honorary post.) Strom responded to this request with an answer similar to the kind he delivered in his early S.C. Senate days. He told the pair that they were "sticking their noses into something that does not concern them." He noted correctly that these individuals did not hold public office and that the pair should pay attention to the more important duties that faced them.

At that point, Culbertson demurred and suggested that there might have been some members of the CIO among Strom's Colonels. (The CIO Culbertson referred to was the labor organization which is now part of the AFL-CIO. At that time, they were separate organizations, and the CIO was the more radical.) Culbertson asserted that the CIO and the FEPC (Truman's civil rights body) stood for the same thing.[1] This was an attempt to paint Thurmond as a supporter of radical labor factions and a hypocrite. As Culbertson was relatively unpopular and a junior member of the legislature, his calls for disclosure were never supported by the legislature, but Culbertson did continue to be a source of irritation throughout Thurmond's term as governor.

Strom's troubles with organized labor were not over for the year. Later in July, when Earle R. Britton was reelected as president of the S.C. Federation of Labor, he assailed Thurmond for what he termed a betrayal of labor's interests in the state.[2] Still later in the year, John L. McKinney, a local labor leader who claimed to speak for the Columbia Building and Construction Trades council, said the Dupont Company had not recognized unions at their manufacturing plant at the request of the governor. This charge brought a prompt denial from the state AFL, which praised Thurmond for his impartial handling of the incident.[3]

For Thurmond, however, the first half of the year was no blessing. He had recognized that he needed to woo union-oriented voters. He had tried to do this in his inaugural, but at every turn he had been thwarted by union leaders who supported Johnston.

Another unpromising political situation presented itself in June as Thurmond tried to make further overtures to the black citizens of the state. This incident involved the appointment of a black physician, T. Carr McFall of Charleston, to serve on the Advisory Hospital Council. McFall, a graduate of the Meharry Medical College, had served in World War II and then returned to Charleston to develop a training school for nurses. The S.C. Medical Association nominated Dr. McFall for the Advisory Hospital Council, and in June Thurmond appointed him.

It was the first time a black had ever been appointed to anything by a Democratic governor. Thurmond was called to task for this act by many whites—and despite his public protestations that he had no choice in making the appointment, a good case can be made that he knew what he was doing. He knew most black citizens viewed him unfavorably because of his States' Rights campaign. He also knew that despite his frequent anti-Klan attacks, he was not making any real headway with this potentially large block of voters. By appointing a black to this position, especially in a

situation where he had not selected him directly, he hoped to have
the best of both worlds—that is, to achieve a higher standing in the
black community while not losing significant support among
white voters. There is also room to believe that he made the
appointment because it was the right thing to do. To deny this
qualified veteran this slot would certainly have been difficult but
not impossible. Strom had previously done things he did not
directly support because he thought they were correct. Possibly,
this was one of those times. Whatever his motives, he was to pay
dearly for this appointment. It was one that Olin Johnston would
not let him forget.

At the end of the legislative session, Thurmond chided the
legislators for their unfinished business. At a meeting of the S.C.
Firemen's Association on June 8, he pointed out several major
proposals that were languishing in the legislature: the creation of
a professional State Bureau of Investigation to replace the constabulary, a central purchasing unit, a merit personnel system, the
fish-and-game commission, and an alcoholic treatment clinic, all
measures supported by the governor that had not been enacted.
Without directly suggesting that intra-party politics was at fault,
Strom wanted to make the point that there were still things to be
done.

Every year, even nonelection years, there are opportunities for
politicians and political hopefuls to gather and survey the landscape. One of those occasions occurred at Jolly Street. On August
25, Strom and Olin were both there, making the rounds and lining
up support. Olin said he would run; Strom had nothing to say at
that point. It was all just shadow boxing, however. Both men knew
that Strom was in the race, as did most of the rest of the state. For
the balance of the year, Strom kept up a hectic pace of speaking
engagements. Wherever people were gathered together, Strom
was there. When winter came, there was a brief respite, but it was
the calm before the storm. Olin's friends huddled around winter
fires and planned ways to keep Strom on the defensive. Strom's
friends had planned a few surprises of their own. In between lay
some very important issues for the state.

Almost unnoticed during the 1949 session were some important
items. The voters approved an advisory referendum that allowed
divorce in South Carolina. The new law took effect on March 31,
1949, ending South Carolina's position as the last state to prohibit
divorces of any kind.

Also in 1949 Thurmond had his way when the governor's
unchecked pardon power was eliminated by the legislature. The

pardon issue would play an important part in the upcoming election—not Thurmond's efforts to make it harder to "buy" a pardon, but Olin Johnston's use of pardoning power when he was governor.

Perhaps, though, these successful efforts to transform South Carolina were more significant than the political events that were interwoven throughout them. Strom Thurmond presided over many of the changes that brought South Carolina into the twentieth century. Whether or not he did what he did because of the political ramifications, the state did make some strides while he was governor. The record shows that these advances were more because of him than in spite of him. Even in his final year, with his political future at stake, Thurmond would continue to fight for a better state. And he was often successful.

Now, however, the new year brought the politicians back to the state capital. The toughest battle of his political career was directly in front of him, and Thurmond came out fighting.

Another Year, Another Campaign

If the lines were beginning to blur between politics and government in South Carolina in 1949, the lines were completely erased in 1950. This is not to suggest that Thurmond did not have triumphs—his friends did what they could to help him. But Thurmond had made some enemies and they seemed to be coming out of the woodwork in droves.

The year started on an upbeat note as the state Senate approved Faith Clayton's nomination to the Industrial Commission by a vote of 26–10. Only a day later, though Strom's troubles began. State Senator Robert M. Kennedy, who had supported Thurmond in his states' rights campaign, charged that the Governor was lax in his law enforcement duties. Kennedy said that he knew of "Columbia bookies who take big racing bets" and of a "powerful and wealthy politician" who fixes charges against gangsters. He introduced a resolution to express the displeasure of the Senate.

There was no suggestion that Thurmond was the "powerful and wealthy politician" cited by Kennedy, but several of Thurmond's allies resented the attack and immediately came to Strom's defense. Senator Callison of Greenville, a Thurmond supporter, suggested that the charges, if true, only served to support Thurmond's request for the creation of a more professional state bureau of investigation. Over Kennedy's vocal opposition, his resolution was referred to the Judiciary Committee where it died.

A few days later, Senator Kennedy was at it again, this time attacking Thurmond's sincerity in his support of states' rights. Kennedy reported that Strom had told him that they needed to "soft pedal" any mention of states' rights until after the 1950 Senate election. Kennedy even went so far as to make it known that he had no relationship with Thurmond: "It had been openly believed that Governor Thurmond and I are very close friends whereas as a matter of fact, there has been very little congeniality," he said.[4]

As in many public feuds, this one may have had hidden causes. The issue lurking behind Kennedy's headlines may have been a vacancy that had occurred in the S.C. Secretary of State's office. When William P. Blackwell died, the governor had the power to appoint a replacement, and Kennedy had apparently been interested in the appointment. Thurmond had appointed P. T. Bradham instead, and Kennedy had reacted negatively. But no matter what the background, it was clear to all that the governor was under pressure.

In his first speech to the legislature in 1950, Thurmond outlined the goals he hoped to see accomplished during his last year as governor. Many of these had been suggested before, such as a secret ballot law, higher liquor taxes, a state minimum wage law, and the creation of a state bureau of investigation. Other issues were new, however, such as enlargement of S.C. State College (a predominantly black college in Orangeburg), more farm-to-market roads (rural to urban), and calls for a balanced budget. These were all South Carolina issues, but Thurmond did touch on one issue of national significance: federal aid, particularly for the schools.

Originally, Thurmond had been in favor of this kind of aid, specifically calling for it in his inaugural address. But by 1950 he had reversed himself completely. In his speech, he remarked that "the idea that money which comes from Washington costs us nothing must be exploded . . . it comes from the pockets of the taxpayers of South Carolina. . . . I advocated our support of federal aid to education on condition that control of our schools by left entirely in the hands of state and local employees. . . . What is now transpiring in Washington has made it perfectly obvious that our assumption was wrong, and that not only will federal aid be dangerous to local control of our schools but also restrictions which will be applied under which South Carolina cannot lawfully receive any aid under the provision of the state constitution commanding separate schools for the races." Strom was, of course, completely accurate in this assessment. The federal government did not intend to allow southern schools to continue to be segregated, although the most direct pressure would ultimately come from the courts and not through the pocketbook. He took this issue up again before five thousand members of the S.C. Education Association. Here, however, his belief was countered by J. Paul Beam, the outgoing SCEA president, who supported federal aid.

On February 9, Strom got another legislative victory when the legislature approved implementation of several recommendations from the Reorganization Commission. Under the proposals adopted, eight boards and commissions would be consolidated under the Budget and Control Board composed of the governor, treasurer, comptroller general, senate finance chairman, and the house ways and means chairman. In addition to the consolidation, the proposals created a centralized purchasing system. This was a major thrust of Thurmond's administration, and achieving a major portion of it during an election year was unexpected.

Another victory came later in the session, on April 13, when the legislature ratified a bill that established a secret ballot in South Carolina. This, too, had been an important goal of Thurmond's administration. When he signed the bill on April 20, the state took a major step forward.

Late in the year Thurmond was handed his final victory when the voters of the state repealed the provisions for a poll tax. (A poll tax was generally imposed to prevent blacks from voting.) Despite his virulent opposition to a federal law removing poll taxes Thurmond had consistently advocated repeal at the state level. Now, in his last days as governor, he had helped to make good on another campaign promise issued four years previously.

These were bright spots, certainly, but the real action of the year lay outside of legislative triumphs, because 1950 was a year of politics. The old faced the new, and the voters were to have a series of real choices. In addition to the race between Thurmond and Olin Johnston, another famous South Carolinian would have his name on the ballot: James F. Byrnes, who was seeking a term as South Carolina's governor.

The 1950 Campaign

In a sense, the races in South Carolina had a larger scope than was obvious, in that most of the candidates were really running against Harry Truman. Both Thurmond and James F. Byrnes campaigned against Truman, and both had his disapproval. Another issue that covered the campaign and filled in the cracks as it oozed through the different elections was civil rights. Byrnes was regarded as a kind of savior—surely a statesman of his magnitude could save South Carolina's segregationist policies.

The race between Thurmond and Johnston had similar implications. Although Johnston had proclaimed his support for Truman, he too now ran against him. The contest between Thurmond and Johnston also sank to the level of attempting to establish the greatest support for segregation—while for the first time, South Carolina's blacks had an opportunity to make the difference in an election.

President Truman started 1950 as he had ended 1949—with a thinly veiled dislike for anything or anyone that came from South Carolina. When it was reported to Truman that Byrnes, his former secretary of state, was considering a run for governor in South Carolina, Truman replied with typical bluntness that Byrnes "could do as he damn pleases."[5]

Obviously, Truman was anti-Byrnes, which served Byrnes's purposes well. In the other major race, Strom Thurmond was also faced with a continuing series of snubs from the president and the national Democratic party. Neither Thurmond nor Governor Wright of Mississippi had been invited to a southern Democrat confab at Raleigh on January 28. And when a story was leaked to Drew Pearson that suggested Thurmond might not run against Johnston, Strom sought to lay it at the feet of the president and the party people:

> I am advised that Drew Pearson last night undertook to report from Washington on the political affairs of South Carolina. . . . If it will be any comfort to those who are inspiring these reports from Washington on South Carolina affairs, I can assure them that in our Democratic Primary this summer, the Democrats of our state will be given a clear opportunity to choose between candidates who are following the president and those who are willing to stand up and be counted in opposition to his un-American, communistic and anti-southern program.[6]

Thurmond had not officially announced his candidacy at that point, but this was surely a clue to the people of the state that he would be in the race.

At that time, Truman chose not to publicly intervene in any of the South Carolina elections, declaring that he was not dabbling in South Carolina politics. But later Truman would suggest that he was not certain if Byrnes was a Democrat, and other tricks would be employed by the national party to prevent Thurmond's election.

Locally, John Bolt Culbertson was on the warpath again. First, he predicted that Johnston would sweep the state, declaring, "Strom will spend more money this summer than ever has been spent but it's not going to do him any good." Then Culbertson attempted to paint Strom as a pro-black candidate by suggesting that "Thurmond can speak in negro churches [and] shake hands with negro servants at weddings but Johnston is still going to be elected."[7] Thurmond had done these things as a matter of course, but Culbertson's attack, coupled with subsequent Johnston tactics, forced Strom to continue to move away from the "liberal" tendencies he had once exhibited.

Ironically enough, as the state Democratic party began its precinct meetings on March 25 blacks were elected to Democratic precinct offices for the first time. Spartanburg County had fourteen black delegates. A handful of these black delegates were present on April 19 at the state Democratic convention, which must have been very difficult for them. One of the resolutions adopted at that convention stated: "We deplore the efforts of the leadership of the national Democratic Party to gain the support of minority pressure groups in the large Northern cities by espousing enactment of laws inimical to the best interest of the south and nation." The convention also passed resolutions supporting continued segregation. The black delegates did not vote against either of these sentiments. Obviously there was an element of intimidation, but these first black delegates were also trying to "fit in" as best they could.

This convention was a watershed event in many ways. In addition to the presence of the first black delegates, the convention committee had extended an invitation to Governor Thurmond to speak to the delegates. Normally this invitation was not given to anyone with specific political ambitions. Because of his plans, Thurmond refused the honor.[8]

Throughout the convention, Thurmond remained a campaigning noncandidate, but on April 29, he officially announced to the
people of South Carolina that he would be a candidate for Johnston's
U.S. Senate seat. He warned the people what they could expect
during the campaign:

> Every outside influence that hates and seeks to
> destroy our way of life in South Carolina will
> attempt by every means possible, whether by
> slush funds, or propaganda, or absentee control
> of bloc votes to dominate this election. . . . The
> NAACP and other bloc organizations have been
> encouraged by the rulings of a turncoat federal
> judge [Waring] who has forced into our primary
> thousands of voters who do not believe in the
> principles of the Democratic party of South
> Carolina.

His attacks on Johnston were primarily directed at his support
of Truman and implications that Johnston was a closet Republican
and a supporter of civil rights. Thurmond's approach to Johnston
was summed up in one phrase he repeatedly hurled at South
Carolina's voters: "I will not be one kind of Democrat in Washington and another kind in South Carolina."

For his part, Johnston named his wife, the former Gladys
Atkinson (graduate of Anderson College and former Boiling
Springs teacher), as his campaign manager. His initial strategy
was to run a "Christian campaign" and not to "discuss anything
but Olin Johnston's record and what I have done for South Carolina." And in the early part of the campaign he was confident,
saying, "I'm ready for the race. In fact, I'm looking forward to it."[9]
But Johnston's pious attitude and calm demeanor eventually wilted
under Thurmond's constant attack. Before the campaign was over,
Johnston was anything but happy.

Some Like It Hot

In those days, Thurmond seemed to truly enjoy mixing it up
with his political foes. Looking back, though, one gets the feeling
that he had a personal dislike for Johnston as well as a professional
one. Perhaps he was still resentful of Johnston's early call for
Thurmond's defeat in his bid for reelection to the state senate in
1936. Perhaps he did not like Johnston's two-faced behavior during the 1948 presidential campaign. Another issue rankled Thur-

mond, as well: Johnston's use of his pardoning power while he was governor.

Many South Carolina governors had been accused of misusing their pardon powers. Some had been accused of selling pardons. While Thurmond never publicly accused Johnston of actually selling pardons, he raised a loud hue and cry about the issue. On May 27, he brought the issue up, mentioning that on Johnston's last day as governor, twelve people had been freed from the state prison.

On June 8, while speaking in York, Thurmond made his strongest attack of the campaign on this issue. He accused Johnston of running a "pardon racket," noting that some 3,221 inmates had been released by Johnston (630 pardons and paroles and another 2,591 leaves of absence or "backdoor pardons"). Strom told the crowd of a particular pardon of Johnston's that had gone badly: Dave Dunham, a black man who had been pardoned by Johnston, had soon after attacked a "white couple," killing the man. Strom noted that it was the "pardon racket which ended the life of this young Chester County veteran."[10]

Thurmond compared Johnston's pardon record with his own as governor. Thurmond had granted a total of 126 pardons and sentence reductions, all on the recommendation of the state Parole and Pardon Board. Remember that Thurmond had campaigned for governor on a platform of limiting the pardoning powers of the governor and had seen to it that those limits were enacted. His invective was so strong that his own wife told him, "I almost feel sorry for him (Johnston) myself."[11]

By June 22, Johnston had had enough. His first counterattack addressed the pardon issue and Strom's Colonels. He charged that Thurmond had appointed as Colonels some of the people whom Johnston had pardoned. The Johnston camp also sent out numerous postcards showing Strom standing on his head—Strom was even referred to as "Stand-on-Head." But these were expected barbs with no real effect.

A more ominous note was sounded the same day when an Iowa Senator announced he was launching a Senate investigation into "Dixiecrat" money that might be helping Thurmond. This was more than just one member of the "club" helping out another. It was almost unheard of for Congress to investigate primary spending; this had all the earmarks of a Truman vendetta. Strom had made powerful enemies. (That this was a vendetta is supported by the timing: this "investigation" was called off without any official report or action on July 14, three days after the primary.)

This was not the only money question before the people of South Carolina, however. Late in the campaign, Drew Pearson charged that Republican money was helping Thurmond's campaign. This charge was never substantiated. Thurmond also ran into some trouble during the campaign by attempting to drag Senator Maybank into the picture, though only incidentally. One of Thurmond's issues was that Johnston was a Truman supporter during the 1948 elections, against the wishes of the South Carolina Democrats. By way of comparison, Strom noted that Senator Maybank had supported the efforts of the States' Rights Democrats and his campaign for president. Maybank was politically weaker than Johnston, and not wanting to be stuck in the middle, he told the people of the state that he was having no part in the U.S. Senate campaign—in effect, asking Thurmond to leave him out of it.

The pro-Truman/anti-Truman issue was a viable one in the South. In North Carolina, Senator Frank P. Graham, a Truman supporter, was defeated by a conservative Raleigh attorney in their Democratic primary. Ultra-liberal Senator Claude Pepper was also defeated in Florida for much the same reasons. (Pepper, of course, would reappear in Congress in the House of Representatives and serve for years as an advocate for senior citizens.)

Strom's supporters hoped to keep the trend going and bounce yet another Trumanite. For his part, Thurmond did all he could to keep the issue hot. On June 30 in Spartanburg, Thurmond lambasted Johnston: "My opponent has demonstrated that he thinks more of getting a few crumbs which may drop from the Truman-Pendergast table in Washington than representing the people of South Carolina in the Senate." The Pendergast family ruled Kansas City's (and Missouri's) politics and were reputed to be Truman allies.[12]

Another problem encountered by Thurmond involved organized labor. He had made a play for their support, but as the campaign moved into the unionized areas of the upstate, he found he had worse than nonsupport from these groups—he had active opposition. In Walhalla, a group of textile workers waited for the governor outside the courthouse, apparently looking for trouble. When a constable warned Thurmond to go out another way, Strom took the offensive. Angrily demanding "Where are they?" he strode down the steps to confront them. They were dispersing, however, rather than meet his challenge. Another incident occurred in Greenwood when a group of people tried to force their way into Thurmond's hotel room as they were preparing to leave for a campaign address. The mood of the campaign was angry.[13]

One especially ugly aspect of the campaign involved the issue of race. It was inevitable that race would be injected into the campaign. Court rulings, black involvement in primaries, and pressure to end segregation had most white politicians either backpedaling or taking the offensive—and most took the offensive, there being no middle ground. This set up a situation in which ordinarily decent men sought to "out-racist" each other. The contest between Thurmond and Johnston brought out the worst in both.

The fireworks started on June 26 when Thurmond accused Johnston of sitting by idly while Truman's plan to integrate the armed forces was discussed in the U.S. Senate. To everyone's surprise (because Johnston had not been a vocal advocate of continued segregation), he denied the charge and accused Thurmond of being a liar. Thurmond was on solid ground in his accusation and bristled at the name calling. He offered to meet Johnston "outside" after the meeting and labeled Johnston both a demagogue and a hypocrite. After that, Thurmond campaign ads would repeatedly show a picture of Johnston toasting Attorney General (and former Senator) Howard McGrath, the sponsor of the FEPC legislation and the man who was charged with bringing integration to the South.[14]

As Thurmond's charges about Johnston's laxity in defending segregation began to stick, Johnston began trotting out charges of his own. He reminded the people of the state that Strom had appointed a black physician to the Hospital Advisory Council. The famous Johnston style showed itself very clearly in an ad which ran on July 6. Johnston was quoted from a June 26 speech in Laurens: "I would have suffered my right arm to have been severed from my body before I would have signed a commission for a Negro."[15] This issue became so intense that the S.C. Medical Association wrote letters to the editors of various state newspapers absolving Thurmond of any "blame" in this incident.[16] Johnston also reminded the people that Strom had invited a black man (Governor Hastie of the Virgin Islands) to stay at the Governor's Mansion.

The final indignity came during a last-minute campaign stop in Charleston, where both candidates lowered themselves and "vie[d] for the title of racial segregation's sincerest champion." Both candidates were booed by the blacks in the audience, and at one point, losing his cool completely, Johnston pointed at them and yelled, "Make those niggers quit."[17]

With that kind of campaign crescendo, the primary election on July 11 drew a record crowd of 346,329 voters (including about 60,000 blacks). Johnston won a narrow victory by a margin of 178,088 to 153,554. James F. Byrnes was easily elected as governor and Strom's lieutenant governor, George Bell Timmerman, Jr., was reelected.

In defeat, Strom was congratulatory, if not expansive, in his message to Olin Johnston. The real epilogue to the election was written in a newspaper that most white people never read, the *Lighthouse and Informer.* This black newspaper ran the following front-page editorial immediately after the election: "We think that his [Johnston's] tenure, experience and his already having had his former attempt to throttle the Negro chastised makes him a safer agent of the people than the cocky, verbal filth tossing opponent [Thurmond] who really set the pace for the lowest campaign South Carolina has seen. . . . In Tuesday's election . . . knowing that our people . . . went along with the Senator even though they had to hold their noses and shut both eyes and ears, it is a pleasant feeling to assume that votes from the hands of the very people against whom he stood . . . are largely responsible for his continuing in office."[18] The word had gone out—through the churches, from President Truman, through labor leaders and others—that South Carolina blacks should stick with the devil they knew, and they had.

In his characteristic way, Johnston was said to have put forward his own scenario as to why Strom lost: "Well, the doggoned fellow had to go stand on his head, else he woulda whipped me!"[19] It wasn't that simple. And old "Stand-on-Head" still had a few months left in office, and a few more things to accomplish.

Heading for the Exit

The 1950 primary election was Thurmond's first real defeat in his entire career. In the 1948 presidential election, he carried the state of South Carolina (and three others) over the incumbent, so there was no shame in that effort even though he had not won in any sense of the word.

The 1950 election deeply affected him. This is not to say he was a sore loser, but there was certainly evidence that he felt somewhat cold toward the people of the state. His actions seemed to say that if the people did not want him to serve them in an elective capacity, he might just pack up his marbles and go.

Almost immediately after the election, rumors began circulating regarding his future. No major office would be up for election until at least 1952, and even then, a seat in Congress was all that would be up for grabs. Of course, he could always return to the practice of law or perhaps take up where he left off on the bench. These options did not seem to have much appeal.

In late July rumors began circulating that Strom would be offered a position with the Santee-Cooper power authority. He had always championed the power issue and had regular contact with the board, but in mid-August, he denied that he would accept such a position.[20]

The Anderson *Independent* began reporting another job offer, one more to Strom's liking. The newspaper suggested that Strom was considering rejoining the military with the rank of colonel, even speculating that he might resign from the governorship early to do so. Thurmond did nothing to contradict this speculation and even added fuel to the fire by continually suggesting his availability to serve his country in the escalating Korean conflict. As the days passed, it became apparent that Strom may even have hoped it would happen that way. The S.C. Military District released information that the Third Army Headquarters in Atlanta was expected to form a military government staff section (Strom's previous service) and that it would be activated on November 1 of that year with Strom as its commander.[21]

Even as late as October 28, when asked what he was planning to do, Strom acknowledged that he had been asked to "activate and organize a military government staff section" in the U.S. Army Reserves. The implication was that this was an imminent move that would require his resignation. If it had happened that way, Strom would have left the governor's office dramatically, donning his uniform and going off to serve his country. On October 31, the army confirmed that Strom had been appointed to the post but indicated that, as it was a reserve unit, it would not be mobilized immediately. The next day, the issue resolved itself as an official statement confirmed that Thurmond had not been ordered into active duty. He would be allowed to serve out his term as governor.

All this frantic activity concerning his future did not prevent Thurmond from maintaining an active interest in the affairs of the state. Before he left office, a final incident allowed him to show that he was not in any way affiliated with the radical elements of the anti-civil rights movement. When he learned that a member of the state law enforcement staff had been involved in activities of the Ku Klux Klan, he revoked his commission, stating: "My position on mob rule is well known. I am against it."[22]

Thurmond also devoted some energy to removing another barrier to black participation in South Carolina government: the poll tax. At his urging, a referendum had been placed before the people of the state that enabled them to take the poll tax off the books. In speeches prior to the November 7 general election, he repeatedly urged that the poll tax be revoked. The voters supported his position, and the poll tax was eliminated.

In his final days as governor, Strom was also able to play host at the Southern Governor's Conference, held November 26–28 at Charleston, South Carolina. In their way, by holding the meeting in South Carolina, the rest of the southern governors had put their stamp of approval on Strom Thurmond.

Numerous news organizations also took more formal surveys of Thurmond's effectiveness as governor. Most of them acknowledged what was obvious: he had accomplished almost all the goals he had set for his term as governor. To do so in South Carolina, where the governor's power was almost totally limited to his persuasive abilities, was remarkable. To do so while campaigning for president and the U.S. Senate was even more so. And when you add the component of Strom's public feud with some of the most powerful figures in the legislature, his success was astounding. Even his vehemence in supporting segregation was offset by his efforts on behalf of South Carolina's black citizens to ensure their safety, improve education and economic opportunities, and facilitate their entrance into society.

Strom Thurmond also presided over one of the most honest administrations, up to that point, in the state. There were no major scandals, and not even any minor ones. There were no suggestions that Thurmond ever profited by his dealings as governor—even his critics charged him with excessive ambition rather than with any wrongdoing.

In his final address to the people as governor, on January 10, 1951, he sought to lay out all the positive things his administration had done for the state. He also asked the people to give the governor more power (still an issue in the state today). He singled out South Carolina's elder statesman James F. Byrnes for special praise. Earlier, when excerpts from Truman's biography *The Man of Independence* had accused Byrnes of "failing miserably" as secretary of state, Thurmond had defended Byrnes and commented, "This again demonstrates the low ebb to which the party and our government leadership has degenerated."[23]

Now, in his final address to the people, he called Byrnes "one of the greatest living statesmen of our generation."[24] There can be no doubt that Thurmond had a special affinity for Byrnes. They had worked together back when Thurmond was a young lawyer and stayed cordial over the years. Thurmond's public tribute to his successor was sincere. For his part, Byrnes had an answering affinity for the younger man. The strength of this relationship and its value to Thurmond would be significant in the future.

For now, the Thurmonds were embarking on a new way of life. For the first time in his adult life, Strom would not be on the public payroll. For the first time in her married life, Jean Thurmond would not be living in the Governor's Mansion. Their new situation would require adjustments, but the qualities that had contributed to Thurmond's success in public life—hard work and persistence—would pay dividends in private life, as well. One question would always remain, however: How long would Strom remain a private citizen? Strom had ideas on this, but once again, circumstances would force him to alter his plans.

Chapter 10

THURMOND

AT LARGE

I n January of 1951, for the first time in his adult life, Thurmond found himself in the position of not taking a check drawn from the taxpayers. From his days as a teacher, school superintendent, senator, judge, colonel, and governor, he had always been a public servant. Now his only obligation was to himself and to his wife, Jean.

It must have been strange to him as he spoke with a reporter for the Orangeburg *Times and Democrat* about his future. Thurmond summed up his term as governor: "My ambition while governor has been to give the people honest, clean progressive government" and to "promote integrity and efficiency in government." As to his plans, he said, "I don't know whether I'll ever run for another office. . . . I expect to forget politics except as a private citizen." He did leave one little door open when he said, "I will, however, continue to fight for what I think is for the best interest of our state and people."[1]

After turning over the governorship to James F. Byrnes, Thurmond took a month off and prepared his papers for donation to the South Carolina archives. He also directed his efforts toward earning a living. When the army position had not materialized, he had set about to create a law firm.

He surprised many by deciding not to return to Edgefield. Instead, he selected the "resort" town of Aiken, a pleasant area that was experiencing tremendous growth due to the proximity of the Savannah River Plant. Here, he and his wife rented an apartment while they made plans for the construction of their modest seven-room house.

Strom also made connections with two local attorneys (Dorcey Lybrand and Charles E. Simons) to create the firm of Thurmond,

Lybrand and Simons, with offices on the second floor of a building across from the Aiken Post Office. Sara Fox was hired as the firm's first secretary, and their business was steady, if not spectacular, from the outset.[2] One of the best sources of their business was the Savannah River Plant. To create the plant, the U.S. Atomic Energy Commission had to purchase large tracts of land. Some of the prices offered by the AEC did not suit the owners and they sued for a better price. An example of the success of the Thurmond, Lybrand and Simons effort is demonstrated in the case of Albert and Frank Weathersbee. The AEC had agreed to pay $37,500 for 703 acres of the Weathersbees' land. After a suit, Judge C. C. Wyche awarded the pair $61,500 for the land.[3] This hefty increase demonstrated to the people of Aiken that Strom got results, and he did not lack for business.

Being linked with a well-known politician had its advantages and disadvantages, as Lybrand and Simons quickly found out. One advantage was in the heightened visibility (and added business) that came with the celebrity; a disadvantage was that there was no such thing as a retired politician—politicians were likely to go out of retirement at any time.

By April of that year, Strom's friends were already trying to "drag" him back into public life, at least in a limited way. The vehicle was the Reserve Officers of America, an organization comprising officers of all branches of the armed services who were active in the reserve. Thurmond was a colonel in the reserves and participated in the activities of the ROA. On April 28, the ROA of South Carolina adopted a resolution backing Thurmond for national president of the organization. By May he was giving speeches again, this time on military strength and foreign policy.

His first "major" address of private life was given at an ROA meeting, where he outlined a five-point program for the reserve forces. The main thrust of his speech was that the United States should remain "armed to the teeth" to be able to fight Communist aggression, and that an essential component of that strategy involved increased funds for the military reserve.[4]

The issue of who would lead the ROA was to be resolved on June 20, 1951, at the ROA national convention in Long Beach, California. As luck would have it, the primary contender for the position was an officer with President Truman's backing. Even in Thurmond's private life, the feud continued. And as had happened in the past, Truman's man won. (Fortunately for Thurmond, the Truman magic had played itself out with the ROA defeat, so far as Thurmond was concerned. In the future, Truman's opposition would help more than it would hurt.)

Despite his failure to rise immediately to the presidency of the ROA, this was not to be Thurmond's last involvement with the group. The ROA was to play a role similar to that of the Junior Order of United American Mechanics in that it brought him continued positive publicity, all over the state.

While Strom was in Aiken, he was also active in the creation of the Aiken Federal Savings and Loan Association. He personally handled the application and secured approval from federal officials in Greensboro and Washington. (Thurmond was to serve as president of this banking institution in addition to his practice of law.)

On the political side, there was another interesting development during the year, this time from the Republicans. In September some three thousand Republican leaders (including previous delegates to the national convention) from all over the country were polled regarding their choices for president and vice president in the 1952 elections. There was no clear consensus as to the presidential choice (Eisenhower was not yet officially in the race), but there were some fascinating developments on the vice presidential portion of the question. On the Republican's top-ten list were four southern Democrats: Senator Walter George of Georgia, Senator Richard Russell of Georgia, Governor James F. Byrnes of South Carolina, and private citizen Strom Thurmond of South Carolina.[5] Clearly, even at this date, the Republicans were looking to the previously solid South for support. Thurmond had shown the nation that the South was not solid by his victories in 1948. The Republicans were looking for other openings.

Perhaps the most interesting story to come out of 1951 did not involve politics but rather involved Thurmond in his role as an attorney. The crime was murder, and Strom agreed to defend an Augusta, Georgia, woman named Margie Kennedy. This "sensational" murder case (and Strom's defense of Mrs. Kennedy) was reported all over the country.

The facts, in brief, are as follows: Margie Kennedy had been married for twenty years to John B. Kennedy, a 250-pound former public safety director of Augusta, Georgia, and a leader in the local "Cracker" political party. A parade of witnesses testified that Mrs. Kennedy had been subjected to various kinds of abuse for most of their twenty-year association. Finally, Mrs. Kennedy had grabbed a .22 calibre pistol and shot her husband several times, and when he had tried to run, she shot him again. When she was arrested, she told the authorities, "I shot him, and damn him, I hope he's dead." Fortunately for her, John B. Kennedy did not die immediately. He held on for a few days—long enough for Margie to go to the hospital, talk with her husband, and be with him when he died. After this reconciliation (of sorts), Mrs. Kennedy decided she was sorry she had shot him.

This was only the first part of the bizarre story. Many angles of defense were open to Thurmond, but the one he chose was that Mrs. Kennedy had not really killed her husband, insisting he had died of natural causes. Strom then presented medical testimony verifying that Kennedy had suffered from heart trouble, diabetes, and Bright's disease, caused by chronic nephritis (a form of kidney disease). Strom's chief witness, Dr. Thomas Godwin, testified that "He [Kennedy] could only have been expected to live from one to two years under his existing physical conditions. The bullets that struck him were just the straw that broke the camel's back." Strom himself made the argument that if Kennedy had been healthy, a "few little .22 slugs" would not have killed him. The only thing the defense conceded was that the bullets might have speeded up Kennedy's death somewhat.

The state of Georgia chose to respond with an incredible argument of its own. Rather than debate Mrs. Kennedy's guilt or innocence, the prosecutor spent considerable time trying to establish that Mrs. Kennedy had alcohol problems.[6] The prosecution's climax was when Mrs. Kennedy's daughter, Helen Kennedy Black, admitted under questioning that her father did not give her mother any money because he was afraid she would use it to buy liquor.[7] In the end, it took the jury only four hours to acquit Mrs. Kennedy on what had to be one of the most sensational defenses ever presented. The bells on top of the courthouse tolled at 6:00 P.M. as Mrs. Kennedy walked out to her freedom.

Pictures of Thurmond and his elated client were carried in many newspapers and news publications. Once again, Thurmond was in the limelight—and if the light was not always flattering, it was still illuminating.

The balance of 1951 and the early part of 1952 passed rather uneventfully, with Strom continuing in his legal duties and taking an active role in the development of the savings and loan association. His other interests, the ROA and politics, would begin moving back to the center stage, however. The first indication came with the 1952 S.C. Democratic convention. At that April 16 convention,

Thurmond was elected as a delegate to the National Democratic Convention. Again, as had been the case in 1948, the South Carolina delegates were almost certain their interests would not be represented by the national party's presidential nominee. At first, they were afraid Truman would run again, but even among the other potential candidates, no one pleased the southern delegates. At their state convention, the South Carolina Democrats gave themselves an out, passing a resolution that "the Democratic Party of South Carolina reserves to itself the right to determine its course in the general election, at a subsequent meeting of the delegates of the convention." They suspected even before the national convention that they would not be happy with their party's nominee, and they were determined not to be locked in to that person, whomever it might be.

In May of 1952 Strom's interest shifted back to the ROA when they honored him with a leadership position. The South Carolina ROA elected him as their president, giving him a platform to speak on national defense and military issues. It was a platform he would use extensively over the next several years. Of course, discussions on national issues suggested a larger role at some time in the future—and this suited his needs well.

Strom used his attendance at the national ROA convention in San Antonio to discuss national politics. He expressed his hope that Eisenhower (the Republican nominee) would end up on the Democrat ballot, at least in his state. "I know of no reason why, if the National Democratic candidate is undesirable, an independent state could not make anyone it chooses a candidate," he said.[8]

Strom's place inside the Democratic party appeared to be on thin ice at that point. Prior to the Democratic National Convention, Strom's old adversary, John Bolt Culbertson, appeared before a credentials subcommittee and asked that Thurmond be refused his seat at the convention. Culbertson cited Thurmond's 1948 candidacy for president as evidence. Once again, however, Strom got a little help. Senator Maybank was a member of the subcommittee; Culbertson's appeal was ignored and Strom was seated.

The 1952 Democratic convention was really a Roosevelt show. Eleanor Roosevelt and the Americans for Democratic Action had their candidate, Adlai Stevenson, selected as the presidential nominee. Stevenson was a "New Deal" style liberal and anathema to the southerners.

Franklin D. Roosevelt, Jr., had earlier spoken passionately in favor of a resolution saying no delegate would be seated who did not pledge himself to "exert every honorable means" of seeing that nominees were placed on every state ballot. This resolution, which was adopted, was aimed at the 1948 bolters, and at those delegates who might still have revolution on their minds. In light of South Carolina's instructions to its delegates, Governor Byrnes, who headed the delegation, thought his delegation might be expelled. They did remain at the convention, but when they went home, the mood was not one of unity. Among many southerners there was a real desire to leave the Democratic party—at least the national Democratic party.

Mayor Francis F. Coleman of Mount Pleasant publicly called on Thurmond to lead the state's efforts to make Eisenhower the Democratic nominee in South Carolina, effectively dumping Stevenson from the ticket. One of Strom's allies, former Senator George Warren, eventually headed the South Carolina for Eisenhower movement. Once again, there was rebellion in the air.

From his return from the convention in July through the election in November, Thurmond was very busy. Army reserve duty at Camp Gordon, Georgia, with the 360th Military Government headquarters unit was sandwiched in with his legal and civic duties. In August he agreed to serve as president of the Aiken Community Chest (a forerunner of the United Way). And in October he was back at his role as a defense attorney. In this case, he was able to win acquittal for a man charged with murder when a passenger riding in his car had been killed in a crash.

Thurmond also acknowledged that he was still stewarding over $18,000 contributed to the States' Rights campaign that had come in too late to be spent. He reported that these funds were still on deposit with Security Federal Savings and Loan in Columbia. He had been somewhat forced into revealing that these funds were still intact because of charges that an amount in excess of $15,000 of States' Rights funds had been given to the effort to elect Eisenhower in South Carolina, when in fact no money from this fund had been sent to Eisenhower.

As the presidential campaign heated up, the state's Democratic party was divided into two camps, those favoring Stevenson and those favoring Eisenhower. Surprisingly, Eisenhower had considerable support even among some elected Democratic officials. Governor Byrnes announced his support of Eisenhower and came to be branded by some Democrats in the state as a Republican.

On November 2, Strom Thurmond again climbed out on a political limb and publicly endorsed Ike: "I have followed General

Eisenhower in Europe, and I am following him again in his present crusade. . . . I sincerely believe that General Eisenhower can lead us to an honorable peace [in Korea] and bring our boys home. I will vote the ticket of the South Carolina Democrats (South Carolina for Eisenhower) for Eisenhower."

There was an outcry at Thurmond's statement from state Democrats and from national Democrats. In South Carolina, Edgar Brown predicted a landslide for Stevenson. He was wrong. Brown had also made another speech that would later haunt him. As reported in the Columbia *Record* of October 10, while stumping for Stevenson (and attempting to show how voting for Ike was different from voting for Strom), Brown said, "We voted for Thurmond and Wright four years ago because they were the candidates of the Democratic party of South Carolina and because they were the best Democrats in the race." His acknowledged support of Thurmond's efforts in 1948 would be an issue in a different campaign. Another response to Strom's endorsement came from Minnesota, home of Senator Hubert Humphrey. Humphrey declared that Thurmond's endorsement would hurt Eisenhower.

As the nation went to the polls on November 4, however, the voters gave their ringing endorsement to Eisenhower by awarding him 442 electoral votes and over 33 million votes, while Stevenson won only 89 electoral votes (only about twice what Thurmond won as a third-party candidate in 1948). Eisenhower did not carry South Carolina, but the vote of 172,957 to 168,043 was surprisingly close. Thurmond had opened the door, and now a Republican had carried three southern states (Florida, Tennessee, and Virginia) and came close to winning others.

In what was a fitting (and ironic) tribute to South Carolina, the 1953 presidential inaugural was one of marked contrast with the 1949 event. For when governor James F. Byrnes of South Carolina passed before the new president, Ike rose to his feet and favored him with a big smile and a wave. Compared to Truman's snub at the previous inaugural, it was like a breath of fresh air. With Eisenhower's election, South Carolina was back in the union.

This did not mean that Byrnes and Thurmond (or even South Carolina) were back in the good graces of Harry Truman, however. In a January 17, 1953, interview from Miami, Truman indicated he might want to return to Washington as a member of Congress (as John Quincy Adams had done). He also used this opportunity to express his continued anti-Byrnes and anti-Thurmond sentiments.

Meanwhile, Thurmond's ROA activities gave him a pulpit of his own. In February, in a speech to the Cleveland, Tennessee, Chamber of Commerce, he registered his opposition to international treaties (under the auspices of the United Nations) that superseded the American constitution. He remarked, "I am afraid of world government. It is a dangerous thing."[9]

An opportunity to reassert his populist stance in South Carolina also arose during the early part of 1953. The state legislature had passed a law that would enable resigned state judges to apply for retirement pay. With characteristic Thurmond style, Strom publicly refused to consider the option. Several state newspapers supported his stand.

As Strom became poised to become even more active in national ROA activities, his old supporter from Clemson College, Lieutenant Colonel Leonard R. Booker, was elected president of the South Carolina ROA to succeed Strom. In June of 1953, the national ROA convention was held in Philadelphia. This convention was significant for two reasons. First, Thurmond was elected as the national vice president for the army. Second, Strom found himself in a receiving line, forced to shake the hand of former President Truman, himself a colonel and ROA member. Newspapers all over the country carried the photo of the two men smiling and shaking hands. Thurmond, when queried about the incident, remarked that there was no significance to the handshake, it was "just a greeting of one Reserve office to another."[10]

With all the heightened publicity surrounding Thurmond, the rumor mill in South Carolina became active. There was speculation that he would soon end his not-so-private life and seek public office. Most insiders thought he would seek Senator Maybank's seat in the 1954 elections, but some speculated he might want his old job as governor back. There was ample evidence that Strom was out for something. Using his ROA position as a wedge, he began a national speaking schedule, giving speeches on military issues to ROA audiences as far away as California and Texas. No doubt about it, Strom was after something. It could even have been that he was seeking a political appointment from President Eisenhower.

During this period, Ike was filling numerous military and national defense posts. As a former field commander who had served under Ike, although indirectly, Thurmond certainly qualified. His public support of Eisenhower's campaign in South Carolina, coupled with his general support of Eisenhower's programs also support this supposition. No military appointment materialized, however, and Strom had to content himself with adopting a watchful attitude toward state politics.

The first Thurmond news of the year, 1954, was made not by Strom but by his wife, Jean, who was comfortable with the life in Aiken. She had been involved in a variety of activities, from teaching Sunday school at the First Baptist Church to serving as assistant chairman of the Community Chest drive and chairing the Cotton Festival in Aiken. For her efforts, Jean was elected as the first Woman of the Year by the Aiken Chamber of Commerce.

For Strom, publicity early in the year came from what he did not do. Specifically, he decided not to challenge Burnet Maybank for his U.S. Senate seat and he did not enter the governor's race. As a matter of fact, he did not enter any political race at all. The political climate in the state was relatively quiet that year.

James F. Byrnes was completing his service as governor somewhat discreditably. He had supported a Republican for president, a sin that some in the state would not easily forget. The governor's race was not especially exciting: George Bell Timmerman, Jr., finally got the opportunity to seek the seat after eight years as the lieutenant governor. His opposition was relatively weak, and he easily won the primary. Burnet Maybank had no opposition at all in his Senate race and was apparently headed toward another six-year term.

Thurmond had apparently decided to wait until 1956, when he would have another crack at Johnston. That he was not seeking public office did not mean he was inactive. He continued to seek publicity. In May he received a publicity boost, this time from his friend Governor James F. Byrnes. When Strom's old legal cohort Judge T. B. Greneker had to attend to his mother's illness, Governor Byrnes appointed Strom as a temporary judge of the Eleventh Judicial Circuit—his old circuit. He presided over the session of court held in Saluda and used his "charge" opportunity to praise the calibre of solicitors who had represented Saluda. This allowed him to remind the people of Saluda that J. William Thurmond, his father, had been the first solicitor of the area, from 1896 to 1904. There were no major cases before the court at Saluda, and so Strom's last appearance on the bench proved to be an uneventful one.

Strom spent most of the middle months of 1954 pursuing a higher ROA office. His heightened stature had already enabled him to add his voice to one of the saddest affairs of American government in the 1950s, the witch hunt for Communists by Wisconsin Senator Joe McCarthy. In the middle of the Army-McCarthy hearings, Thurmond was in Boston, speaking to an ROA assembly at the University Club. When asked what he thought of the proceedings, Strom replied, "I have every confidence in Army Secretary Stevens [then under attack by McCarthy] . . . I favor elimination of communism from all positions in government and defense work, and such steps are necessary to do this, including investigation by the appropriate agency. But any investigation should be absolutely free of character assassination, free of head-line hunting and publicity seeking and must be absolutely truth-ful."[11] Once again, Thurmond's sense of decency has asserted itself. The idea of people being convicted without due process in a circus atmosphere appalled him. He spoke out even though anti-communist sentiment was strong at the time.

Thurmond's ROA position also enabled him to see a missing element in the coordination of national defense. He was one of the first to urge the creation of an Under Secretary of Defense with Reserve responsibilities. In June, at the national ROA convention in Omaha, Nebraska, his devotion to the cause of reserve officers and their mission was rewarded: he was elected the national president of ROA. Not only was he elected, he was elected without opposition—the first time anyone had not been opposed for the post. In his acceptance speech, he outlined a fifteen-point program designed to enable the reserves to better accomplish their duty. Its chief components were a better pay structure for reservists, better facilities and equipment, and the equalization of rights between reservists and regulars.

On July 15, President Eisenhower invited him to the White House to speak about the defense needs of the country. At that meeting, Thurmond reiterated his key points and made a strong case for his proposals. He made quite an impression on the national leadership in a short time. On July 20, he testified before the Senate Armed Services Committee and urged Congress to "stop this business of kicking around" the reservists.[12]

And later in July, the U.S. attorney general appointed him as a delegate to the national Conference on Citizenship to be held in Washington September 15–17. To all the world, it appeared that Strom was settling into the role of dignified elder statesman, perhaps in line for a future appointment. But, as always when Strom appeared ready to settle into a role, something happened that was to alter his course abruptly.

On September 1, 1954, U.S. Senator Burnet Maybank died of a heart attack in his sleep at his Flat Rock, North Carolina, summer home. His death set off a political scramble that would test old friendships and strengthen old resentments. Strom was going to get another chance at the elusive U.S. Senate seat.

A Successor to Maybank

Burnet Maybank's career was meteoric. His first election success was his race for an alderman's spot in Charleston. He followed this up with service as mayor of the historic city, and then, in 1938, he defeated Wyndham M. Manning to be the first Charlestonian elected to the governorship since the Civil War. In 1941 he was elected as a U.S. Senator and had been reelected in 1948 over a field of candidates that included Third District Congressman William J. Bryan Dorn. In 1954 Maybank was the recipient of a free ride in the Democratic primary, and since the Republicans did not make even a token opposition, he would have been elected easily in November.

When he died on September 1, the South Carolina Democratic party was faced with the dilemma of putting someone into that slot. Without a sanctioned candidate on the ballot, all sorts of extremes were possible, including the election of a Republican. But how to fill the vacancy? A full six-year term was at stake—had this been a nomination to fill two years of a term, it might have been less of a problem for the party.

While he was a state senator, Strom Thurmond had helped draft a law that was designed to empower party leaders to select a candidate in cases such as this. One aspect of this law was that candidates had to be selected and certified by the state election commission at least sixty days before the election. There were ways around this law, though, that would have allowed for a primary election to select a candidate, and this proved to be an issue throughout the campaign.

The day after Maybank's death, the press speculated on who would be chosen to succeed him and assumed the nominee would be selected under the "Thurmond law," which enabled state Democratic party executive committee members to make the selection. Three names that immediately came forward were those of Strom Thurmond, Donald Russell (a former law partner of Governor Byrnes and president of the University of South Carolina), and Governor Byrnes. Coupled with this speculation came the first rumblings of a second course of action—a primary to nominate Maybank's successor. State executive committee member Jesse S. Bobo of Spartanburg suggested that a primary was desirable. If an individual were nominated and then resigned his nomination after the filing date, the party could hold a primary prior to the general election. This course of action was discussed by state Democratic party Chairman Neville Bennett and S.C. Attorney General T. C. Callison.

By September 3, however, the idea of a primary had been discarded, and the speculation returned to what the executive committee would do. By now, the list included Edgar A. Brown, national executive committee member and state senator; Marion Gressette, another Barnwell County leader; and Neville Bennett, the state party chairman. Senator Brown made a public statement regarding the inclusion of his name: "I could not refuse [the senatorship]," he said, if it were offered.[13]

The Charleston *News and Courier* suggested that Brown was likely to get the nod even though Governor Byrnes and Chariman Bennett supported a primary. Byrnes was emphatic that a primary should be held, even before he knew who might be nominated by such a scheme. On September 4, the day of Senator Maybank's funeral, Byrnes was informed that the executive committee of the party was likely to select a candidate. Byrnes's reply was, "If the committee does, it will cause a political revolution in this state and I'll help the revoluters."[14]

Later that day, Senator Maybank's funeral was held in Charleston and attended by almost every politician of note in the state. As the funeral procession moved solemnly from the church to the cemetery, Edgar Brown's car was seen to pull out of line and head toward Columbia, where the executive committee was meeting.[15] The only business before the executive committee was how to handle the Maybank situation. After some discussion, Rembert Dennis moved that the committee should appoint Maybank's successor. A motion to table this motion was lost by a vote of 29 to 18. With the committee on record as desiring to appoint the state's next U.S. senator, all that remained was to name the person. Once again, Dennis had the floor, this time nominating Edgar Brown, reminding the group that Brown was a man who had "served you faithfully and well through the years and who deserves the Senatorship." Another delegate gave Brown the credit for holding the state in the Democratic column in 1952. When the vote was taken, Brown was nominated by a vote of 31 to 18. And he was profoundly moved, saying, "I feel as humble as I did in the old days when I was a youngster in old Aiken County."[16] And indeed, he should have been grateful. This group of men had handed him something that he had not been able to win outright in two previous tries in 1926 and 1938.

In the aftermath of the executive committee's decision, there were two general responses from the people of South Carolina. The first response was that Brown's nomination was a good one. After all, he was eminently qualified to serve and he was known all over the state. The state's newspapers, however, took a dim view of the fact that thirty-one people could select a U.S. senator and began a furious, coordinated tirade against his nomination. As this attack continued, the people of the state became energized.

One of the first to speak up was an old friend and ally of Strom Thurmond. Mount Pleasant Mayor Francis Coleman called the nomination a disgrace and suggested that Strom be a write-in candidate. Of course, running as a write-in would be difficult: write-in candidates have almost no chance in any election. But for the people of South Carolina, this was virtually the only option open. (The state Republican party considered putting someone up so the people would have a choice, but the Republicans were splintered into several factions and this proved unsuccessful.)

The action quickly heated up after the committee's announcement. Two hundred and forty-six citizens of Marion telegraphed Strom and asked him to run. Greenville Representative Preston S. Marchant proposed Burnet R. Maybank, Jr., as a possible write-in candidate. He also suggested that whoever was elected should pledge to resign in time for a primary in 1956. Representative Dorn, a distant runner-up to Maybank in 1948, publicly opposed the committee's actions, and it was suggested that he might offer to be a write-in candidate.

On September 6, Governor Byrnes showed his distaste for the Brown nomination by appointing Greenville businessman Charles E. Daniel to fill the vacancy, with his appointment to expire on January 2, 1955. Like Byrnes, Daniel had supported Eisenhower in 1952. Byrnes's action was significant because if he had appointed Brown to fill the vacancy, he would have endorsed the executive committee's decision. And if he had appointed any other of the senatorial hopefuls, he might have killed their chances. His appointment of Daniel was perfect strategy. Byrnes was a master of political strategy; he demonstrated his talent more than once during this election.

On September 8, Strom Thurmond announced that he would be a write-in candidate. He declared that he was a Democrat, a South Carolina Democrat, that he would support the Democratic party where he could. But, underscoring his support of President Eisenhower, he indicated that "partisanship should stop at the water's edge."

Meanwhile, others in the state continued to keep things hot for Brown and the executive committee. Former state senator J. M. Lyles, of Fairfield County and a member of the executive committee, publicly charged that the "Barnwell ring" still controlled the state. The Charleston County Citizens League voted to oppose the Brown nomination and endorsed Thurmond. A special meeting of Democrats in Edgefield County asked the committee to reconsider their stand on a primary and went on to endorse Thurmond. A straw poll at Baron DeKalb High School in Westville gave Strom a huge margin as the teens voted 39 to 15 for him.

At that point, there began, inexplicably, a series of actions by people inside and outside of South Carolina that would dramatically assist Thurmond's efforts. First came a statement from national Democratic party Chairman Stephen Mitchell that the party would support Brown's nomination. This gave Thurmond the opportunity to remark, "the national Democratic party has never been able to dictate to the people of South Carolina as to how they should vote and I'm sure it cannot do so today."[17]

The national party had already been rejected in 1948 and almost rejected again in 1952. If they had really wanted to help Brown, they would have stayed out of it. Only a few days later Edgar Brown repudiated the help of the national party, declaring, "It won't be necessary for him [Mitchell] or any other outsiders to campaign for me . . . The issue here is loyalty to the Democratic party."[18] When Mitchell was confronted with questions about the South Carolina race only a few days later, he had gotten the message, at least temporarily. His rather terse reply was, "I have no further comment on that thing at all." But he did comment one more time—with disastrous results for Brown.

Meanwhile, the people in South Carolina continued to have their say: the Sumter County Democratic executive committee unanimously condemned the state committee's actions and endorsed Strom (this time with one dissenting vote). In Greenville County, the local executive committee voted 42 to 15 to ask the state committee to reconsider.

Governor Byrnes took advantage of a brief respite in anticommittee activities to suggest that they examine their decision to hold a primary in light of the obvious support for one and to allay bad feelings. That same day, Congressman Dorn took himself officially out of the race. In a speech to the Columbia Jaycees, Dorn noted that he had prepared himself since childhood for the office of U.S. senator but that he was willing to "forget personal ambition for the sake of patriotism and good will."[19]

In his autobiography, Dorn gave a slightly different version of his decision not to run. By his recollection, shortly before Maybank's death, Thurmond had invited Dorn to Aiken to attend an American Legion meeting. Taking Dorn aside, Thurmond had supposedly said to him, "You realize that someday both of these seats will be coming open. Now, Bryan, Maybank's seat is yours. You ran for it before. But Johnston's seat is mine." Dorn recalled, "We weren't making a deal, but we shook hands on it as though that is the way it would be."[20] But after Thurmond's announcement, Governor Byrnes and others called Dorn and suggested that he not run.

Although Dorn was out, Marcus Stone, the perennial candidate, tossed his hat into the ring and so did Heyward Brockington. Brockington quickly withdrew, however, leaving only two write-ins: Thurmond and Stone. In reality, it was a two-man race between Brown and Thurmond. When it started, it appeared to be an uphill battle for Thurmond, but his spirits were buoyed by widespread public wrath at the committee's tactics, and his chances were aided by that crafty old politician Jimmy Byrnes. The combination of these two factors put Strom in the driver's seat.

While a write-in challenge may not have seemed like much of a threat to anyone outside the state, Senator Brown and his supporters recognized the potential damage of the effort from the beginning. On September 16, state party Chairman Neville Bennett pledged that "wherever opposition to a Democratic nominee develops, every assistance will be given to the Democratic nominee by the Democratic party. We will protect the Democratic party and Democratic candidates against attacks from without and sabotage from within."[21]

Note Bennett's repetition of the word *Democratic* in this statement. This call to party loyalty was to be the chief issue of the Brown campaign. In their eyes, the party had picked its nominee and party loyalty alone should dictate support of a nominee. The people, however, were beginning to have second thoughts about blindly supporting the party that had been presenting them (at the national level, at least) with a series of unsatisfactory candidates.

The same day Bennett took to the press to sound the trumpet for party loyalty, some party regulars were warming to the support of the senator. Weyman H. Busch, an Aiken County deputy sheriff, wrote to Senator Brown, declaring, "I am proud that we have a real Democrat running for the U.S. Senate, one that we can trust and one that most of the good people of the state can put their faith in. . . . The Sheriff's office of the County here is behind you 100%."[22]

As the party faithful became energized, Brown and his organization began corresponding with supporters and potential supporters all over the state. When Brown wrote Busch back, he speculated, "We ought to beat them good in Aiken County."[23]

Meanwhile, Governor Byrnes continued to call for a primary. In another public statement, Byrnes went out of his way to let the people know he had nothing against Brown personally. He said, "On that day [Maybank's death] no meeting of the state committee had even been called so no person can justly say that my advocacy of a primary election was due to the personality or political record of any individual." Byrnes and Brown had a long-standing political relationship that had become personal over the years. Brown had even had Byrnes serve as the best man at his wedding. But the actions of the committee had really incensed Byrnes, and true to his word, he began to actively help the "revoluters"—one revoluter in particular.

Byrnes had picked up on the notion of having whoever was selected as the U.S. Senate nominee resign near the end of his term to force a primary in time for the next general election in 1956, and he encouraged Thurmond to make that pledge part of his campaign. This would entail the necessity of resigning the office if he won, but it would firmly endear him to the voters in the current election. Over the advice of many of his friends and his wife, Thurmond agreed to make the pledge and made major headlines with the statement on September 18. The newspapers in the state had already been somewhat favorable to Strom's candidacy, and with this announcement, almost every newspaper in the state fell in line behind him (the notable exceptions being Wilton Hall's Anderson newspapers, the *Independent* and *Daily Mail*.) The united voice of the state press infuriated Brown and his supporters to the point of labeling most of the press as "Republican minded" as part of their efforts to paint Thurmond as a non-Democrat, supported by other non-Democrats.[24]

To further emphasize Strom's "outsider" nature, Senator Olin Johnston publicly endorsed Brown for Maybank's Senate seat.

There had been some speculation that Johnston might be secretly supporting Thurmond in hopes that he would not have to face him again in 1956. Johnston's support of Brown immediately drew a negative response from various South Carolina citizens. One such letter, written immediately after Johnston's announcement (and dutifully forwarded to Brown), suggested that there were already fourteen votes against Brown and that "In closing I wish to state that I consider myself a better Democrat than Edgar Brown or anyone who supports him in this coming election."[25]

Others thought their rights had been abridged and were given favorable attention by the newspapers of the state. Citizens in Charleston, Aiken, Calhoun, Lancaster, Horry, and even Anderson County went on record as opposing the committee's actions. Many of them also indicated some level of support for Strom Thurmond.

While Strom was making speeches hammering away on the theme of voters' rights, one upstate daily, the Greenville *News*, made a point of asking Senator Brown if he would step down so a primary could be held—the state attorney general had indicated it was still not too late to do so. Brown took his time in responding, and when he did, his response was not warmly greeted. In a prepared statement delivered on September 30, Brown declared: "I would be a traitor to the Democrats of South Carolina who are supporting me as the Democratic candidate . . . and would be aiding and abetting those who for years have sought to control the Democratic party of South Carolina and who, having failed, now seek to [w]reck it if I gave any consideration to the suggestions of the Republican minded Greenville News that I withdraw from the race." Brown went on to defend the committee's actions and his own actions based on the short amount of time left for filling the vacancy. He concluded this statement by campaigning against Eisenhower, who was not on the ballot.[26]

Brown's defense did not convince the voters. In fact, this entire incident was an example of the ineptitude with which Brown ran this race. Numerous opportunities lay before him to counter the Thurmond threat. He could have agreed to resign and allow a primary, or he could have matched Thurmond's pledge to resign within the first two years of the term. Instead, Brown clung to his coveted prize—the nomination as the Democratic candidate.

The official party counterattacks against Thurmond relied on some inept tactics, as well. Neville Bennett went before the people to ask that Thurmond bring a lawsuit to test the legality of the committee's actions. This would have served the party because the courts would have upheld the actions of the committee—they were legal. Strom had not said they were not; his argument was predicated on fairness. In a speech in Sumter, he had said, "This is not a political campaign, it is a crusade for the right of the people to express their own choice." In this way, Strom was saying that a vote for him was more than just a vote for him; a vote for him was a vote for their rights. Even some who did not personally support Thurmond agreed with that argument.

Brown also continued his campaign blindness by refusing to meet with Thurmond in public debates. An outstanding leader with high popularity ratings could snub challengers calling for debates (as Thurmond himself would do later). But Brown was already charged with being afraid to face the people, so this seemed to justify the initial charges. Brown went so far as to skip a Spartanburg League of Women Voters meeting where Strom was also to appear.

Then, making matters worse, the national Democratic party chairman Stephen Mitchell made another statement that deeply offended South Carolinians. In a comment that was reported widely in South Carolina, he said, "They may have a different level of education down there but in Illinois if a man had his name printed on a ballot and if the people had a choice of marking an "x" by his name or writing in the name of J. Strom Thurmond, the man with the printed name would win."[27]

This kind of "help" for Brown was all Thurmond could have hoped for. How condescending of the Yankee to suggest that South Carolinians could not write. The response was swift, carried by South Carolina newspapers responding to the challenge. Strom rekindled the old dislike of northerners with his response: "Evidently this friend and supporter of the committee thinks that the people of South Carolina cannot write. . . . They will let this Chicago lawyer know that South Carolinians resent his interference in the politics of this state."[28]

On October 12, the error was compounded by the Democratic Senatorial Campaign Committee when they sent $2,500 to help Brown in his race against Thurmond. The final, crippling blow to Brown's campaign was delivered by Strom's old adversary Harry Truman and his military aide Harry Vaughn. On October 15, the state press carried word that Truman had endorsed Brown and declared him as the "real" Democrat in the race. Then, General Vaughn (retired) had further complicated the mess with one of the most inane statements ever made in public: "Harry Truman has been a 'regular' so long, he can forgive small things like rape and murder but he can't forgive a guy who goes back on his party." Surely Vaughn did not mean to suggest that a U.S. president considered party loyalty a higher power than the law. Yet that was exactly what Vaughn said, in an effort to "help" Edgar Brown.

Within a couple of days, word was leaking out of Brown's camp that if he were elected in November he might try to force Senator Daniel into resigning before January so Brown could have the seat. The underlying theme was probably that he wanted to rid the Senate of an Eisenhower supporter as quickly as he could, but in the state press it just looked like another monumental campaign goof.

By mid-October, Brown felt forced to tie the write-in effort firmly to the Republican party. In a speech delivered to the Columbia Chamber of Commerce, Brown charged: "The write-in campaign being waged against the legally certified nominee of the Democratic party for U.S. Senator, presents but one question— whether the people of the State desire to replace a great Democrat, Burnet R. Maybank, with a Democrat or replace him with a 'write-in' ally of the Republican Party."

Race was to be the pivotal issue for almost all southern candidates during the 1950s (and into the 1960s), and Brown tried to make the most of it in the Senate campaign by attempting to tie Thurmond into the Republican initiatives that dealt with integration. "Our way of life in the South is in danger of being destroyed unless a Democratic controlled Congress can stem the tide of Republican race mingling." His hope was that by linking Thurmond with the Republicans, he could run against a series of Eisenhower administration decisions that had not set well with many South Carolinians. In his speech, Brown cited farm issues and the executive order that President Eisenhower initiated abolishing segregation in all industrial plants. Brown then launched a forceful attack on Republican foreign policy.[29]

All this might have been helpful if he had been running against a Republican, but Thurmond was an avowed Democrat. And unlike Truman, who could not do enough for his candidate, President Eisenhower wisely stayed out of the race, insisting it was a race between two Democrats.

As Brown became more desperate, he sought the help of other Democrats in the state. Former Governor Ransome Williams issued a statement criticizing Thurmond for failing to pay adequate respect to Truman's vice president, Alben Barkley, when he had visited Columbia. (Strom had not invited Barkley to the Governor's Mansion when Barkley was in town.) Williams closed his statement with "He [Strom] has rebelled against our two-party system, yet he has the unspeakable nerve to ask Democrats to support him, a self-nominated, partyless write-in candidate."[30]

Another blow delivered on behalf of Brown came from Alex S. Salley, a retired South Carolina state historian who sought to justify Brown's nomination on previously similar actions. In his address to the people of the state, Salley noted that the "Executive Committee had a long standing precedent. In 1886 General Arthur N. Manigault had been nominated by the Convention for the post of Adjutant General. He died before the election. The executive committee met and nominated Mr. M. L. Bonham for the place. No perpetual candidate had his jealousy aroused by this honor paid to Mr. Bonham, and so there was no whine that this was a 'dangerous precedent.'"[31]

These two slaps at Thurmond showed how desperate Brown was becoming. Neither of these men had any great influence with the people of the state. They delivered messages in support of Brown because they were the best he could find. Many of the other elected officials in the state were afraid to publicly support the actions of the committee. So it was left to outsiders, political lightweights, and Brown himself to deliver the message.

Even Brown's message was relatively weak. Rather than campaign on his strengths (years of legislative service, and so on), Brown tried to hinge everything on party loyalty. This was the same party loyalty that had been strained, stretched, and broken completely in 1948, and sorely tested again in 1952. Brown was calling on something that was not really there.

On October 19, Brown publicly proclaimed that Thurmond protested Brown's nomination only because the committee had not given it to Thurmond. This weak charge had almost no impact coming so late in the campaign, and it was brusquely thrust aside by Thurmond, who said he had always wanted a primary.

Governor Byrnes held his views of the race between Thurmond and Brown to himself. On October 23, however, he nailed perhaps the last nail into the Brown coffin with his public endorsement of Thurmond. Seeking to clear up any misunderstanding, Byrnes said, "I want my position to be clear. I would not vote for any person in South Carolina nominated by the Committee under the circumstances in which this nomination was made. I have told friends who asked me privately and I now say publicly I shall write in the name of Strom Thurmond."[32]

In addition to this affirmation of support, he also lauded Thurmond's previous service: "As Governor, on many occasions, I have had to read the files as to transactions during Strom Thurmond's term as governor. From the records of this office I know that as governor he was honest, forthright, capable and courageous. Strom Thurmond is clean in his personal life as well as in his public life. No one of us is perfect. Certainly Strom Thurmond has made mistakes. But there never has been even the breath of scandal as to his service. . . . There has never been even the slightest suspicion of Strom Thurmond ever using public office for personal gain."[33]

As the campaign entered its final week, Strom flung back the charge that he had deserted the Democratic party by proclaiming that Brown had deserted the Democratic party in 1948 by voting for him. Brown countered by calling Strom's charge a "tissue of lies"—the same phrase that he had used regarding Thurmond in the 1946 governor's race—and added that "I have no respect for him and have never voted for him at any time for anything."[34] When Thurmond then produced a copy of a speech in which Brown acknowledged that he had supported Thurmond, Brown countered that when he said "we voted for Strom Thurmond" he was speaking for the Democratic party as a whole.[35]

The whole thing was hopeless. No matter who was right (and Strom was, apparently), Brown's denial and then subsequent evasions only further confirmed that he was not to be trusted. The final Brown public relations fiasco revolved around an old friend and enemy of Strom's: state Senator Robert M. Kennedy. The Brown people dug up copies of Kennedy's previous feud with Thurmond and put his name on an ad supporting Brown. At that, Kennedy suddenly reappeared as a Thurmond friend, denying he ever had endorsed Brown and giving Strom a warm endorsement.[36]

November 3, 1954 was election day in South Carolina, and unlike most general elections in South Carolina, this one was well attended. Some disturbances were reported during the day, such as when Barnwell County Sheriff Jeff Black struck a Thurmond supporter and ordered him to leave the polling place. In most places, though, voting proceeded without incident—but slowly. In areas where there were voting machines, foot posture could tell those watching from outside how people voted (short people who voted flat-footed were voting for Brown; it they stood on their toes they were writing in Thurmond).

Counting took a lot longer, too, but the results were obvious almost from the moment the polls closed: a massive Thurmond victory. When the final tally was in, Thurmond had received 143,444 votes to Brown's 83,525. When Thurmond faced the people later that evening, he was very humble, congratulating the people of their "great victory" and repeating his pledge to resign in time to create a primary in 1956.

The reaction was jubilation for Thurmond and a resigned coldness for Brown. Brown's attitude was not helped any by the hate mail he received as he was hearing the results. One telegram read, "Congratulations on your defeat. You asked for it and I helped you get it."[37]

Brown and the committee had completely underestimated the feelings of the people. They had also underestimated the power of the press. Their almost unanimous voice constantly pounding on the voters had been decisive. Helped by his "friends" and blinded by his own ambition, Brown had also contributed to his defeat. Despite the setback, Brown was a consummate politician, and by December 3, was corresponding with his friends around the state, thanking them for their help. By then he was beginning to see at least part of the reason he had lost. "We fought a good fight but the Republican segment of the press abused the power of the free press to distort the truth and mislead the people by building up the false issue, to wit: the disenfranchisement of the people, and kept the same alive by feeding it on lies and prejudice. The news columns were closed to our side."[38] This last part, at any rate, was true.

It was a few days before the miraculous nature of what had happened really sank in on Strom and the people of South Carolina. History had been made in this campaign. Never before had a write-in candidacy produced a winner at this level of government. Strom was riding high in personal popularity in the state. Governor Byrnes must also have felt some vindication in Strom's election. If there was any Byrnes referendum buried in the Brown-Thurmond campaign, Byrnes had won it handily. Now, with the election behind him, it was up to Thurmond to make the most of his opportunity.

Chapter 11

THURMOND GOES TO WASHINGTON

The 1954 Senate campaign was decided on one issue—the selection of Edgar Brown as the Democratic nominee by the party's executive committee. Brown spent little time talking about other issues, and Thurmond spent less time than Brown. When the people of South Carolina elected Strom Thurmond, they did not know what to expect. If they thought about it at all, they assumed that he would be interested in the same things as senator that he was as governor, but they could not be certain.

The nation as a whole was experiencing both peace and prosperity. Internationally, the mushrooming Cold War was a cloud on the horizon. The chief national issue was race relations, spurred on by a series of court decisions that struck down segregationist laws. The most famous of these court decisions was *Brown v. Board of Education of Topeka et al.* This decision, delivered on May 17, 1954, by the U.S. Supreme Court, ended legally segregated schools. Southern politicians were seething at this decision and continued to look for ways to legally preserve segregation. In South Carolina, agriculture was still important. So as he contemplated his upcoming duties as a U.S. senator, Thurmond could have expected to be involved in those three issues, as well as many others.

He was eager to begin his duties. Almost immediately after his election, rumors began circulating that Senator Charles E. Daniel, who had been appointed, would resign so Thurmond could take his seat early and gain a little seniority over the other incoming freshman senators. (In the battle for committee seats, seniority is a key factor, so this move would have made some sense.) Senator Daniel, however, appeared slightly miffed at the suggestion that he resign and stated that he had no plans to do so before January 5, 1955, when his appointment officially expired.

By Christmas Eve 1954 (perhaps at the urging of Governor Byrnes), Daniel had changed his mind, and resigned his seat in the U.S. Senate so the "Honorable Strom Thurmond" could get a seniority edge for the benefit of South Carolina. Thurmond quickly set up his senatorial staff, appointing Governor Byrnes's press secretary, Alex McCullough, as his administrative assistant. Shortly thereafter, he appointed Harry Dent as his press secretary, and Richard Dusenberry as his personal assistant. He completed his office staff by hiring Loretta Conner, Dorothy C. Hope, Jean Quarles, and Sarah Jones Steppe.

When it was time to leave South Carolina for Washington, Strom and Jean decided to drive rather than fly. Strom was so excited that at one point he made Jean stop the car so he could jog off some nervous energy. Once he arrived in the nation's capital, he continued to exhibit this high energy level.

One of his first meetings as a senator came on January 4, 1955, when the Senate Democratic Caucus met to conduct pre-session business. These meetings were used to map out legislative strategy and to settle some routine "housekeeping" issues. The most important issue at this particular meeting involved the selection of the secretary to the majority, since the Democrats had a majority in the Senate.) This person (who was not a senator) assisted the Democratic Senate leader in his administrative duties. The selection of this officer had South Carolina implications: Bobby Baker of Pickens, South Carolina, was the leading candidate. Baker had managed Edgar Brown's Senate campaign against Strom, but Strom was in no mood to carry the feud to Washington.

Thurmond supported Baker and indicated that he did so because having him in the position of secretary to the majority would be beneficial to South Carolina. After ten days as a senator, Thurmond was already turning into a statesman.[1] Baker was elected to the position and served in government at the national level until a scandal during the Johnson administration forced his return to private life.

On January 5, Thurmond was sworn into the U.S. Senate by the vice president of the United States (also the presiding officer of the Senate), Richard M. Nixon. In the first few days of Thurmond's term as a senator, it was difficult to tell which party he belonged to. Within a week of being sworn in, he was at the White House, conferring with President Eisenhower. A scant week later, the president nominated Thurmond for a promotion to brigadier general in the reserve (which was granted on February 8 of that year).

And when he had the opportunity to speak to the Southern Society in New York City, Thurmond told the audience that "an aroused electorate cannot be considered a sure thing for any political party." While this may have sounded innocuous, his reference was clear—the South was no longer in the bag for the Democratic party. Even though he had run as a Democrat and come to Washington as a Democrat, there was a lingering feeling that he was not necessarily a party man.[2]

In the aftermath of the senatorial campaign, many thought Thurmond might find a cool reception awaiting him in the U.S. Senate. After all, he was an outsider: he was elected over the "regular" Democratic nominee but was not Republican. During the election, Senator Brown had charged that Strom was "neither fish nor fowl" and that he would be ineffective as a senator.

As has been the case so many times in Thurmond's life, though, fate intervened to lessen the impact of his choice. In this case, the deciding factor was the closely divided U.S. Senate. The 1954 election saw the Democratic party regain control of the House of Representatives. They regained Senate control, too, but by a very slim majority. So slim, in fact, that Independent Senator Wayne Morse (formerly a Republican) proved to be the swing man. (Morse negotiated some desirable committee assignments in exchange for agreeing to organize with the Democrats.) But the margin of control was very small and every vote counted—a fact well known by Senate Majority Leader Lyndon Baines Johnson of Texas. Johnson knew he could not afford to alienate any of his charges, and he made it clear from the outset that conciliation would be his path. Even before Thurmond reached the Senate, Johnson and Senator Richard Russell of Georgia had made public statements to the effect that Thurmond would get "good" committee assignments, the real essence of power in the Senate. A senator on the right committees could wield significant influence over legislation in those areas. In those days, freshman senators were often assigned to relatively unimportant committees, such as the District of Columbia Committee (the committee that oversees the administration of the nation's capital) or the Post Office Committee.

Thurmond's appointments were a little better than average, all things considered. He was placed on the Interstate and Foreign Commerce Committee, the Public Works Committee, and the Government Operations Committee. These were not his first choices but neither were they his last.

With his well-known vigor, Thurmond dove into the routine of the Senate and was accorded some very quickly conferred responsibilities. In mid-January he was appointed to a Government Operations subcommittee studying some of the recommendations of the Hoover Commission. (Former President Herbert Hoover chaired this blue ribbon panel that made recommendations to streamline the federal government.) Strom's reputation for streamlining South Carolina government was certainly a factor in this important appointment.

On January 26, the absence of Vice President Nixon and most high-ranking Democratic leaders enabled Thurmond to serve as the president of the Senate for about an hour. This honor is seldom accorded totally green freshmen and almost never so soon in a senatorial term. If there were signs that he was unwelcome in the Senate, they were well hidden.

In addition to the conferred honors, Thurmond reached out for additional responsibility—first by way of a speech. The Senate is a tradition-bound institution where custom is a powerful force. At that time, the understanding was that freshman senators did not make Senate speeches during their first year of service. They were to be seen and not heard, to a certain extent. But more than one Senate tradition was tested by the impetuousness of Strom Thurmond. Although he was aware of the custom, he took the floor in his first month in office and gave a six-minute speech supporting Eisenhower's plans for the defense of Formosa (Taiwan) against attack from Communist China. Thurmond characterized this defense "not as an act of aggression but a step toward preservation of peace."[3]

The whole issue of China and its relationship with its neighbors was constantly before the Congress in those days. Another issue, one that remained through President John Kennedy's administration, involved two island neighbors of China: Quemoy and Matsu. There was speculation that China might annex these islands with military force, and when President Eisenhower refused to be hemmed in as to specific defense plans for these islands if they were attacked by the Chinese, Strom Thurmond came forward again to applaud him. On foreign affairs, Ike had a friend in Strom.

Domestically, it was another story, however. The 1954 *Brown v. Board of Education* decision overturned the concept of "separate but equal" contained in *Plessy v. Ferguson*, which was decided in 1896. When the court overruled its previous decision, it created turmoil all over the country, particularly in the South. Republican

President Eisenhower was to prove as firm as Democratic President Truman in his desire to end segregation—going so far as to federalize the National Guard in Little Rock, Arkansas, to ensure integration of Arkansas schools. For this reason, many southern Democrats who tended to support Eisenhower's foreign policy found themselves fighting him on domestic issues. (For their part, South Carolina's legislators also disapproved of much of Ike's farm policy, as well.)

Racial questions were constantly before Congress at that time. In the middle of the efforts to keep the Supreme Court out of racial questions was Strom Thurmond. Congress had the power to set limits on the kinds of cases that could be appealed to federal courts, and Thurmond introduced a bill that would have kept the racial issues out of the Supreme Court and in the more localized district courts, where friends of segregation would be more likely to sit on the bench. This bill had the public support of most southern leaders, including Governor Timmerman of South Carolina and Strom's old nemesis and current Senate colleague, Olin D. Johnston. And when Ike sent the name of John M. Harlan to the Senate for confirmation as a U.S. Supreme Court justice, Thurmond was one of eleven senators to vote against his confirmation. Strom's opposition was due, in part, to his concerns regarding Harlan's views on civil rights.

But if Thurmond was against federal involvement in matters of racial discrimination, he went out of his way to suggest that the federal government should play a role in reducing sexual discrimination. In February of 1955 he coauthored a bill with Senator John M. Butler, a Maryland Republican, that would amend the Constitution to read: "Equality of Rights under the law shall not be denied or abridged by the U.S. or any state on account of sex." Strom was one of the first to take a public stand on this issue, and he did so in the early 1950s, long before the Equal Rights Amendment was passed by Congress and sent to the states.[4] Strom had always supported women's interests: throughout his career in public life he had advocated greater responsibilities and opportunities for women. After his marriage, he moved even further as a supporter of women's equality. (This piece of legislation was thought at the time to convey more property rights to women and to allow them to serve on juries. Its original authors did not envision the sweeping changes later accorded to it. Strom continued his support of this legislation, and when it was presented later as the Equal Rights Amendment, he supported that.)

Meanwhile, an intra-party squabble was heating up again between national Democrats and South Carolina Democrats. In March of 1955 Harry Truman came back to the Senate to visit his old friends. Thurmond left the Senate floor to avoid him. A short while later, Democratic Chairman Stephen Mitchell declared that former South Carolina Governor James F. Byrnes was "personally obnoxious" and should be barred from the 1956 Democratic National Convention. Part of this flap came about because South Carolina Democrats had selected a night to honor Byrnes that conflicted with a dinner in honor of Texas Congressman and House Speaker Sam Rayburn. This conflict was not intentional, but it forced many politicians to choose between honoring Byrnes or honoring Rayburn. In the end, every South Carolina politician except Senator Johnston, state Senator Brown, and two congressmen decided to honor Byrnes.[5]

In May it was reported that both of South Carolina's senators had supported President Eisenhower on 62 percent of the votes. This support was chiefly in foreign affairs issues; on the domestic front, southern congressmen, in general, were becoming more and more antagonistic to Ike's civil rights moves. The furor over civil rights caused Eisenhower to retreat slightly on one issue rather than lose some of his valuable southern support.

The issue involved a military reserve bill that incorporated many proposals endorsed by the ROA to strengthen that portion of the service. Congressman Adam Clayton Powell, a black representative from New York, had added an amendment to the bill that would have made segregation in reserve units illegal. This amendment caused southern legislators to move to block passage of the measure. In an effort to remove the southern obstruction and have the law enacted, President Eisenhower made a public statement defending his record of fighting against segregation, both in the military and out of it, but emphasizing that national defense should not be jeopardized by a contest over this amendment. He urged that the bill be passed as it was. He suggested that the antisegregation measures should be taken up and debated on their own merits. Senator Thurmond heartily approved of the president's stand on this issue, both because he supported passage of the legislation and because it was well known that southern congressmen had been able to prevent most stand-alone civil rights legislation from coming to a vote.

Later in June Thurmond once again went to bat for the president on a national defense issue. In this case, the Democratic majority wanted to reduce the size of the Marine Corps, over the president's objections. Majority Leader Lyndon Johnson suggested to Thurmond if he wanted a seat on the powerful Armed Services Committee, he would support the move. Once again, though, Strom stood up for his convictions. He confronted Johnson with the threat and said, "Let's get one thing straight right now. I've got to vote my conviction."[6] When the votes were counted, Ike lost by a vote of 40 to 39, and Thurmond's standing with the Democratic leaders was sinking. This incident is important because once again, Thurmond had placed conviction above ambition. As a World War II veteran, brigadier general in the reserves, and ROA president, Thurmond was a natural for the Armed Services Committee, and he wanted the post. When it was offered in exchange for a vote that he found repugnant, he refused it. Especially repugnant would have been the "deal" aspect of this offer. In his public service, he had not operated that way, and LBJ's notorious political "oil" grated on Thurmond.

The balance of Thurmond's first year in the Senate found him involved with two major issues—the continuing battle over integration and alcohol. The first issue erupted when President Eisenhower sent the name of Simon E. Sobeloff to the Senate for confirmation as a judge for the Fourth Circuit Court of Appeals. This court handled appeals from South Carolina, and Thurmond came out against Sobeloff because "he has been a strong advocate of integration of the races in the public schools."[7] Due in part to his opposition (and opposition from other southern legislators), hearings before the Judiciary Committee were postponed.

Shortly after that incident, the Fourth Circuit Court handed down a decision that made it impossible to maintain segregation on buses traveling in the state. At this attack on segregation, Thurmond was moved to state that efforts to maintain segregation would continue, despite the court order.[8]

But his response was weak on that issue compared to the offensive he mounted toward the end of the year. In November Thurmond said he would propose legislation that would eliminate the tax-exempt status for organizations that originated lawsuits to which they were not a party. He said this measure was aimed at some thirty-five thousand organizations that did not pay taxes. Alert observers digested the information and recognized it as an attack against the NAACP. The NAACP had made great strides for blacks by suing various states and institutions and challenging segregation and discrimination wherever it was found. These suits were coming before more favorable judges as time went on. Strom's effort to eliminate the NAACP's tax-exempt status could have ended most of its activities. Even with this effort, at the end of the year, he vented his growing frustration with the federal courts. He suggested that he was ready to impeach all nine of the U.S. Supreme Court justices.

The only other major issue Thurmond addressed that year involved alcohol. Here, he reaffirmed his position and urged the Civil Aeronautics Administration to ban the sale of alcohol on all commercial and military flights. If nothing else, he was proving to be consistent.

The alcohol issue was important to him, but the main issue before Congress—ending segregation—was a growing threat to the white southerners' way of life. As segregation barriers came down one after another, the feeling among southern whites was beyond anger and heading toward desperation. Thurmond recognized that the issue would not go away, and he was determined to continue his fight to prevent further federal intervention. His efforts would be complicated, however, by a promise he had made to the people of South Carolina.

While campaigning in 1954, he had promised to resign so there could be a primary. As a man of his word, he intended to resign, but that meant an interruption of his Senate service. Thurmond knew something drastic would have to be done to combat further federal intervention in the South's way of life—and as always when something needed to be done, he was willing to do it. Before he resigned, he threw himself into the preparation of a document that he hoped would explain the South's position on race relations. The document's official name was the "Declaration of Constitutional Principles," but it came to be known as the "Southern Manifesto."

The "Southern Manifesto"

In his 1956 State of the Union message, President Eisenhower recommended that Congress appoint a bipartisan commission to investigate charges that blacks were being subjected to "unwarranted economic pressures." This proved to be the opening shot in a conflict that resurrected arguments almost two hundred years old regarding the nature of our federal union. For his part, Thurmond set the tone in his response to the president's remarks when he said, "I regret that the President has been persuaded to recommend

the establishment of a commission to interfere in matters
reserved by the Constitution to the control of the individual
states."[9]

Thurmond's response was in keeping with his views on the
founding of our nation and the intended balance of power between
the states and the national government. Our system of government
is known as federalism, which means two distinct levels of government serve the people on different issues. Our national government
was created when representatives of the original thirteen states
met to create a plan to strengthen the anemic national government
that existed after the Revolutionary War. The states agreed to
surrender certain powers to the national government, but they
intended to keep the national government from ever becoming so
strong that individual liberties were lost. (For that reason, they
included the provision that all constitutional amendments must be
ratified by the states.) Specifically, the framers of our Constitution stipulated that all powers not expressly conferred on the
national government in the Constitution are reserved to the states
or to the people. This stipulation is directly stated in the Tenth
Amendment to the Constitution, part of the Bill of Rights that
many states insisted on before they would ratify the new Constitution.

In the view of many conservatives, if an item is not directly
referenced in the Constitution, the national government has no
authority to enact laws in that area. Others hold that the Constitution grants the national government many powers indirectly. This
argument began in President Washington's first Cabinet, when
Alexander Hamilton suggested that Congress had broad powers
and Thomas Jefferson argued that it did not. This debate continues
to this day, but in the 1950s and 1960s, the argument revolved
specifically around the question of segregation. There is no mention anywhere in the Constitution directly regarding integration,
and southerners used this omission to defend the practice.

As Thurmond and others called on the national government to
refrain from further interference in state issues, many people were
gathering to show their continued support for segregation. In a
speech in Myrtle Beach, Lieutenant Governor (later a senator of
South Carolina) Ernest F. Hollings said that "public schools are for
education, not integration."[10] And Senator James Eastland of Mississippi was joined by many South Carolina politicians and four
thousand others at the Township Auditorium in Columbia at a
meeting of the Citizen's Council. The sole purpose of this meeting
was to unite against integration.

In February the South Carolina legislature harked back to another constitutional argument and passed an "interposition" resolution. Interposition was first proposed secretly by Thomas Jefferson in response to a series of bad laws passed by the Federalist party in the late 1790s. The thrust of interposition was that states can interpose (and suspend) operation of federal laws in their territories pending an inquiry into the constitutionality of the laws. This argument was picked up by John C. Calhoun of South Carolina in response to a series of tariff laws that almost destroyed his state's economy. Thurmond, in his subsequent support of federalism principles and strict interpretation of the Constitution, placed himself directly in this line of political succession. The main articulation of the modern argument in favor of interposition (and against federal pressure to integrate) was called the "Declaration of Constitutional Principles," or the "Southern Manifesto," and Senator Thurmond was intimately involved in its production and presentation.

The actions on this declaration began early in 1956 when Thurmond approached other Southern senators suggesting that they issue a declaration of their views regarding the U.S. Supreme Court's desegregation decision of May 17, 1954 (*Brown v. Board of Education of Topeka et al.*). In this decision the court had construed the Fourteenth Amendment regarding "equal protection of the laws" as prohibiting segregation in public schools. Senator Thurmond found a strong ally in Senator Harry Byrd of Virginia, and he immediately set to work producing the first draft of the work.

In his first draft, Thurmond attacked the Supreme Court for its "disregard" of the historic background of the segregation issue: "Only by following the intent of the framers of the [Fourteenth] amendment and the people who ratified it could the Court hope to arrive at a constitutional decision. But . . . the Court did not follow the constitutional intent in the school cases. Instead, the Court sought the opinions of modern-day sociologists and psychologists."[11]

Thurmond's key point in this draft was that since the Constitution does not mention education, "public education is a matter for the States and the people to control." He then went on to list eight declarations that ranged from reliance on the Constitution as the supreme law of the land to calling on his Senate colleagues to join in approving a resolution that would make clear to the Supreme Court that "equal protection is provided to all citizens where separate but equal public facilities are maintained."[12]

This first draft was subsequently reworked by Thurmond and presented as a second draft to a meeting of southern senators that was called by Senator Walter George of Georgia, the senior southern senator. There was some delay in getting this meeting set, as some of the senators thought the issuance of a manifesto would be useless. But because of Thurmond and Byrd's insistence, Senator George called the meeting for February 8, 1956, in his office.

At this first meeting, Thurmond's second draft was presented to a committee for further study and consideration. This committee consisted of Senator Richard Russell, chairman; Senator John Stennis of Mississippi; and Senator Sam Ervin of North Carolina (later to gain fame in the Watergate hearings). When this committee did not report back in a short time, Thurmond and Byrd again agitated for action. Another meeting was held, and this time Senator Spessard Holland of Florida, Senator Price Daniel of Texas, and Senator William Fulbright of Arkansas offered a draft that was considered along with a draft from the Russell committee. The new draft was not as strong as either the original Thurmond draft or the Russell committee draft, and another committee was formed under Russell's leadership to draft yet another document. This time, Thurmond was on the committee along with Russell, Stennis, Daniel, and Fulbright.

The committee presented its final draft to Senator George, who sent a copy of the completed draft to Congressman Howard Smith, who circulated it among interested House members and tried to obtain as many signatures as possible.

In the final draft, many of Thurmond's original ideas were maintained. The "Declaration" stated: "The original Constitution does not mention education. Neither does the Fourteenth Amendment nor any other amendment. . . . The very Congress which proposed the [Fourteenth] Amendment subsequently provided for segregated schools in the District of Columbia." The Declaration went on to trace the origins of the doctrine of "separate but equal" to an 1849 case, *Roberts v. City of Boston* and then demonstrated how many northern states had maintained separate school facilities. The declaration also defended the *Plessy v. Ferguson* decision in 1896, which encapsulated the "separate but equal" concept, and pointed out that as late as 1927, Chief Justice William Howard Taft (also a former president) had noted that the separate-but-equal principle is "within the discretion of the State in regulating its public schools and does not conflict with the Fourteenth Amendment."[13]

The "Declaration of Constitutional Principles" stopped short, however, of endorsing a resolution reaffirming the separate-but-equal principle. Instead, by this document, the signatories pledged to "use all lawful means to bring about a reversal of this decision which is contrary to the Constitution and to prevent the use of force in its implementation."[14]

Nineteen southern senators and ninety-four southern congressmen signed the final document before it was presented to the Senate by Senator George on March 12, 1956. (Senate Majority Leader Lyndon Johnson and House Speaker Sam Rayburn were not asked to sign. Because of their leadership positions, neither man could afford to sign, but it would have been difficult for them to face their constituents if they had refused to sign.) Thurmond took the floor after George to support the action, and he declared that the South would "fight to the end" to defend segregation. His speech was followed by Senator Wayne Morse of Oregon, who denounced the action of the southerners.

Support of the "Declaration" proved to be the last straw for South Carolina's black voters as far as Thurmond was concerned. Despite being couched in constitutional language, the "Declaration" ran counter to the interests of black South Carolinians, and they have not forgotten it.

Thurmond's boldness in taking such a major leadership role also rankled some senatorial veterans. Traditionally, a Senate junior did not take that kind of action—but Thurmond had done it and he was prepared to accept the consequences. Consequences would have to wait for a while, however. In a March 3 letter to Governor Timmerman, Thurmond had resigned his seat in the Senate, fulfilling his promise to the people. His intention was to resign as of April 4. Governor Timmerman accepted his resignation and appointed Strom's friend, Greenville's Thomas A. Wofford (who handled the defense for the Willie Earl lynching trial), to serve as an interim senator, through January of 1957. Wofford's stated ambition was to make at least one speech in the Senate.

Toward the end of March, as Thurmond served the remainder of his notice, he was elected as a delegate to the Democratic National Convention and nominated as the national committee member to face Edgar Brown. In a gesture of goodwill, Strom withdrew in favor of Senator Brown.

Thurmond kept up his attacks on integration, and in late March he charged that communists were behind efforts to create racial turmoil. As proof, he cited information from the Ohio attorney general's office that communists were trying to enlist members of the Labor Youth League in a campaign for federal intervention in the segregation issue.[15]

Meanwhile, Thurmond's resignation was not producing any great rush of challengers for a primary. A political neophyte, Frank R. Thompson of Anderson, placed his name in the ring and then withdrew it some thirty seconds before it would become official. This would not have been a serious attempt to unseat Thurmond anyway, but as it was Strom had no opposition and was guaranteed to return to the Senate.

When his resignation took effect, Strom rejoined his old law firm and participated in a victory for a client in a land condemnation suit that was tried before George Bell Timmerman, Sr., Strom's old opponent for the Eleventh Circuit judgeship and now a federal court judge.

Anyone who thought Thurmond would take it easy during this interim was bound to be disappointed. As always, Strom stayed busy, doing what he liked best: making speeches and attending meetings. His speeches were generally against further intervention in local issues. He also took time out to attend the funeral of Fielding Wright (his former running mate). Getting further involved in local issues, Thurmond agreed to serve as the honorary chairman for the S.C. Association for the Mentally Ill's annual fund drive.

These activities took a back seat to the turbulent political situation of the times. Nationally, the Democrats were searching for someone to defeat President Eisenhower. In South Carolina, the issue again was whether the state party would support the nominee or not. Prior to the national convention, seven state Democratic leaders issued a public statement that they would work within the party framework. This was not the same as saying they would actively support the party's nominee, but it was a pledge that they would not participate in third-party activity. After their statement, Thurmond made a statement of his own. He decried their actions and pointed out that guaranteed adherence to the national party's rules would eliminate one of South Carolina's most effective weapons in the fight to lend more weight to southern opinions.

Prior to the Democratic National Convention of 1956 in Chicago, Thurmond (and several others) had indicated that they would not support another try for Adlai Stevenson. The picture was further muddled because Stevenson did not have enough committed delegates coming into the convention to be nominated. Adding to this unpromising situation was former President Truman's intention to endorse a candidate of his choice: former New York Governor Averell Harriman (a New Dealer).

Naturally, Truman's choice pleased no one in South Carolina, so the state delegation nominated Governor Timmerman as a favorite son. On the first ballot, Timmerman received eighteen of South Carolina's votes, while Stevenson received two and Harriman none. Despite maneuvering from various convention elements, Stevenson was nominated for a second try at Eisenhower.

The convention then attempted to placate the South again, this time by choosing Senator Estes Kefauver of Tennessee as its vice presidential nominee. Once again, however, Thurmond and most of the rest of the South Carolina delegation were not appeased.

The state Democratic party met after the national convention to decide what to do and opted to remain behind Stevenson's nomination. (There was not as much pro-Eisenhower sentiment as there had been during the previous election, and no one appeared ready to offer any challenge to Stevenson.) The move to stay in the fold was strongly endorsed by Senator Olin Johnston, but the decision was not unanimous. Former Governor Byrnes and Senator Thurmond wanted an independent slate of electors who would not be tied directly to any party. When their efforts failed to sway the convention, the action was carried on outside the party apparatus. Former S.C. Supreme Court Justices Gordon Baker and Eugene S. Blease joined the efforts, and an independent slate of electors was placed on the South Carolina ballot. One of the eight electors was Strom's old law partner, J. Fred Buzhardt, and another was his old friend-enemy-friend Robert M. Kennedy.

Thurmond traveled to the Far East in October, toured military installations, and met the Republic of Korea's President Syngman Rhee. All in all, Strom's self-imposed exile was relatively pleasant, although he was no doubt champing at the bit to return to Washington, where he could have a more significant impact.

The November elections posed no difficulty for Strom. He did not even have token Republican opposition. Olin Johnston, whose six-year term was up, did have Republican opposition. Leon Crawford, South Carolina's only Republican mayor (who served in Clemson), had been selected to oppose Johnston. Crawford received a $2,500 contribution from the Republican Senatorial Campaign Committee and a few thousand votes from the people of South Carolina, but it was far from enough.

The real election news of the year was in the vote totals for the presidential campaign. Nationally, Eisenhower was easily re-elected over Stevenson, but in South Carolina the people demonstrated their unhappiness with the Democratic label. Stevenson received 132,358 votes and was awarded South Carolina's electoral votes, but the Independent slate garnered 86,801 votes, and Eisenhower received 75,082 votes on the Republican slate. Once again, as in 1948, the Democratic nominee for president had not won a majority of South Carolina's votes. Sooner or later, a Republican might just carry the state.

With the election over, it seemed a simple matter to get Thurmond back into his Senate seat. On October 28, Senator Wofford wrote to Governor Timmerman resigning his seat, effective November 7. Upon his election, Strom immediately returned to Washington and was reinstated on the federal payroll. Strom's presumptuousness may have irritated Governor Timmerman, and it set off an unexpected battle between the two.

Timmerman's contention was that the interim appointment had been through January 3 of 1957 and that Wofford's resignation entitled the governor to appoint someone to fill the remainder of the vacancy. Thurmond countered that Senate rules stipulated that when an election is held to fill a seat held by an appointee, the victor immediately assumes the Senate seat after the election.

Timmerman was not pleased with that interpretation and suggested, publicly, that he would be pleased to appoint Thurmond to the vacancy, but if Thurmond did not accept, he would give it to someone else. Their feud simmered in public until November 13 when Thurmond accepted Timmerman's appointment.

As later events would prove, Thurmond had a legitimate case, but he was also in a difficult position. First, he did not want to be part of a petty squabble. Second, he was in the same position he had been in after his first election to the Senate. He needed to enter the Senate a few days prior to the opening of the term to have a seniority boost over the incoming crop of freshmen senators. By resigning, he had lost the seniority he had built up, and in a sense, he was starting from scratch.

His seniority was not all he had lost. His decision to resign had cost him over $13,000 in lost salary. In 1956, that was a lot of money to walk away from. But whatever the short-term cost in seniority and income, Thurmond had won the hearts and minds of South Carolina voters. In a way, this resignation was the ultimate act of faith for a politician. The voters could have rejected Strom in a primary (or even in the general election). Strom accepted that risk. But the people had no intention of defeating Strom. His actual resignation verified their trust, and he won the balance of the six-year term on his own. He would not go before the voters again until 1960.

Another question making the rounds at the end of that year caused considerable speculation, however. In the 1956 elections, the Democrats held on to control of the U.S. House of Representatives, but their grip on the Senate was a tenuous 49 to 47 (there were only forty-eight states at that time and ninety-six senators). A switch of one vote would mean a 48-to-48 tie, and with Vice President Nixon casting the deciding vote, the Senate could be organized by Republicans. When the political pundits looked around at potential party-switchers, one name headed their lists: Strom Thurmond of South Carolina.

He had bolted the party before, and there might be substantial rewards from the president if Thurmond were to switch. His recent feud with Democratic Governor Timmerman might just have been the last straw. As 1956 ended, many people thought Thurmond's defection was sure to come and waited to see what would happen in the new year.

Chapter 12

BACK TO THE SENATE

J anuary of 1957 found Strom Thurmond in the same position as in January of 1955—he was coming to Washington as a freshman senator from South Carolina. He had some assurances that he would not be treated as a total newcomer, but his fate was still up in the air. This was further compounded by the rumors that Thurmond would switch parties. In 1957, however, while he may have been ready to leave the national Democratic party, he had nowhere to go. There was too much talk regarding new Republican integration initiatives for Thurmond to cross the line. The rumor was that President Eisenhower would personally present a call for a wide-ranging integration law.

Because Thurmond was still in the Democratic fold, he was given an additional committee slot by the Democratic leadership. He was placed on the Committee on Labor and Public Welfare (and he was retained on the Government Operations Committee and the Interstate and Foreign Commerce Committee). Within a few weeks of his committee assignment, he was appointed chairman of the Labor and Public Welfare's Subcommittee on Veterans Affairs. This gave him a little more visibility and demonstrated that he was not exactly an outsider in one of the world's most exclusive clubs.

This appointment also launched Thurmond on perhaps his most significant area of public service—veterans' benefits. One of his first actions was to back a bill that would enable more veterans to apply for National Service Life Insurance. This was only the beginning of his advocacy of veterans' issues; his diligence on their behalf made him one of the Senate's foremost experts on the subject. Yet his work with veterans has never received much public note, mainly because it was done in the relative anonymity of subcommittee meeting rooms, and as such, received little media coverage.

Before the Senate tackled important business, it took time to chastise Governor Timmerman of South Carolina for meddling with one of its own—Strom Thurmond. The Senate passed a resolution stating that Thurmond had been a senator since election day (and was not therefore dependent on Timmerman's appointment). By this act, the Senate reasserted that it was the ultimate judge of its members. Timmerman's reaction was to take another shot at Thurmond. Timmerman said he was surprised that Thurmond, an ardent states' righter, would take part in an effort to usurp a power held by a governor—the right to appoint the successor when a vacancy occurred. Timmerman suspected Thurmond of being behind the resolution. Thurmond responded that the resolution was the product of the Senate leadership and that he had not even been notified in advance of its preparation.

After this bit of diversion, the Senate liberals immediately set about trying to ease the way for their planned assault on segregation by introducing a measure that would limit Senate debate. One of the weapons often employed by the minority on major issues is their right to "talk" an issue to death. This process is known as a filibuster, and often the Senate will agree to suspend consideration of an issue that is under filibuster threat in order to get on with its other business. At that time, a senator was allowed to maintain the floor until such time as sixty-six senators (two-thirds of the total membership) voted to impose cloture (suspend debate). If cloture was voted, the business of the Senate could proceed.

The liberals wanted to change the rules so that a simple majority vote could impose cloture. They knew a Senate filibuster could tie up civil rights legislation indefinitely. Rules changes had been proposed before, but the Senate had always held on to its right to talk.

The first attack on the filibuster rules was turned back—this time with the help of Majority Leader Lyndon Johnson. From the standpoint of the southerners, the defense of the filibuster rules could not have come too soon. President Eisenhower proposed a sweeping civil rights law with four objectives:

> Protection of the right to vote.
> A program of assistance to protect other rights.
> The creation of a Civil Rights Commission.
> The creation of an additional Civil Rights Division
> within the Justice Department.

Most offensive to the southern senators was the part of the proposal that applied civil rights to areas outside of voting rights. This part, known as Section Three, came under the most intensive attack from the southerners. Southern pragmatists had concluded that defending the practice of locking blacks out of the electoral process was untenable, but they hoped to maintain segregation in other areas, especially in education.

After the introduction of President Eisenhower's initiatives, though, there was a lull as the Senate transacted other business. Lyndon Johnson did not let the civil rights bill come up immediately; he wanted to hold it until the Senate was facing an adjournment or pressed up against some other deadline so he could prevent lengthy debate.

So the work of the Senate continued for a time. On February 14, Thurmond introduced legislation calling for a balanced federal budget. It was not the first such call, but it is interesting that the budget deficit then was only a few billion dollars. Nevertheless, this is another position that Thurmond has held, without swerving, throughout his Senate career.

February also saw the appointment of Greenville attorney Clement Haynsworth by President Eisenhower to serve as judge of the Fourth Circuit Court of Appeals to succeed Armistead M. Dobie. This was a small victory for southerners, as Haynsworth could be counted on to preserve states' rights wherever he could. (Previously, Ike had appointed a Maryland liberal, Sobeloff, and his appointment of Haynsworth was the other part of the package.)

While the president and the legislators had slowed their action on civil rights, the judicial branch of the federal government increased its pace. After several delaying tactics by the people of Arkansas, the federal courts added their own fuel to the already burning civil rights fire by ordering immediate compliance with the integration order at the schools of Little Rock, Arkansas. Arkansas had other ideas.

Trouble in Little Rock

September 1957 was a turbulent month in Arkansas. The federal court's order to immediately integrate Little Rock's schools had hit the town like a tidal wave. Little Rock's schools were operating under a previously approved plan that gradually integrated their schools over a six-year period beginning in 1957. When the League of Central High School Mothers applied for an injunction (and got one from a state court on August 29), the federal court of Judge Elmer D. Davies overturned the state court's injunction, ordered immediate compliance, and triggered the controversy.

The white people of Little Rock believed a state court decision should not be swept away so easily. The state's governor, Orville Faubus, agreed. As governor, he had repeatedly pledged to fight integration in every conceivable way. The federal court order gave him his chance. In an unprecedented action, Governor Faubus called out the Arkansas National Guard, not to protect the black students who were to enter Little Rock schools but to prevent their entry. Faubus expected that the federal marshals with orders to enroll the black students would not confront the National Guard.

President Eisenhower reacted immediately. Using his powers as commander in chief of the country's armed forces, he federalized the Arkansas National Guard, placing them under his orders. Then he sent in additional troops (including the 101st Airborne) and more federal marshals. Governor Faubus (and two National Guard officers) were summoned to appear before the federal court of Judge Elmer D. Davies on September 20. On September 25, as a crowd of angry white people shouted their defiance, federal marshals escorted the first black students into the white public schools of Little Rock. All this occurred shortly after President Eisenhower's civil rights proposal came to the Congress of the United States.

Thurmond and the Civil Rights Fight of 1957

Senator Thurmond was already incensed by the actions of the federal government, even before the events of September. On June 26, he accused the federal courts of tyranny and introduced a bill to curb judicial power by eliminating school segregation and state sedition cases from their appellate jurisdiction. He followed up this effort with a July 11 speech to the Senate in which he declared: "Every citizen of this nation should be concerned with this combined effort by a part of the executive branch and members of Congress to force through the Congress this so-called 'civil rights' bill. . . . The real purpose is to arm the federal courts with a vicious weapon to enforce race mixing."[1]

By this time, as well, the House of Representatives had already passed Eisenhower's proposals in their original form. All eyes turned to the Senate, which had always thwarted previous efforts to enact civil rights legislation. The first target was the previously mentioned Section Three. Most southern lawmakers were willing to grudgingly accept the measure if it did *not* include the provisions that extended civil rights to areas other than voting. After some discussion, on July 24, the Senate deleted those provisions—hoping that this compromise would speed passage.

Thurmond, however, had yet another amendment. He insisted that all cases involving civil rights should be heard by juries—not just judges. (Few southern juries, if any, would find in favor of integration.) Other aspects of this requirement, such as the constitutional principle that Article VI of the Bill of Rights guarantees the right to a jury trial, made Strom's argument persuasive—and the jury trial provision was added.

These two provisions necessitated a conference committee between the House and the Senate to iron out the differences between the two versions of the bill. Eisenhower's Justice Department, and Republican and Democratic congressional leaders hammered out a compromise that deleted Section Three and modified the jury trial amendment to allow federal judges to *decide* which cases would go to juries. This effectively maintained judicial control, but because Section Three was eliminated, most southern legislators were willing to accept the compromise—or not fight it too much. They hoped that acceptance of this bill would ease civil rights pressures; some even feared that if this bill were not passed, even harsher measures would follow. But Thurmond insisted that civil rights issues should be decided by a jury, and he was willing to keep on fighting, with or without the support of his southern senate colleagues. On August 27, by a vote of 279 to 97, the House of Representatives approved the compromise and sent it to the Senate, where LBJ was confident of passage.

In South Carolina, state Senator Marion Gressette, chairman of the state's Segregation Committee (a committee set up by the state government to fight integration efforts) had telegraphed Senator Thurmond and Senator Johnston and urged that they consider a filibuster. "Since the object of this legislation is to make the South an oppressed minority, we feel this fight should be carried to the limits of unlimited debate, the U.S. Senate's historic last resort for defense against unfair and unwise legislation."[2]

On his own, Thurmond had already attempted to kill the compromise measure by making a surprise motion to send it to the Senate Judiciary Committee. This effort had failed by a vote of 66 to 18. In the process, Strom had irritated LBJ by not giving him advance notice of his intentions. As usual, Strom was willing to do something—even if that something proved to be unpopular with his peers.

A Record Filibuster

On the evening of August 28, when Strom stood up to speak, no one expected him to try to hold the floor for long. As time went on, however, the Senate realized it was in for a filibuster. Thurmond had decided to educate his Senate colleagues on the virtues of jury trials. He had been preparing himself for several days for just such an occasion.

As he spoke, his two chief aides, Alex McCullough and Harry Dent, sat beside him, handing him reading material. Up in the visitors' galleries were two very interested observers—Strom's wife, Jean, and Clarence Mitchell. Mitchell was the director of the Washington chapter of the NAACP. When he recognized Thurmond's efforts as a filibuster, he issued a statement saying it was "a demonstration of very poor sportsmanship—its obvious this is just an exercise in futility at this point."[3]

Thurmond might have expected support from some of his fellow southerners. Certainly some of them felt as strongly as he did about the proposed legislation, but within a few hours it was clear he would have no help. He was in it alone.

The Senate filibuster record was held by Wayne Morse, who had spent twenty-two hours and twenty-six minutes opposing an effort to prevent offshore oil lands from being given to the states (Morse thought they should be retained by federal government). Strom's motivation was to do the best he could to block the legislation, but he probably wanted to break the record as well. When he saw he had no support, the latter was all that kept him going.

After Strom held the floor for a few hours, he did receive some help, but not from his Southern Democratic friends. Republican Senator Barry Goldwater of Arizona, no friend of segregation but a friend of Strom's, asked permission to have the floor without Strom giving up his right to continue. He held the floor long enough for Strom to get a short break.

Strom got another break when Republican leader William F. Knowland interrupted him to ask several lengthy questions (and to lecture him on the futility of his effort). But by and large, Strom continued his one-man assault throughout the night and into the morning, speaking to a skeleton crew of three senators, none of whom paid him any attention.

As morning neared, Strom's temper flared slightly as he called down some of his colleagues who were talking, albeit softly, on the Senate floor. He also used this time to dispel the idea that he was speaking against blacks. He said, "I want to see every man vote . . . every man who is qualified."

As Strom droned on, Senator Paul Douglas of Illinois, one of integration's strongest proponents, set a pitcher of orange juice down on the lectern next to Strom and departed. Perhaps Douglas was hoping the orange juice would put extra pressure on Strom to quit (via his bladder)—perhaps it was a genuinely helpful gesture. No matter, Strom took a few sips and continued, unaffected.

That afternoon, Jean Thurmond spoke briefly to the reporters, noting that "he never looked happier. I know he is really enjoying this. He doesn't seem the least bit tense and he doesn't look tired to me." When Jean's brother asked her why she didn't try to get him to stop, she said that the only person who could make Strom stop was Strom.

These public statements were not exactly matched by private actions, however. Jean had already sent her husband a note: "We all agree you're on the top now. Suggest you stop now—to go on would weaken your position. You're wonderful! Jean." And Strom's assistant, Harry Dent, had written: "Everyone thinks you should wind up. Lyndon wants to swear in Proxmire when you finish."

But Strom had no intention of quitting just then. He did permit William Proxmire to be sworn in as Wisconsin's newest Senator—without giving up his right to the floor. And later he got a two-minute break as twelve Italian deputies were introduced. His last break of the day came when LBJ interrupted him to ask for approval of some amendments that were uncontested.

Earlier in the day, President Eisenhower had remarked through his press secretary, somewhat sarcastically, that he had expected a busy day but since the Senate was tied up he had decided to play golf. And Strom talked on.

That night, after twenty-four hours and eighteen minutes, Strom ended his one-man crusade against the bill, and it was passed by a vote of 60 to 15. Thirty-seven Republicans were joined by twenty-three Democrats in voting for passage. All those voting no were southern Democrats.

With the Senate's approval, on August 29, 1957, Congress enacted the first civil rights legislation in eighty-two years. After the vote, some southern senators expressed their displeasure with Strom's actions. Strom insisted that it had been clearly understood that each Senator was free to follow his conscience and oppose the bill in his own way. As always, Strom's way was a hard road.

Strom Fights On

Strom Thurmond's time in the U.S. Senate has confounded friend and foe alike. On the one hand, he could always be counted on to espouse some conservative positions, such as his perpetual stand in favor of states' rights. On the other hand, he often advocated progressive measures, as in his sponsorship of an equal rights amendment for women. After the record filibuster, and in the midst of an ongoing assault by Senate liberals on southern institutions, it would have been natural for Strom to become a one-note Senator, sounding off only on his pet issue. Throughout its history, the U.S. Senate has had many such members—people elected to office on one issue who knew nothing else.

But Thurmond in 1958 and 1959 continued to set an erratic course between conservatism and progressivism. True, most of the time he was on the conservative side, but there were occasional forays over to the other side. Even more interesting is the dichotomy between his voting on domestic issues and foreign issues. He had initially supported Eisenhower, but his enthusiasm for him continued to wane in the face of Ike's relentless march toward civil rights. Thurmond repeatedly criticized the president in those areas as well as the president's farm policy and his views on international trade. Thurmond advocated protection for the American textile industry (which is based predominantly in the South), and the president adamantly refused to have much to do with the notion of American trade barriers.

But in national defense and foreign affairs, Thurmond continued to publicly support the president, often in direct contrast to the wishes of the Democratic leadership. When votes were tallied, no senator supported Eisenhower's direction in foreign policy more than Strom Thurmond.

Even in his early days in the Senate, when the demagogic demon often grips those in politics, Thurmond was active in a broad range of issues. He demonstrated some of his breadth of interest in the first few days of the 1958 legislative session. On January 8, he cosponsored a bill with Senator Goldwater that would have established a national right-to-work law. South Carolina (and most Southern states) had such a law, the main purpose of which was to prevent union shop contracts, which required all employees hired by a company to belong to the union.

The next day, January 9, Thurmond proposed the creation of a U.S. Science Academy. In the face of Soviet advances in rocket technology, he wanted a place where the best of science was

encouraged and taught. He wanted to see this academy administered by the Department of Defense because of "the vital role the
academy would play in our national defense and security programs." As part of the Defense Department and as an aid to
national defense, it would be constitutional.

On January 23, Thurmond introduced more legislation, this
time a bill to examine the relative powers of the federal and state
governments as well as the relative powers of the three branches
of the national government. He sponsored this legislation because
he feared the centralization of power at the federal level; he
suggested that the usurpation of power by the federal government
was "law by law, decision by decision, [creating its version] of the
uniquely American version of the totalitarian state."[4]

For all his frantic activity, Strom had to face another fact of life
in the first month of the new year. His mother had become ill and
Strom was summoned from Washington to be with her. On January 30, Mrs. Thurmond died at University Hospital in Augusta,
Georgia. Her loss was not unexpected, but her death had an impact
on Strom. He was close to only a few women, two of whom were
his mother and his wife. His mother's death was the first real loss
since his father had died more than thirty years earlier.

When Thurmond returned to the Senate, he returned with a
vengeance. Senator Pat McNamara of Michigan resigned his seat
on the Special Labor Rackets Committee, organized to investigate
the growing corruption in organized labor. This committee promised to be the kind of assignment that could add stature to a career,
and Thurmond was slated for the open spot on it. There was just
one catch. The Community Facilities Loan Act had a provision
allowing the secretary of labor to establish a "prevailing wage
rate" for all federal contracts. This meant that local contractors
doing federal work would have to pay their employees whatever
the secretary said, despite local wage market conditions. Thurmond was against that provision and intended to say so. The
Democratic leadership did not want the provision opposed because it had the support of organized labor. Would he back off,
they wanted to know?

The answer, of course, was no. Thurmond was opposed to the
provision and gave an address against the bill. As a result, he was
denied the seat. It went to another promising young senator who
helped to draft a bill that earned a lot of publicity: John F. Kennedy.

Thurmond then turned his attention to other issues, starting
with a particularly offensive ad for beer in which a three-year-old

boy asked for "Miller High Life" and cried when he couldn't get it. Thurmond favored a law that would ban interstate liquor advertising and used this ad as one of his examples. This campaign was, of course, rooted in his temperance beliefs.

Another interesting development resulted from Alaska's request to be admitted as a state. Strom was opposed; his reason was that Alaska's admission would "set a precedent for the admission of other non-contiguous areas, the customs and traditions of which would have non-American roots." Strom also stated that Alaska would need "extraordinary federal aid." Alaska's subsequent discovery of huge oil reserves invalidated that criticism.

His real opposition, however, was predicated on the "non-American" portion of the complaint. Moves were then underway to admit Hawaii, as well. Both states had large non-white populations, and their representatives were not expected to support Southern positions. (This argument was somewhat reminiscent of Southern opposition to the creation of new states in the mid-1800s, when the South feared, correctly, that admitting nonslaveholding states would eventually tip the balance of power away from the South.) Despite Thurmond's opposition, Alaska was admitted.

As 1957 drew to a close, Strom was working on a possible appointment to the committee that he had a real desire to serve on—Armed Services.

Another Year, Another Civil Rights Bill

The first business before the Senate in 1958 was not committee appointments. Senate liberals had picked this as the year to make a major push for civil rights legislation, and they knew Senate Rule 22 was their greatest obstacle. Rule 22 required that debate could not be halted on a bill unless sixty-six senators voted for cloture. The liberals correctly thought that if they made it easier to limit debate, they could pass their legislation more easily. Their plan was to revise Rule 22 so that debate could be limited if simply a majority of the Senate voted to stop debate.

When they heard that this measure was in the wind, seventeen southern senators, including Thurmond and presided over by Senator Russell, met to plan a strategy to defend Rule 22. In this effort, Senate Leader LBJ was both an ally and a nemesis. He was pledged to getting some reform in the Senate rules, but he could not afford to alienate the restive southern senators. So he advocated that the rule be changed so that two-thirds of those present could vote to limit debate. Russell and the rest were opposed to any change and were unwilling to accept any compromise. But by a vote of 72 to 22, the southerners lost.

Happily for Thurmond, his fight to preserve Rule 22 had not cost him anything. He had stayed reasonably in line during the rule change fight—no filibuster at any rate—and LBJ allowed him to move on to the Armed Services Committee. There was a cost, however: he lost his place on both Labor and Government Operations. Thurmond's increasingly vocal criticism of Walter Reuther, the United Auto Workers chief, may have caused his ouster from Labor.

As expected, the rule change was followed by another civil rights proposal. This one sought to make mob action a federal crime (which would allow greater federal control over law enforcement) and sought incentives for school districts that implemented integration (which would expand federal control over local education). Thurmond could take some grim satisfaction in pointing out to his southern colleagues that the 1957 civil rights law had not been the end—in fact, it was just the beginning.

At that point, Senator Harry F. Byrd of Virginia, Richard Russell of Georgia, and Thurmond (along with most of the rest of the southern senators) joined together to oppose every facet of the bill. With their opposition, the latest civil rights attempt was stalled at almost every turn. Later in 1958, still with nothing accomplished and tempers frayed over the issue, Thurmond and New York's liberal Republican Senator Jacob Javits were both ordered to their seats when during a furious Senate debate each made disparaging remarks about the other's state.

Although Thurmond did nothing earth-shattering, 1958 may have been one of the most pivotal years, in many respects, for him. Events during the year served to push him towards a fundamental reassessment of his political orientation. The action centered on two poles: conservative Republican Senator Barry Goldwater of Arizona and liberal Democratic Senator John F. Kennedy of Massachusetts.

Kennedy, Goldwater, and Thurmond

Thurmond had no vendetta against Senator John F. Kennedy, but Kennedy's position on issues dear to Strom caused increasing friction. The first instance resulted from a bill Kennedy sponsored regarding racketeering in labor unions. (Remember that Kennedy became involved in this issue after Thurmond was denied a seat on the rackets subcommittee.) Kennedy authored a bill that addressed the racketeering issue, and the legislation was presented to the Senate. At that point, Senator John L. McClellan of Arkansas added a seven-point program described as a "bill of rights" for the working man, intended as a backdoor approach to a national right-to-work law. Kennedy already had his sights set on the 1960 presidential campaign, and he knew these provisions would hurt him with organized labor—one of his biggest supporters. So he fought the amendment. Strom Thurmond played a major role in aiding Senator McClellan, and when the vote came on the McClellan amendment, it was adopted by a vote of 47 to 46. Thirty-two Republicans and fifteen Democrats (most of them southern) joined to support the amendment. Forty-four Democrats (including the other major presidential hopeful, LBJ) voted against the amendment, aided by two Republicans.

This was one of a series of votes in which Republicans linked with conservative southern Democrats. May brought another incident that would have long-term ramifications in Strom Thurmond's future. In a speaking engagement in Greenville, South Carolina, Senator Goldwater took time out of his prepared text to compliment Strom: "I do not usually go around extolling Democrats, but I think South Carolina's Strom Thurmond is one of the most outstanding men in America, and I pray that God will send us more like him."[5]

While senatorial courtesy has been refined to an art form, this lavish praise of Thurmond went above and beyond the call. On the one hand, the Democrats seemed to be leaning further left (on all issues, not just integration); on the other hand, Barry Goldwater, speaking for the Republicans, was full of praise for Thurmond, man of the right.

Other wedges were soon driven between Thurmond and his mates. In July the AFL-CIO, America's premier labor organization (with strong ties to the Democratic party), issued its first blacklist of people whom they hoped would be defeated in the 1960 elections. Strom Thurmond's name was one of seven on that list. As one of the Democratic party's most loyal (and vocal and wealthy) supporting groups, the AFL-CIO was demonstrating that perhaps the Democratic party had no place for Strom Thurmond.

Then, later in July, Senator Kennedy clashed with Thurmond on one of the areas nearest and dearest to Thurmond's heart—patriotism. The issue this time was the National Defense Education Act, which provided loans to persons attending college. Senator

Kennedy wanted the loyalty oath provisions dropped from this program, but Thurmond was adamant that they remain. In an impassioned address, Strom declared: "I do not know of any quality I would rather attribute to me than that I am a loyal, true, patriotic citizen. If a person does not love his country . . . I say that he has no business getting a loan from the government of the U.S. Furthermore, I should like to see him indicted, apprehended and punished, because he is dangerous and a menace to society."[6]

Leaving aside Strom's last statement (an example of his after-thought statements that have often overshadowed excellent points), this issue illustrated one of the keys to Thurmond. He always loved his country and devoted a lifetime to serving it. Further-more, he did so not only behind a desk but also on the battlefield, so any comment he ever made on the subject of patriotism de-served some attention. To Thurmond, this effort by Senator Kennedy represented yet another attempt by some liberals to say that it was somehow all right not to love your country. Strom blanched at the thought (and beat Kennedy again on this issue by a vote of 49 to 42). As an aside, Strom often referred to people as "patriots" and "true patriots"; viewed in this light that was about as high a compliment as he could bestow.

But these were all political battles, and while Thurmond felt strongly about them, victories and defeats did not seem to have much effect on him. A defeat did not suggest that he might be wrong—simply that he had not educated others properly in the correctness of his position. Victories were viewed as less than sweeping, too, because he recognized that another battle would soon crop up. In these kinds of battles, he had some control: he could lecture, apply logic and reason, even rant if it was appropri-ate, with some hope of obtaining a favorable outcome. Whereas in some situations in life none of these actions had any value; some foes would not listen to your arguments and you had to stand by helplessly and accept their judgments. For Strom Thurmond, that type of situation was exceedingly difficult to bear—especially if it involved the one person he cared most about.

Early August of 1959 saw the beginning of the saddest story in Strom Thurmond's life. And he had no choice but to stand by helplessly as it unfolded.

Strom with James F. Byrnes (1947)

With Florida Governor Caldwell and eventual Vice Presidential running mate, Governor Fielding Wright of Mississippi, at Southern Governors' Conference in Miami in 1947

Jean Crouch (nine years old—1935)

Jean Crouch modelling uniforms at Winthrop with two others in 1947

Jean Crouch with parents in October 1947

Strom and Jean at Furman-Carolina game in 1947

Wedding portrait (1947)

Strom with Edgar Brown at the 1948 Democratic National Convention in Philadelphia (July 1948). Note Thurmond's button supporting Ben Laney for President.

Private citizen Thurmond and Jean in front of their new home in Aiken
(January 1952)

"The Gladiators." Olin D. Johnston broods about losing the state to Barry Goldwater while Thurmond rejoices in his personal vindication—November 3, 1964

Strom and Nixon together in 1968

Strom and his new bride, Nancy, being greeted by Judge and Mrs. Pace at a party in honor of the newlyweds on December 29, 1968

Chapter 13

A PERSONAL TRAGEDY
... AND MOVING ON

W hen Jean Thurmond arrived in Washington in 1955 with Strom, her first questions concerned what she would do to occupy her time. She had been active in South Carolina, and she hoped to be able to be involved in Washington. With a few weeks of her arrival, Jean was active in the social life normally associated with congressional spouses. She joined the Ladies of the Senate, which met every Tuesday to sew, knit, and fold bandages for the Red Cross. She was also a member of the 84th Congress Club, which was composed of the spouses of members of Congress elected for the first time in 1954. Jean was also a member of the International Neighbors Club, which drew its membership from residential Washington and the diplomatic corps, as well as from Congress. These activities kept her fairly busy, and she was rewarded for her hard work by serving as the chairperson of a 1957 luncheon honoring Mrs. Eisenhower.

Her greatest contribution, however, came in her dealings with constituents. A steady stream of South Carolina people visited Washington, and Jean often played host to them, taking them on tours of the capitol and entertaining them at lunches and dinners. During her five years of entertaining, Jean's face became familiar to all kinds of people connected with Congress, from elevator operators to the members themselves.

This routine was valuable to Strom, and Jean enjoyed it. But if it was exciting, it was also tiring and for that reason, Jean was not aware that the chronic fatigue she began experiencing in the spring of 1959 was a symptom of a serious condition. Later, after representing Strom at the Watermelon Festival in Hampton, on a hot July day, she complained of having the "worst headache I've ever had in my life." On another occasion, she drove into the back of a truck. The accident was not serious, but Jean could not remember how it happened. These incidents were warnings of worse times to come.[1]

In early August, after a day of entertaining constituents, Jean Thurmond went home to the Potomac Plaza apartments to relax in front of the television and to wait on her husband to come home to dinner. As she watched the evening news, she had the most severe fainting spell of her life, and barely managed to reach the bedroom before she collapsed on the bed. When she regained consciousness, she called her husband's office and Strom left for home immediately. When he arrived at 7:30 that evening, Jean was barely able to answer the door. She recovered during the night, but the next morning, after Strom had returned to the Hill, Jean had another attack.[2]

Strom was determined to get the best possible care for his wife and she underwent a series of tests at the National Institute of Health in Bethesda, Maryland. Jean was admitted as a patient after successive attacks led to partial paralysis on the left side of her face which spread so that she dragged her left foot as she walked. The physicians knew she was having seizures but they did not know why. After extensive testing, they decided on brain surgery to determine the nature of the problems. On September 17, 1959, a tumor with no indication of malignancy was removed, but the paralysis persisted after the operation.

Strom's position as a general in the Army Reserve required him to go to Fort Leavenworth, Kansas, so on October 11, Jean returned to South Carolina for a visit with her parents. Her situation did not improve. When she returned to Washington for a post-operative examination, she found a letter waiting for her from Strom (who was still in Kansas).

He said he feared the stress of their lifestyle and the demands it placed upon her were somehow a factor in her illness. So he offered to give it all up for her. "If it is your desire that I resign from the Senate, if this will facilitate your recovery, I shall carry out your wishes. You mean everything to me and I shall follow the course that is best for you.[3]

Jean, of course, had no intention of allowing her husband to resign. She must have suspected that her illness was very serious and that his job might someday be all that he would have left. Strom's letter showed how seriously he took the situation, but it was apparent to many friends and observers that the possibility of Jean's death—the ultimate defeat—never occurred to him. Jean herself demonstrated her own feelings in November as her health continued to fail. She spent her time trying to convince those around her that she had lived a good life and she was willing to accept whatever plan God had for her.[4]

As November drew to a close, the doctors allowed Strom to take Jean back to her family again. On Thanksgiving Day, they made the trip. By the middle of December, she spent most of her time sleeping. In late December, when Strom was helping Jean stand, she fainted and Strom placed her back in bed, and in that moment, he had an inkling of the real situation. His wife was dying and he could do nothing about it. Tears of sadness and frustration flowed from him as he looked at the most important part of his life slipping away from him.[5]

On January 3, 1960, Jean's condition was so serious that she was flown back to the National Institute of Health. After allowing her a day to recover from the flight, the surgeons operated again, and this time they found a growing malignancy. After the surgery, Jean lapsed into a coma. Throughout the night and early into the morning, Strom and Jean's family kept a vigil. The surgeons had no encouraging news—Jean was dying. Thurmond remained unable to deal with it. When her chief surgeon, Dr. Maitland Baldwin, told Strom of her death at 8:35 on the morning of January 6, Strom was incredulous, "This can't be true! I can't believe it!"[6]

Jean Thurmond, only thirty-three years, his beautiful, devoted, loving wife, was gone. When she died, part of Strom died with her. Jean was buried on January 8, 1960 in Aiken, South Carolina. Her funeral was attended by several U.S. senators and their spouses, including Senator and Mrs. Lyndon Johnson. Other dignitaries and almost all of South Carolina's leaders were there, out of deference to Strom and to say goodbye to a lady who had impressed them.

With tragedy at its outset, 1960 was one of the worst years Thurmond ever faced. Certainly some things that had seemed important could have become irrelevant in the face of the tragedy of his wife's death. One approach would have been to just quit, to drop out of public life—maybe even out of life, itself. But that was not Thurmond's way. His solution to most problems in his life had always been activity. After a brief period of private mourning, he plunged back into the routine he knew—it was his catharsis.

Moving Forward

Strom's first public act of the new year was to create a permanent endowment at Winthrop College, where Jean had been a student and he had been a trustee. His desire was that Jean would never be forgotten by the people of South Carolina. At its creation, the Jean Crouch Thurmond Scholarship would provide about $200 per year in income to be used to aid in a young woman's education. This was the first permanent scholarship ever given in honor of a Winthrop graduate.

Given the nature of government, Strom also had other things to divert his attention, specifically the transcendent issue of the times. The new year—and election year—brought out the civil rights urge in politicians of both parties. Vice President Richard M. Nixon, the Republican front-runner, espoused a strong civil rights stance. Senate Democrats such as John Kennedy and Lyndon Johnson were also on that bandwagon. In his position as majority leader, LBJ had the most opportunity to make political hay out of the issue, and southern senators were geared for the fight.

By early 1960 the southern senators were organized into a type of "SWAT team" that was to be prepared to react at all times to keep civil rights legislation bottled up in committee or off the Senate floor. One member of their group was always to be on the floor to act as a lookout and control valve. They knew that new civil rights legislation would be coming because LBJ had promised to bring a civil rights bill to the floor. Because of his ambition to be president, LBJ knew he had to secure the passage of a new civil rights law. He understood that the other southern senators were arrayed against him, so he awaited his chance and then displayed the trickery he had become famous for as the Senate leader.

A civil rights bill should nominally have something to do with civil rights. You would not expect an innocuous bill on the environment, for example, to contain civil rights provisions. One of the major problems with enacting civil rights legislation, however, is that it had to be approved by the Senate's committee system. Many of the powerful Senate committees (including the Judiciary) had southern chairmen. This made it almost impossible even to get civil rights legislation onto the Senate floor.

As majority leader, LBJ often went before the Senate and asked that bills be placed on the Senate calendar by unanimous consent. One objection would prevent a bill from being admitted to the calendar. In order to get a civil rights bill on the floor, LBJ called up a minor bill having no relationship to civil rights and asked unanimous consent that it be placed on the calendar. When no objections were voiced, Johnson then announced that it was the civil rights bill. This meant that civil rights legislation could be added to the bill by amendments. Senator B. Everett Jordan of North Carolina was the South's man in the Senate when the move was taken, but since there was no indication that the bill had anything to do with civil rights, Jordan did not object. Johnson's chicanery had succeeded in placing the civil rights bill before the Senate, but at the expense of some trust by his Senate colleagues. Senator Richard Russell of Georgia accused Johnson of "lynching of orderly procedures."

The civil rights issue of 1960 was the enactment of additional provisions guaranteeing blacks easier access to the electoral process in southern states by enabling federal courts to appoint referees to register black voters in areas where voting discrimination had been proven. The bill also ended up with federal provisions against hate bombings and those who attempted to interfere with school integration efforts. Once again, civil rights proponents were attacking segregation by putting more authority in the hands of the federal government.

Thurmond opposed these efforts as a further infringement on the rights of states by the federal government. In the debate on this bill, he also sought to educate the Senate on the differing nature of race relations in the North and South.

> Just as there are in this country two main and quite distinct cultures, a northern culture and a southern culture, so there are in this country two different species of genus segregation—In the south, the separation of the races—this is the more accurate term, though for the sake of habit and convenience we shall continue to say "segregation"—is a matter of public policy, regulated by law as well as by custom. Segregation in the south is honest, open, and above board. . . . While, in the North there is almost always an actual physical, geographical separation, in the South it is not necessary. . . . Northern segregation is founded on hypocrisy and deceit.

He pointed out that in the North, there was de facto segregation in the suburbs, and he reiterated that southern segregation was "human and honest."[7]

Of course, Thurmond's efforts at "educating" the senators were ineffective. The measure was approved by a margin of 71 to 18; the only dissenting votes came from southern senators. After the bill had been passed, Strom gave public credit to LBJ for saving the South from a punitive bill. (Thurmond was supporting LBJ for president, but he commented that if Barry Goldwater decided to run for president on either ticket, "he would sweep the South.")

There were two other major events in the spring of 1960. In March President Eisenhower nominated Thurmond for a promotion from brigadier general to major general. Also in March Thurmond announced his desire to be reelected to the U.S. Senate.

His announcement was followed closely by the surprise announcement of eighty-year-old Columbia attorney R. Beverly Herbert that he would seek Strom's seat. He chose to make his first attempt at public office for oblique reasons. Herbert said he thought Thurmond was a good senator and did not think he himself had any chance of winning, but "I am running . . . because it is the best chance I see to say things I think should be said." One of the things he thought should be said was that the NAACP had the backing of the Communist party.

Throughout the brief campaign, Herbert expounded the principle that no one was telling the whole story about the NAACP. Thurmond virtually ignored his opponent and was easily reelected in the June 14 primary, gathering 273,795 votes to only 32,136 for Herbert. This campaign was almost a noncampaign, and it demonstrated Thurmond's political strength in the state. No one of any stature had even considered opposing him.

The only other action of the year was in the contest for president. Thurmond was once again elected as a delegate to the Democratic National Convention, held in Los Angeles that year. The 1960 contest pitted LBJ's political craftiness against John F. Kennedy's activism. There was some Kennedy support in the South Carolina delegation, but under unit rule, all twenty-one votes were cast for Lyndon Baines Johnson, who Thurmond called "the best friend of the South among the present candidates." As history tells us, this was another lost cause. When the ballots were totaled, Kennedy had secured a majority. When efforts were made to make Kennedy's nomination unanimous by the convention, the bitter South Carolina delegates refused.

This convention also passed a civil rights plank. After Kennedy selected Johnson as his running mate, he pledged to "placate an angry Dixie." But Strom Thurmond, who was both a student of the South and of history, knew the value of those words. In 1828, after his election as president, Andrew Jackson had sought to "easy the southern mind" regarding some tariffs opposed by John C. Calhoun and others. As time wore on, Jackson did nothing, and Thurmond suspected that Kennedy's pledge would have similar results.

Immediately after the convention, Thurmond predicted the possibility of another third-party movement, although this time he had not thought of being on the ticket. He was so quiet on where he stood that Governor Fritz Hollings challenged Thurmond on his position in the election. Thurmond replied, "I hope Senator Kennedy's pledge at his news conferences to push for enactment of all points in the 'civil rights' plank in January will serve to alleviate the Governor's lack of understanding about my refusal to be in the bag in this election."[8]

The political situation clouded considerably when Alabama and Mississippi voted to make their electors independent—that is, not pledged to either the Republican or Democratic candidates. The dissatisfaction with both the national candidates—Kennedy and Nixon—was not restricted to the South. Some people in New Jersey attempted to create a Goldwater-Thurmond ticket and get it placed on the ballot. *Newsweek* even hinted that Thurmond might be pro-Nixon. (*Newsweek* was right: Thurmond later acknowledged that he had voted for Nixon.)

In the midst of all this, Thurmond went to Japan to participate in an inter-parliamentary meeting. When he returned, he found that Senator Goldwater was urging the South to come over to the Republican party. Thurmond also found that his statements (and those of James Byrnes) were appearing in South Carolina newspaper ads for the Nixon-Lodge ticket.

The South Carolina presidential vote was representative of the national vote, with Kennedy edging Nixon out by a narrow margin of 198,129 to 188,558. This was the closest that South Carolina had come to supporting a Republican slate of electors since the disputed election of Rutherford B. Hayes over Samuel Tilden in 1876. In the aftermath of the election, Thurmond took to the stump and declared that northern Republicans and southern Democrats working together in the Senate had "saved this country."[9] An alliance was again stirring.

In presidential elections the official vote of the electors is a formality. In presidential election years, the electors gather in their respective state capitals to cast their votes for president and vice president. As has been mentioned previously, these electors are not bound to follow the wishes of the electorate of their states, though most of the time they do. On December 20, 1960, the electors of Alabama and Mississippi conferred a small honor on Thurmond by awarding him fourteen electoral votes for vice president (Richard Russell had received their fourteen votes for president). This made Thurmond the only person ever to receive electoral votes for both president and vice president as a third-party candidate. Once again he made history. With a new six-year term under his belt, it was highly probable that he would get the opportunity to make a little more.

A Change in Focus

It is inconceivable that communism and democracy can exist side by side in this world. Inevitably one must perish.

—Lenin

In today's world it is difficult to understand the relationship between the United States and the Soviet Union in the early 1960s. In America, we tend to forget the words of Lenin and other Soviet leaders whose goal was world domination. But in 1960, some Americans were vividly aware of the avowed goals of communism, and they were anxious that the rest of the nation be aware, as well. Among these was South Carolina's junior U.S. senator, Strom Thurmond.

Under Eisenhower's presidency, Thurmond had always felt relatively confident about the nation's will to defend itself. Thurmond recognized that Kennedy's election might portend a change in American foreign policy, and he was uneasy about the path that change might take. His fears seemed justified early in the Kennedy presidency.

Less than two weeks after Kennedy was inaugurated, Arthur M. Schlesinger, Jr., a Harvard professor and Kennedy speechwriter, remarked that the best defense against communism was the welfare state. While Schlesinger made efforts to distance his remarks from the president, Thurmond thought such a remark from a Kennedy advisor was ominous: the president had surrounded himself with people who had no intention of defending America's position. Rather than maintain the traditions that had made our nation great, Thurmond thought, they intended to move our system closer to communism. And if this was the position of many of Kennedy's advisors, it must be Kennedy's as well. Thurmond responded to Schlesinger's remark with: "Not only is the welfare state no defense against Communism, but there is a serious question as to whether, in practical sense, the welfare state is even an alternative to Communism. . . . Welfare statism is like Communism in its mistrust of individual liberty and in its reliance on state control."[10]

As the first days of the new order progressed, Thurmond was alarmed to see more and more signs that the Kennedy administration was determined to undermine America's will to win the Cold War with the Soviet Union. The final straw came on July 21, 1961, when Thurmond read in the Washington *Post*, that "a Senate Foreign Relations Committee memorandum has warned that right-wing propaganda activities by military officers may create 'important obstacles' to President Kennedy's programs."[11]

To Thurmond, the implications were immediately clear: the Kennedy administration had decided that armed forces personnel were not to be allowed to suggest that America was in the right or that the Cold War was a contest to be won. When he finished reading the article, Thurmond removed his glasses and rose to his feet as if he had heard a call to another campaign. This was outrageous—were America's military personnel supposed to assume a defeatist attitude? He had to find out. He sent a staffer over to Senator William Fulbright, the chairman of the Foreign Relations Committee, with a request for a copy of the memo referred to in the *Post* story. When his staffer returned empty-handed, Thurmond himself made the trip to see Senator Fulbright and was told that Fulbright was not there and no copies were available. Next, Thurmond wrote to Fulbright: "I am writing this letter to personally request that I be provided with a copy of this memorandum within the next hour as I would like to read its contents and possibly comment on it before leaving Washington after lunch."[12]

Shortly thereafter, Fulbright replied: ". . . the [story] states clearly that this was a private memorandum to the Secretary of Defense. . . . The memorandum is in no way a committee memorandum. . . . Since it is a private communication to the Secretary of Defense, I have not felt that it is necessary to make it available to anyone else."[13]

These letters observed the Senate's rules on decorum, but there was real animosity. Senator Thurmond was enraged that such a memo should be written, with or without the committee's sanction—and he was rambunctious enough to request to see the memo without delay. For his part, Senator Fulbright was irritated with Thurmond's ultimatum-like request, and in any event, he was "unwilling to open my private files in response to so impertinent a letter."[14]

An underlying reason for Fulbright's reluctance may also have been that he understood the consequences of his actions and knew only too well what Thurmond's response would be to the comments contained in his memorandum. When he continued to refuse to supply it, Thurmond used other sources to come up with the document, and the consequences were every bit as bad as both Thurmond and Fulbright suspected. Without naming Fulbright as the author, Strom stated, "I can well understand why anyone connected with this document would be fearful of public disclosure of the entire contents."

The memo contained two passages Thurmond found particularly irksome:

> In the long run, it is quite possible that the principle problem of leadership will be, if it is not already, to restrain the desire of the people to "hit the Communists with everything we've got." . . . Pride in victory, and frustration in restraint during the Korean War, led to MacArthur's revolt and McCarthyism.
>
> Fundamentally, it is believed that the American people have little, if any, need to be "alerted to the menace of the Cold War." Rather the need is for understanding the true nature of that menace, and the direction of the public's present and foreseeable awareness of the fact of the menace toward the support of the President's own total program. . . . There are no reasons to believe that military personnel generally can contribute to this need beyond their specific technical competence.[15]

The essence of these statements was that Fulbright was concerned that "education programs" and speeches conducted by the military might damage the president's efforts to soften his stance toward the Soviet Union. In response to Fulbright's memo, Secretary of Defense Robert S. McNamara announced new restrictions on speeches by top military men. Officers' speeches were supposed to contain references only to military matters and to steer clear of any foreign policy implications.

At a press conference held on July 21, Thurmond assailed the actions and called the memorandum "a dastardly attempt to intimidate the commanders of the U.S. Armed Forces and prevent those commanders from teaching their troops the nature of the menace of world Communism."[16] His further response was to demand an immediate investigation into the exact nature of this attempt to "muzzle" the military, with a look at the deeper implications of the new thrust in foreign policy being espoused by the Kennedy administration. Fulbright, in his effort at damage control, launched the countercharge that Thurmond was attacking the fundamental American belief that the military should have civilian control. This patently false argument was repudiated by Thurmond on numerous occasions and was borne out by his conduct throughout the dispute.

Thurmond's attempt to convince the Senate to hold hearings on the matter fell on deaf ears, initially. He spoke to the Senate repeatedly during July and August in efforts to force an investigation. He also used the media (when he could get their cooperation) to promote the investigation. He was joined very early in his efforts by two conservative Republican senators, Karl E. Mundt of South Dakota and Barry Goldwater of Arizona. The impact of Thurmond's speechmaking was felt by the Senate as some seventeen thousand telegrams (most of them favorable to Strom's position) flooded the Armed Services Committee. Finally, on September 6 and 7, 1961, the Armed Services Committee heard testimony from Defense Secretary Robert McNamara. Thurmond kept his examination polite, but he was insistent, and he uncovered a remarkable fact—some fifteen hundred speeches of military leaders had been censored. Strom immediately asked to see the speeches so that he could determine what kinds of statements were being purged, and after some assistance from Senator Richard Russell, he got them.

On September 18, while he was deep in his study of the speeches, Thurmond took the floor to give a lengthy speech of his own, again requesting a full investigation. When the Armed Services Committee met, they granted Thurmond's wish by a vote of fifteen to one. The scope of the investigation was narrowed into three phases of inquiry:

1. A study of the practices and procedures
    relating to the policy review or censorship of
    public speeches of military personnel for the

purpose of determining whether they are
established and administered properly and
whether there have been abuses or improper
practices in the administration thereof.

2. An examination of the military troop infor-
    mation and education program to determine
    the effectiveness of the existing program, the
    scope of the desired program, and the ques-
    tion of what could and should be done to
    strengthen the program and make it more
    effective.

3. A study of the proper role of military person-
    nel in informing, educating and alerting the
    civilian population as to the menace of the
    Cold War (or anti-Communist seminars) and
    the military external information program in
    general.[17]

The investigation was to take place before the Preparedness
Investigating Subcommittee, which had Senator John Stennis of
Mississippi as its chairman. Other subcommittee members were E.
L. Bartlett of Oklahoma, Henry Jackson of Washington, Leverett
Saltonstall of Massachusetts, Margaret Chase Smith of Maine,
Stuart Symington of Missouri, and Thurmond. A series of delays
kept the subcommittee from starting work until January 23, 1962.
When it did begin, Thurmond had done his homework and was
prepared to show that the Defense Department (and State Depart-
ment) were regularly deleting references that were unfriendly to
the Soviet Union or communism from the speeches of military
officers.

Thurmond pointed out ten examples and went on to add: "This
pattern of censoring out penetrating phrases on Communism is
relatively consistent wherever such material is submitted. There
appears to be complete consistency in the deleting of any use of the
word 'victory' or the word 'war.'"[18] The bottom line of Thurmond's
assertion was that the Kennedy administration was pursuing a
"no-win" foreign policy (Thurmond coined this phrase). As Thurmond hammered away at the attitude that underlaid the actions of
the censors, the liberal elements of the press (and Kennedy's staff)
began taking shots at him. The most serious charge was that
Thurmond was on a McCarthy-type witch hunt for Communists in

the government. This was patently false: Thurmond was not after individuals, merely the assumptions that underlaid the policies. But these attacks were designed to direct the focus off the actions and issues and onto Thurmond himself—and he was an easy target.

When the subcommittee began soliciting testimony from witnesses, the first order of business was a lengthy statement from former president Eisenhower who noted that "I have yet to meet the American military officer who viewed himself as budding Napoleon, or even a Rasputin, and I suggest it is worthy of note that in recent world history the three major dictators, Hitler, Mussolini, and Stalin, came from civil life. . . . I question the desirability of requiring the topmost government officials, whether military or civilian, to submit their proposed public statements for what amounts to censorship of content."

Others (such as Robert A. Lovett, defense secretary under President Truman) disagreed with Ike's comments. Most damaging to Thurmond's case was the fact that no senior miliary men would admit to an outright "muzzling." Later in the hearings on January 30, Thurmond presented incidents in which the testimony of military officers had been censored prior to testifying before at least three congressional committees. That the executive branch would attempt to edit the information the Congress received was a gross insult to the legislative branch. As the subcommittee became more aroused over the imperious tactics of the executive branch, President Kennedy acted. On February 8, he pulled the plug by declaring that the information was to be withheld under the doctrine of executive privilege. Since most of the materials regarding censorship were in the control of the executive branch, this effectively ended this area of inquiry. (Because he was a popular president, this bit of stonewalling was allowed to stand.)

With this avenue capped, Thurmond sought another means of getting at Kennedy's foreign policy and found it in the person of Undersecretary of State George Ball. When it was uncovered that the State Department had the major censorship responsibilities, Ball was called on to provide justification as to why various phrases were censored.

Ball responded on March 29, 1962, by sending speeches grouped into five chronological periods: the U-2 incident and the abortive Paris summit of May 1960; the inauguration of President Kennedy; early 1961, including Yuri Gagarin's space flight and the Bay of Pigs; the Vienna summit between Kennedy and Kruschev in June of 1961; and events surrounding the beginning of the Berlin crisis in June and July 1961. Ball's explanation for the State Department censorship was that "relations between the United States and the Communist Bloc were in a particularly sensitive and critical state."[19]

One example of the censorship included a speech by General G. H. Decker, in which he said, "*Aggression* and subversion in Africa, Asia and Latin America are timely examples of the means used to pursue their [communist nations] aim of world domination." In this example, the word *aggression* was replaced with *intervention* because "the methods used by the Communist nations in the areas referred to had not been officially labeled by the United States Government as aggression. It was deemed particularly inopportune to have a United States official make this charge at a time when the new administration [Kennedy's] was attempting to develop its avenues of communication with the Communist Governments."[20]

Another involved a speech by General Herbert B. Powell, in which he said, "The basic challenge, of course, stems primarily from *rampant Communism* intent on achieving its declared goal of world domination." The State Department substituted a *foreign ideology* for *rampant Communism* because "the characterization of Communism as 'rampant,' could be taken as implying an acknowledgement on the part of this Government that, contrary to fact, the Communists were making substantial gains."[21]

The best (or worst) example of this censorship involved the phrase "victory on each of the four battlefields of the Cold War," which was deleted. The State Department's justification was that "the word 'victory' has a militaristic and aggressive ring less suited than the substituted phrase describing our national objectives. It implies an 'all or nothing approach' leaving no room for accommodation."[22]

Strom finally had his proof. In their own words, the State Department had admitted that they were pursuing a "no-win" foreign policy. He had been at least partially vindicated.

As the investigation moved into the other two phases, the only other fireworks came from the appearances of General A. Edwin Walker. Walker had been relieved of his command of the 24th Division in Germany on April 17, 1961, for allegedly violating the Hatch Act, which prohibits partisan political activity. His troubles stemmed from the "pro-Blue" information program he installed to train his troops on the nature of communism. Thurmond had cited Walker's case (and early on had offered him office space). The press hoped to link Thurmond to Walker, and called the hearings the Walker hearings because it was assumed that Walker would play a large role in them. In his testimony, Walker insinuated that some members of the administration were Communists. He later punched an annoying reporter, and his case went down in flames.

The investigation officially ended in October, 1962. The subcommittee's work had been extensive: they had heard sixty-seven witnesses in thirty-six days of open hearings, and they submitted a ninety-thousand-word report. Thurmond issued a separate, minority report of eighty-five thousand words. In the end, the subcommittee did not fully subscribe to Thurmond's opinions, but there was agreement in some areas. Specifically, the subcommittee agreed that "although the Subcommittee is convinced that a system for prior review and clearance of military speeches is altogether proper and desirable, the record of the hearings reflects that the actual operation of the present system has left much to be desired." Thurmond had proved his point, and he had gained the respect of other senators with his tenacity.

The "military muzzling" incident is notable for reasons other than its demonstration that, in some ways at least, President Kennedy was pursuing a "no-win" foreign policy. This was Thurmond's first major foray into foreign relations, and as such, it marked a slight change in his focus. Since his election to the Senate, he had been almost totally concerned with domestic issues, particularly the question of integration. Now Thurmond had begun his move away from that position. He would still make occasional statements and continue to be involved to lesser degrees in civil rights issues, but from this point forward, it became less and less important with him.

Now that he was focused on foreign affairs, he used his sources, both at home and abroad, to closely examine America's enemies. When he trained his sights on Cuba, he brought the country a startling revelation. On January 15, 1962, Strom Thurmond told the nation about a suspected buildup of Soviet missiles in Cuba—months before President Kennedy acknowledged the buildup and decided to do something about it during the "Cuban Missile Crisis" in October.

Thurmond took President Kennedy to task for his advocacy of the Nuclear Test Ban Treaty, going so far as to urge the Senate to adopt a resolution in opposition to any such treaty before Kennedy's treaty was presented to them. (The Senate has the responsibility to "advise and consent" on all treaties.) Thurmond failed in this effort, but he was able to secure an unfavorable report from the Preparedness Investigating Subcommittee, which voted 5 to 2 against the treaty on September 9. On September 24, 1963, however, the Senate did approve the treaty.

Thurmond was not through with defense issues. He was an early proponent of the creation of an antiballistic missile system and actually forced a closed-door "secret session" of the Senate to allow for a frank discussion of America's lack of defense preparedness under President Kennedy. Thurmond was not initially successful in his efforts to create an antiballistic missile defense system, but he persisted. Finally, in 1966, funds were voted to begin preproduction engineering on a defense system against incoming missiles.

No doubt Senator Thurmond was genuinely concerned about these issues. His total immersion in military matters immediately after his wife's death, though, may have been a tonic for his grief as much as anything else. Indeed, many observers felt that he would not have undertaken these "crusades" (or would have approached the subjects differently) had Jean been alive. Without her around to soften his stance and divert him, he became totally consumed.[23]

Now, too Thurmond was being forced to reexamine his beliefs in many areas. When he looked at the national government, he found more compatibility with the membership across the aisle—with the Republicans—than among the Democrats, many of whom were espousing expanded federal intervention in all facets of life and a "no-win" foreign policy. For years, he had been an excellent conservative and a poor Democrat. Fast-moving events would force him to make one more far-reaching decision, and the catalyst would be Senator Barry Goldwater.

Chapter 14

THE WINDS OF CHANGE

B eginning in the summer of 1963, protests from black Americans took an increasingly active form. Previously, the challenge to the practices and institutions that prevented
blacks from participating in the benefits of American society had
been through lawsuits. As blacks became impatient with the slow
pace of these changes, leaders such as Dr. Martin Luther King, Jr.,
of the Southern Christian Leadership Conference and James Farmer
of the Congress of Racial Equality organized "demonstrations" to
emphasize the need for immediate change.

In the South, these demonstrations took the form of sit-ins at
segregated lunch counters and protests at other blatantly discriminatory practices. In the North, the protests centered on de
facto segregation that existed in jobs, schools, and housing. Most
of the demonstrations took place in the South, however. One of the
first major demonstrations was in May of 1963, when thousands of
blacks demonstrated against segregation in Birmingham, Alabama. Several "freedom marches" followed in other cities. The
culmination of these efforts came on August 28, 1963, when a
racially mixed crowd of some two hundred thousand people
marched on Washington, D.C. At this gathering, Dr. King shared
his hope for the future in his "I have a dream" speech.

Shortly after the Birmingham protest, on June 18, 1963, new
civil rights legislation was introduced in Congress by the Kennedy
administration. The primary provisions of this legislation dealt
with prevention of segregation in public accommodations and
facilities. After the legislation was introduced, Senate Majority
Leader, Mike Mansfield, a Democrat from Montana, determined
where to send the legislation to assure its best chance of passage.
Normally, legislation of this type was referred to the Judiciary

211

Committee. But Mississippi's Senator James Eastland was chairman of that committee, and the legislation, therefore, was not likely to see the light of day. A second alternative was to use the portions of the bill relating to interstate commerce and send it to the Commerce Committee. There was only one discernible obstruction on the Commerce Committee: Strom Thurmond. Mansfield was confident that Thurmond's objections could be overcome.

When the hearings began, President Kennedy promptly sent Attorney General Robert F. Kennedy to testify on the bill. When he had an opportunity to question Kennedy, Thurmond immediately launched into a comprehensive review of the Constitution and the provisions of the bill, in an effort to establish that the proposal was unconstitutional. Since the Kennedy administration had chosen to make its case on the "interstate commerce" aspect of the bill, Thurmond repeatedly asked the attorney general to define exactly which types of business would be covered by the law and how much "interstate commerce" they had to do to be covered under its provisions. Kennedy refused to be pinned down, and his refusal convinced Thurmond that Kennedy had no real grasp of the constitutional issues that underpinned the legislation.

For several hours, Kennedy submitted to a thorough grilling by Senator Thurmond. The climax in the questioning occurred when Thurmond offered a child's booklet, "What Everyone Should Know About the Constitution," to the attorney general with the suggestion that he study it. One senator later recalled that Kennedy "didn't know whether to laugh or cry."[1]

Despite some very strong pro-civil rights sentiment in the Congress, the Kennedy civil rights measure stalled. The tragic November 1963 assassination of President Kennedy moved Lyndon Baines Johnson into the White House, and he quickly adopted Kennedy's legislation as his own. The House of Representatives adopted the measure on February 10, 1964, and it reached the Senate on February 17. This time, the southern Democrats responded as a unit—there was no need for Thurmond to make a lonely stand. Senator Richard Russell of Georgia organized a filibuster that began in March and lasted for weeks. (On March 18, prior to the beginning of the filibuster, Thurmond argued the southern position on national television on the "CBS Reports" program. His opponent in the debate was Senator Hubert H. Humphrey. Thurmond acquitted himself well in the exchange—but, of course, made no headway with Humphrey.)

In July of 1964, the southern filibuster was ended, and the Civil Rights Act of 1964 was passed. Even in defeat, however, Thurmond refused to give up. Prior to final passage he proposed some thirty-six restrictive amendments, all rejected by the Senate. For all intents and purposes, the Civil Rights Act of 1964 marked the end of Thurmond's strident segregationism. The law, itself, was a powerful weapon in ending segregation. In addition to requiring equal access to public accommodations and facilities, the act forbade discriminatory voter registration tests, barred discrimination by employers and unions, and provided for withholding federal funds from state and local programs that were not integrated. After this legislation, most of the visible signs of segregation disappeared.

For Strom Thurmond, the passage of this legislation may have also signaled another change. The fight against it was the last time he led opposition to civil rights efforts. He continued to be opposed to other measures that impacted on civil rights, including the Civil Rights Act of 1968, but his opposition became less and less vocal. This is not to suggest that Thurmond became a vocal civil rights proponent, but he began moving into what passes as neutrality for him. Before he reached that stage, however, he had another opportunity to oppose some of President Johnson's civil rights initiatives. He hoped he could do so by doing nothing, but he ended up doing a lot more than he counted on. The incident in question was Strom's famous wrestling match with Senator Ralph Yarborough of Texas.

Thurmond Versus Yarborough

The cause of the Thurmond/Yarborough scuffle was President Johnson's appointment of former Governor Leroy Collins of Florida to serve as the director of the Community Relations Service (CRS). The CRS was to handle some racial disputes and provide mediation. Collins raised Thurmond's ire by making a speech in South Carolina that many white southerners regarded as "grossly unfair and insulting."[2]

When Collins came before the Commerce Committee for confirmation hearings, he found an unhappy Strom Thurmond facing him. Thurmond questioned Collins in great detail for over three hours. When Committee Chairman Warren Magnuson of Washington tried to call a vote on the nomination, however, Thurmond removed himself from the committee room, thus denying Magnuson a quorum and preventing action on the nomination.

Thurmond repeated the move and was doing so again on another day when Senator Ralph Yarborough started to enter the room and "playfully" pulled Thurmond toward the door. In turn, Strom pulled the 190-pound Yarborough away from the door and suggested a deal. If Yarborough could pull Thurmond in, Thurmond would stay—but if Thurmond could keep Yarborough out, Yarborough would stay out. Initially, Yarborough dismissed the challenge as a joke but when Thurmond repeated it, he decided to take him up on it. The men handed their coats, pens, pencils, and papers to a Thurmond aide and the grappling began. Thurmond grabbed Yarborough's legs, threw him to the floor, and pinned him there. Ever the sportsman, Thurmond let him up; then he threw Yarborough to the floor again and sat astride him. By this time the halls were filling with members of the media. Capitol police refused to allow any pictures to be taken, but there were many witnesses. Thurmond maintained his perch, occasionally asking Yarborough if he intended to keep his end of the bargain. Yarborough decided he could not be party to an effort to prevent a quorum so he remained on the floor, occasionally struggling to free himself. One senator on his was into the meeting did his best to break the duo up. Finally, Senator Magnuson ordered the men to stop, and they did. By that time enough senators were present to constitute a quorum with or without Thurmond, so he went in too and cast the lone vote against Collins. The final vote was 16 to 1 to confirm.

Once again, Thurmond's actions had simply gotten out of hand. His advisors lectured him at length on why he should never do things like that, only to have their efforts weakened by calls from constituents congratulating him on his wrestling "victory." The residents of the state of Texas buried their senator under a mountain of Wheaties™.[3] This wrestling match had no effect on the country, nor did it have any lasting effect on Strom Thurmond. It showed poor judgment by the two sixty-one-year-old U.S. senators who rolled around on the floor. But Thurmond continued to exhibit the depth of his conviction and the lengths to which he would go to stand up—or lie down—for what he believed in.

If the people of South Carolina thought that Thurmond's headstanding and wrestling demonstrated his independent spirit, they were about to get an even greater demonstration. The political situation in 1964 was forcing a realignment in national politics—especially in the South. The issue was not primarily race, although that was part of it. The real issue revolved around the power of the federal government—concerning which Thurmond had generally maintained that less is better. To demonstrate his adherence to that principle, he made the political decision of his lifetime, at the urging of his old friend Barry Goldwater.

Thurmond: Republican?

When his wife Jean was alive, Strom was friendly, professionally and socially, with Lyndon Johnson, who was then majority leader of the U.S. Senate. When Johnson ran for president in 1960, he had Thurmond's support. After the death of President Kennedy, Thurmond had issued a statement praising Johnson and acknowledging him as "one of the most experienced and capable leaders I have ever known." But after Johnson became president, Thurmond noticed a decidedly liberal turn to his politics.[4]

Strom had previously predicted that there would be a political realignment in America, with liberals dominating one party and conservatives dominating the other. When he issued his call, he must have thought that southern conservatism could still reassert itself in a leadership role in the Democratic party. But years of liberal presidential nominees, including Truman, Stevenson, and Kennedy, had begun to convince him that the party he had known and been part of for his entire life was changing. And while the Democrats were hurtling pell-mell toward a full capitulation to liberalism, the Republicans appeared headed the other way, toward conservatism. Beginning with his service in the U.S. Senate, Thurmond had seen that many of his views were closer to those of the Republican party than those of his own party.

The only area where there was an apparent divergence in Thurmond's views and the Republicans' was in the area of civil rights. The Republicans had always favored civil rights, while Thurmond still represented the traditional southern view. Still, the Republicans tended to view civil rights somewhat differently than many of their Democratic counterparts. Republicans favored slow, steady change with local leaders directly involved in the transition, while many Democrats seemed to favor radical, immediate change directed by the federal government. These differences were fairly obvious and, as such, southerners could find some comfort in the Republican view.

The real issue here, to many, was no longer civil rights but the concept of federalism. Thurmond believed the federal government had no right to involve itself in areas not expressly mentioned in the Constitution. He asserted that new federal initiatives should be preceded by a constitutional amendment. In this belief, he found many friends in the Republican party and few in his own.

Nowhere was this difference emphasized more than in the 1964 presidential election. In July the Republican party nominated Barry Goldwater as their standard-bearer. Goldwater was an Arizona conservative who served with Thurmond from his early days in the Senate and often supported him in his fights (not civil rights, but in other issues such as the military muzzling incident). In addition to their friendship and working relationship, Goldwater also demonstrated that he was a strict constitutional constructionist and that he was against further federal involvement in areas without constitutional approval.

The Democrats were intent on nominating Johnson to serve a four-year term of his own. Since assuming the presidency, LBJ had espoused several civil rights measures, called for a "war on poverty" that would take the federal government into new areas, and appeared headed toward control of local government through programs to "revitalize" cities and "upgrade" educational systems. These were decidedly liberal measures and would place large grants of additional power in the hands of the federal government.

Strom was so distressed with this liberal trend in his party that he used his position as a delegate to the Interparliamentary Union meeting in Europe as an excuse not to serve as a delegate to the Democratic National Convention in August in Atlantic City, New Jersey. He knew he would find no happiness there. Events bore out his suppositions.

When President Kennedy died and Johnson assumed the presidency, the vice president's slot was vacant. Johnson, therefore, had an opportunity to name his running mate for the 1964 election. Out of the many possible choices Johnson chose the one sure to upset the most southerners—Senator Hubert Humphrey of Minnesota, one of the Senate's most liberal members. To Thurmond and many other southerners, this was the last straw for the Democratic party.

At that point, three options were open to Thurmond: keep quiet; endorse Goldwater and remain a Democrat; or endorse Goldwater and switch to the Republican party. Strom was solid in the affections of his state's voters. He could easily have kept quiet, or in the climate that prevailed, he could even have publicly endorsed Goldwater and remained a Democrat. But being Strom Thurmond, the urge to do what was right forced him to do some real soul searching.

Thurmond and his aide Harry Dent traveled across the state to seek out advice. Most of the people they talked to suggested that he just keep quiet. The opposition to any public comment or party switch was so intense that Thurmond briefly considered doing nothing. But Strom Thurmond had consistently demonstrated the desire to do what he felt was right without any regard for his own best interests, and he did so again.

While having dinner with Dent, Thurmond decided he would have to go all the way—to endorse Goldwater, campaign for him, and switch to the Republican party. He drew up a statement for public release and set up an appointment with Goldwater for September 12. At that meeting, Strom laid out his position and asked Goldwater what would help him the most. Goldwater told him that his support would be welcome but his switch to the Republican party would be most important. Thurmond then produced his statement and asked Goldwater to review it. After reading it, Goldwater told him, "Don't change one word. That's one of the finest statements I've ever read."[5]

Strom decided to address the people of South Carolina on Wednesday, September 16 at 6:15 P.M. and to be present for Goldwater's visit to Greenville, South Carolina, the next day. (While he was making arrangements to change parties, President Johnson's wife, Lady Bird, called to invite him to ride on the "Lady Bird Special," a campaign train that would carry her throughout the South. Strom declined, citing his need to make some fundamental decisions.)

The story of his decision to change parties actually broke on September 15 on the CBS Evening News broadcast with Walter Cronkite. A day later, standing before a giant picture of Barry Goldwater, Strom Thurmond faced the people of the state and, using the speech he had shown Goldwater, informed them of his historic decision.

He put forward some of his basic philosophy when he quoted, "For evil to triumph, it is only necessary that good men do nothing." As always, Thurmond was prepared to do something. He vented his frustration with the national Democratic party, declaring: "The Democratic Party has forsaken the people to become the party of minority groups, power-hungry union leaders, political bosses, and big businessmen looking for government contracts and favors."

As he continued his speech, he attacked the actions of the Democratic party on domestic and foreign issues. On domestic issues, Strom declared:

> The Democratic Party has converted the Government from a servant of the people to a master of the people. . . . The Democratic Party has invaded the private lives of people by using the powers of government for coercion and intimidation of individuals. . . . The Democratic Party has rammed through Congress unconstitutional, impractical, unworkable, and oppressive legislation which invades inalienable personal and property rights of the individual. . . . The Democratic Party has encouraged, supported and protected the Supreme Court in a reign of judicial tyranny, and in the Court's effort to wipe out local self-government, effective law enforcement, internal security, the rights of the people and the States, and even the structure of the State governments. The Democratic Party is converting our Constitutional Federated Republic into the same type of disciplined and submissive servant of an elite power group as it has made of the Democratic Party itself.

On foreign policy, he said, "the Democratic party, as a custodian of government, faltered at the Bay of Pigs and in the Cuban crisis of 1962 . . . has sent our youth into combat in Vietnam, refusing to call it war, and demanding of our youth the risk of their lives without providing either adequate equipment or a goal of victory."

He then went on to propose an alternative—Barry Goldwater and the Republican party. He closed his address with a statement of personal courage.

> To my friends who have conscientiously advised me against this step, because of a sincere belief that I could best serve the country by following a course designed to keep myself in office, I can only say that I fully realize the political risk involved in this step and that my chances for

> reelection might, because of this step, go down
> into oblivion. But in the final analysis, I can only
> follow the course which, in my heart and con-
> science, I believe to be in the best interest of our
> State, our country, and the freedom of our
> people. I have chosen this course because I
> cannot consider any risks in a cause which I am
> convinced is right.[7]

The next day, Thurmond introduced Goldwater to a crowd of some twenty-five thousand South Carolinians in Greenville. Thurmond then embarked on a vigorous campaign schedule that took him as far away as Burbank, California, but mainly centered on southern locations.[8]

Although he campaigned in other southern states for Goldwater, Thurmond realized that his party switch and endorsement made it imperative for Thurmond himself that Goldwater carry South Carolina. In a sense, the 1964 presidential vote in his state would be a referendum on Strom Thurmond. Many prominent Democrats, including Senator Olin Johnston, vowed to campaign all the harder for Johnson. For that reason, Thurmond spent most of the last two weeks of the campaign in South Carolina, working hard to make sure it was in Goldwater's column on election night. Harry Dent organized a massive rally in Columbia, South Carolina, on October 31, the Saturday night before the election. Many southern politicians, including former Governor James F. Byrnes and Congressman Albert Watson, were on the program, as well as Senator Goldwater himself. (This rally followed a Johnson visit to the state on October 26.)

When the voting was over, history had been made. Goldwater had carried South Carolina by over 92,000 votes, and other southern states had gone for Goldwater, as well. Most of the credit went to Strom Thurmond. (With the exception of the southern states and his home state of Arizona, Goldwater won no other electoral votes.) Goldwater was not successful, but his candidacy had ended almost one hundred years of blind loyalty by southerners to the Democratic party. By his courage, Strom Thurmond had helped to change the course of history.

Courage of this sort is often rewarded. The Republican party was not in power, but it did what it could to thank Thurmond for his efforts. In joining the Republican party he lost no seniority on the Armed Services Committee (he was given Goldwater's place), and he was transferred from Commerce to Banking and Currency, which was almost equal in status to Commerce. He was also accorded the honor of a spot on the Republican Policy Committee.

With characteristic vigor, Thurmond immediately set about building South Carolina's Republican party. At that time, it had able leadership in Drake Edens, but Strom envisioned even bigger things, such as expanding the staff to include a professional executive director. In a November 25, 1964, letter Strom offered to let the party have the services of Harry Dent and to assist in putting on a dinner to raise additional funds.[9] His offer ran into some hesitation on the part of the state's Republicans, however, and on December 3, Strom withdrew his offer and decided on the course that would ultimately benefit him the most.[10] He began building his own organization in South Carolina, one that was independent of both political parties. (The initial rejection of Dent's help was only temporary, however. When the South Carolina Republicans got together, they elected him as their state chairman.)

Thurmond's switch from the Democratic to the Republican party could not have been completely unexpected. For years he had given signs that he was, at best, independent. Now, in many ways, he truly was. He had cut his ties with the Democrats but there was no real Republican party in South Carolina to affiliate with. This made no difference in day-to-day interactions, but it could be critically important in the hard-fought reelection campaign that was sure to come.

A Republican Senator

Throughout 1965, Strom Thurmond did battle with his new enemies—the national Democratic party. President Johnson came under attack for his calls for increased federal involvement in local issues, as well as his lame foreign policy, specifically as it related to his conduct of the Vietnam war.

Thurmond was also involved in efforts to defend the Taft-Hartley legislation against attempts by President Johnson and Senate liberals to water down its provisions. Taft-Hartley regulated labor unions, and one section (14b) was targeted for removal by friends of organized labor. Thurmond was vociferous in his support for the legislation, and his position found support among many in South Carolina because of its right-to-work position. A black Easley resident wrote to Strom: "I urge you to vote against repeal of Section 14(b) of the Taft-Hartley Act . . . and I will vote for you in our great State in the coming election."[11]

Thurmond took a leadership role in efforts to save Section 14(b) and was successful. Interestingly, he had always maintained that the federal government had no legal role in setting labor policy because it was not specifically referenced in the Constitution. But when pressed for further explanation, he acknowledged that once the federal government was involved, there was an obligation to do the best that could be done with it.

Back in South Carolina, several political events were shaping up. Albert Watson, the Democratic congressman from the Second District (the Columbia area), had decided to switch parties, giving the state two Republican officials in Congress. A big development was the death of Senator Olin Johnston in the spring of that year. When he died, Governor Donald S. Russell resigned and was appointed to the Senate seat by Robert E. McNair, who had been Russell's lieutenant governor. Russell's action, tantamount to appointing himself to the U.S. Senate, produced another opportunity for the Republicans to make a strong challenge for the seat—which they did in 1966.

As Thurmond worked at building his own organization, the real beginnings of the South Carolina Republican party were also in motion. Buoyed by the Goldwater victory, Thurmond's switch, and that of Watson, Republicans in the more progressive parts of the state began recruiting candidates to run for the state legislature and other local offices. They even began talking about putting up candidates for other statewide offices, which had long been routinely conceded to the Democrats.

Thurmond's first consideration, obviously, was his own reelection, and as usual, he devoted considerable energy to the task. Without a state Republican organization to support him, he had to build his own organization. Sometimes he recruited Republicans, other times Democrats. Even as a Republican, he demonstrated the independence that his constituents had come to expect—and admire.

Another side to his campaign efforts was the extensive fundraising that he began immediately after the 1964 presidential election. Using an organization known as Thurmond Speaks, Strom traveled around the country espousing his brand of bedrock conservatism. His ideas were popular with many people outside the state and found an enthusiastic audience among military retirees. His war record, his ROA leadership position, his seat on the

Armed Services Committee, and his work for veterans made him a logical candidate to support. Contributions began flowing in from all over the country in January of 1965. One contributor who donated $1,000 via California Senator George Murphy wanted Strom to know that he considered him "a really great American and a great Conservative."[12] Throughout this campaign (and subsequent ones), Thurmond was able to draw on vast sums of money from these sources.

As 1966 drew near, Thurmond obviously expected the Democratic party to put up a strong challenge, but—as had happened so many times in the past—fate and circumstances intervened. Most important was Donald Russell's self-appointment to the U.S. Senate. Popular former Governor Ernest F. (Fritz) Hollings would have been a likely challenger to Thurmond, but with Russell's action (slightly reminiscent of the Edgar Brown fiasco), that seat appeared easier to capture than Thurmond's seat. The upshot was that Hollings decided to challenge Russell in the Democratic primary. That left Robert McNair, a popular lieutenant governor who became even more popular while serving as governor. He, too, would have mounted a serious challenge to Thurmond, but his ascension to the governorship with less than two years remaining in the term allowed him to run for a full four-year term in 1966, which he did.

With Russell, Hollings, and McNair already locked into statewide races, the Democrats were casting around for a suitable challenger for Thurmond. The first to step forward was state Senator P. Bradley Morrah, Jr., of Greenville County. In his opening statement, delivered on April 11, 1966, Morrah declared that Thurmond had been ineffective and he declared his own moderation: "I'm no extremist in either direction." Morrah, however, did not exactly radiate confidence in his decision to oppose Thurmond. He decided to seek reelection in his state senate seat that year, as well.

Morrah's timid stance was bound to provoke other Democrats to enter the primary. Acerbic John Bolt Culbertson, who had grown into the state's foremost liberal voice, did so. In his statement, Culbertson blasted Morrah as being as conservative as Thurmond and suggested that Morrah should get in one race or the other. The Democratic primary was set for June 14, and their differences would be settled there.

Meanwhile, state Senator Marshall Parker of Oconee County switched to the Republican party to run against the winner of the

Russell/Hollings matchup; state Representative Joseph O. Rogers of Clarendon switched to the Republican party to run against McNair for governor; and Dr. Inez Eddings, the Richland County superintendent of education, switched to the Republican party to run for state superintendent of education. And Albert Watson was already on the ticket, running for reelection to Congress as a Republican. People were coming out of the woodwork to run as Republicans, but the question remained as to how effective they would be.

Thurmond continued his own intense pace throughout the filing period. By the time of the Democratic primary, his organization was almost complete: a finance committee had been put together, and almost every county in the state had a Thurmond volunteer chairman. In addition, Thurmond political staffers were combing the state, uncovering friends and identifying enemies daily. The Thurmond organization also benefited through numerous friends inside the Democratic party structure. Opposition campaign memos were often sent gratuitously to Thurmond.

The only part of Thurmond's campaign that was not functioning smoothly was his relationship with his advertising firm, Bradley, Graham and Hamby. This all-female firm had assisted him in previous campaign endeavors and appeared ready to help again. A difficulty came up regarding the campaign of Marshall Parker, who wanted the help of Bradley, Graham and Hamby in his race. Dolly Hamby wrote to Strom asking his advice on whether to get involved in the race, saying, "I am reluctant to take on any other statewide candidate for fear of spreading myself—and the agency—too thin. . . . I know that Marshall Parker wants our help. However, my instincts and judgement tell me to go only with you at the statewide level. . . . If you have any strong conviction or desire for us to help Marshall, just let me know and we will give it more consideration."[13]

On May 19, Hamby again wrote to Strom, this time with a concern over a growing difference of opinion with Harry Dent and to communicate her reluctance to help with the Parker campaign.[14] The relationship continued to deteriorate and as a result, Bradley, Graham and Hamby bowed out of assisting Strom in his race on June 27, 1966.[15] Lowe and Hall, a Greenville advertising firm, stepped in and finished the campaign.

These were all minor issues, however, as Strom's main interest continued to be on his own race. In the June 14 Democratic primary, the people chose nominees for both U.S. Senate races.

State Senator Morrah easily outdistanced Culbertson by a margin of 131,545 to 91,934 for the right to face Thurmond. Meanwhile, in the contest for the remaining two years of Johnston's term, Senator Russell was defeated by Fritz Hollings by a margin of 165,657 to 105,679.

It is interesting to note the discrepancy between the total number of people voting in the Morrah/Culbertson race (223,479) and the number voting in the Russell/Hollings race (271,336). Some 50,000 fewer people voted in the race to oppose Thurmond. This should have given the victor, Bradley Morrah, some cause for concern even at that early date.

After his primary victory, however, Morrah went on the attack. First he reminded the people that he had earned the right to run through a primary rather than becoming the hand-picked candidate of a convention, as had Strom Thurmond. Because there were no contested elections, the Republicans did not have a primary, instead selecting all of their nominees through a vote of the delegates at the state convention. Morrah then attacked Thurmond's effectiveness as a senator. He noted that of ninety-eight bills introduced by Thurmond as the sole author and twenty-one others where he had been the principal cosponsor between 1955 and 1965, only one had passed. And he noted that in 1966, of the seven sole and seven cosponsored bills Thurmond introduced, the only one that passed was a resolution honoring Winston Churchill. Morrah had seized upon this as a weakness, and he sounded this charge throughout the campaign.

For his part, Strom ran the kind of campaign he always ran—virtually ignoring his opponent and instead, concentrating on his own record and accomplishments. He was able to pull off his own coup of sorts by getting several senators to publicly endorse his reelection bid. The Republicans included Senator Everett M. Dirksen of Illinois, Senator George Murphy of California, Senator John Tower of Texas, and Senator Karl Mundt of South Dakota. These were to be expected, but in addition to these Republicans, Thurmond was also able to capture the public endorsements of several prominent southern Democrats, including Senator Richard B. Russell of Georgia, Senator Stuart Symington of Missouri, Senator John Stennis of Mississippi, and Senator Herman Talmadge of Georgia. To publicly endorse a member of the opposition was relatively rare and was testimony to the high regard these men had for Strom. (Thurmond also benefited from a visit to the state by former Vice President Richard M. Nixon, who was working hard for Republican candidates and preparing a path for his second try for the presidency in 1968. At a Columbia appearance, Nixon praised Thurmond and attacked President Johnson.)

Thurmond officially opened his campaign headquarters at 1616 Taylor Street in Columbia on August 2, 1966. William C. Plowden, Jr., of New Zion served as the chairman of the "Re-elect Thurmond Committee." Other officers were Dave L. Hughes of Newberry as finance chairman and Henry G. Chandler of Clinton as campaign director.[16]

As the campaign passed Labor Day, the traditional kick-off, Thurmond focused on one of his easiest targets—President Johnson. In September he said that LBJ had "turned traitor not only to the South but to America."[17] Senator Morrah tried to inject himself into this schism by calling Thurmond to task. He suggested that Thurmond should either begin impeachment proceedings or retract his statement and apologize to Johnson.[18] Strom did neither— he kept up his attack on Johnson (although he did clarify his statement by insisting that he meant Johnson had "failed to uphold constitutional principles")[19] and continued to ignore Morrah.

Thurmond also called for a formal declaration of war in the Vietnam conflict. Again, Morrah inserted himself by claiming that the declaration could mean the "sudden and brutal" deaths of American POWs. In October Thurmond went on to criticize Johnson for his handling of the action, declaring that the North Vietnamese could be beaten within ninety days if the United States would quit fighting with its hands tied behind its back and commit the resources necessary to win. This accusation brought an injured squawk from Johnson, who accused Thurmond of "harassing" him.[20]

Morrah's difficulties were compounded when Greenville attorney and former U.S. Senator Tom Wofford declared himself a write-in candidate for Morrah's state senate seat.

While Strom continued his attacks on Johnson and the national Democrats, he was not idle in South Carolina. Lowe and Hall collected and spent some $80,000 between August 11 and October 31. The list of promotional items included outdoor advertising, 10,000 calendar cards, 40,000 bumper stickers, 200,000 brochures, 25,000 flyers, 250,000 sample ballots, and time and production on newspaper, radio, and television ads.[21] Lowe and Hall covered the state with the Thurmond story during the sixty-day campaign.

And the results were comforting. Polls commissioned throughout the campaign showed Thurmond with a large lead in every part of the state at every education level and every age level. Some polls showed Strom with at least a 15-to-1 lead; others showed a 2-to-1 or better lead.

The Morrah campaign continued to have hope as late as a month before the election, counting on a large black vote. One memo stated that Fritz Hollings, Robert McNair, and the Democratic party had given thousands of dollars, and that this money was "purely for transportation [of blacks to the polls] on election day." The same memo also carried some bad advice, as it advised Morrah not to "worry too much about Tom Wofford." The Morrah strategy for the final stretch of the campaign was to continue to hit Thurmond on his ineffectiveness as a legislator—specifically, the number of bills he had passed. The memo closed with: "It's within grabs Bradley. Even the so-called pros, of which I personally don't think there are any, even they say with conviction that we've got a chance. . . . If you win you can cross the Potomac and say who's Lyndon and Fritz who? If you come close, that puts you and Fritz as the big Democrats in the state."[22]

As Thurmond and Morrah headed for their showdown, the other races between Democrats and Republicans were also getting some attention. Despite his early enthusiasm for Marshall Parker, many speculated that Thurmond was not supporting him in his race against Fritz Hollings. The Hollings/Parker race was not run so much against each other as against Washington. Hollings asserted that the nation needed a stronger Congress to check the expanding powers of the president, while Parker declared that Hollings gained favor with his friend Bobby Kennedy with his attacks on Johnson. As the campaign drew to a close, Parker's supporters began clamoring for a formal endorsement by Thurmond. Just a few days before the election, Thurmond gave Parker one of his rare endorsements, but it appeared to be too little, too late.

Other Republican candidates were also fighting for their political lives, even with a popular Thurmond at the head of their ticket. While incumbent Republican Albert Watson seemed headed for victory, the candidates for governor, lieutenant governor, and superintendent of education were not faring well. Better news came from some of the local elections: it appeared that Republicans might actually capture a respectable number of seats in the state legislature.

On November 8, 1966, the people of South Carolina went to the polls and confronted a new era. Everywhere they looked, they saw contested races on the ballot. State Democratic leaders had warned the people about a Republican attempt to gain control of the state on Thurmond's coattails. As people voted, many made the fundamental decision to vote Republican at the state and local level for the first time in their lives—the catalyst, of course, being Strom Thurmond.

When the votes began to roll in, the result of the Thurmond race was immediately clear-cut. After jumping out to an early lead, he coasted to a resounding victory by a margin of 271,297 to 164,955. Morrah also lost his state senate seat to Wofford. For all intents and purposes, Morrah's political career was ended by his decision to challenge Strom Thurmond. Other would-be challengers have been scared off by that lesson.

In the other U.S. Senate race, Fritz Hollings narrowly defeated Parker by a margin of 233,790 to 212,032. Thurmond's late endorsement had not been enough—indeed, the feeling in the state was that a strong, early Thurmond endorsement would have elected Parker. In the other races, Democrat Robert McNair defeated Rogers by a wider margin of 255,854 to 184,088. Democrats also won the other contested state races by similar margins. One Republican bright spot was that Congressman Watson was elected over his challenger by a margin of 48,742 to 27,013.

Even brighter news was that six Republicans had been elected to the state senate. These were the first Republican senators elected to the South Carolina Senate since Reconstruction. Further, seventeen Republicans were elected to the state house of representatives. These were important elections for the future of the South Carolina Republican party because they showed that Republicans could win at the county level. (These elections also served to highlight an important difference between the South and the rest of the country. Republicans won in the more progressive, urban areas of the state—around Charleston, Columbia, and Greenville. The rural areas continued to vote heavily Democratic. The Republican party in the South is built around the urbanized areas and this was in direct contrast to the Republican strength elsewhere, in the northeast especially.)

As for Strom Thurmond, he could look back at 1966 as the final step to invincibility. He had carried the state as an independent, a Democrat, and a Republican. Now, with his political future seemingly secure—with a new six-year term under his belt—Strom had the leisure of looking around him and setting a new course. He could look to greater involvement in the Republican party, certainly.

The 1968 presidential election was fast approaching, and Strom knew the South was prepared to play an important role in that future. Personally, he could stop worrying about proving anything to his constituents and concentrate on the struggles that were important to him—preservation of constitutional government in the United States of America.

Almost immediately, this new focus allowed him to take a different approach toward South Carolina's blacks. Soon he would be making bold moves to secure their favor. As had happened after the 1946 governor's election, his new sense of security enabled him to look to his personal needs, as well.

Chapter 15

THURMOND BECOMES A STATESMAN

There can be no doubt that President Lyndon Baines Johnson was exceptional at getting legislation through Congress. In addition to his previously mentioned success in civil legislation, Johnson had a knack for getting the Congress to adopt wide-ranging programs in almost any area he thought was important.

Johnson's legislative triumphs in 1966 and 1967 include the following: food for India, child nutrition, creation of the Department of Transportation, rent supplements, child safety, narcotics rehabilitation, highway safety, mine safety, bail reform, increased minimum wage, urban mass transit, air pollution control, partnership for health, increased social security payments, public broadcasting, college work-study, and food stamps. Suddenly it seemed that there was almost no area of life beyond federal control. President Johnson seemed to think the federal government was the cure for almost every ill—and he had no problem with adding taxes to pay for these cures.

Here, in its bluntest form, was the logical extrapolation of Alexander Hamilton's arguments for an all-powerful, "energetic" government. It was also the antithesis of the beliefs of Strom Thurmond. This may have been the worst time of Thurmond's professional life, as he saw the federal government enact one piece of liberal legislation after another, each one going further in granting excuses for federal intrusion than the last. Perhaps much worse than the bare fact of the new intrusions was their effectiveness. They were failing miserably, and even Johnson knew it. Late in his presidency, Johnson confided to his old foe Barry Goldwater that he knew he had failed, he just did not know why.

The failures were glaringly obvious at home—riots in the ghettos and demonstrations on the college campuses. Very little could be found that was right anywhere in America. Obviously, something had to change. Thurmond and many others decided that a good place to start was with the occupant of 1600 Pennsylvania Avenue.

The first question revolved around Johnson: Would he seek reelection in 1968? As his support crumbled, Johnson realized he could not win, even if he captured his party's nomination. His withdrawal from the race left three contenders: Robert F. Kennedy; Hubert H. Humphrey, Johnson's vice president; and Senator Edmund Muskie of Maine. These three voices were decidedly liberal, and although all promised to be different from Johnson, their cure for America's ills appeared to be more of the tonic that many believed had made it sick. The assassination of Robert Kennedy and subsequent collapse of Muskie's efforts put Humphrey in the driver's seat, and he was selected as the Democratic standard-bearer at the riotous Chicago convention.

On the Republican side, Richard Nixon was the front-runner. He had built up considerable support by traveling over the country, working for Republican candidates. Other hopefuls were Nelson Rockefeller and Ronald Reagan. These three men represented an ideological divergence, with Reagan on the right, Nixon in the middle, and Rocky on the left.

Nixon pinned his hopes on capturing the South—first to secure the nomination and then to win the election. A key component for both was the senior Republican statesman, Senator Strom Thurmond of South Carolina.

Thurmond Makes a King

In 1968 there was another Republican presidential candidate who pinned his hopes on southern delegates at the Republican National Convention in Miami. Ronald Reagan entered the convention as an unannounced candidate, but the California governor was certain that his brand of conservatism would set well with the South. Reagan's thinking did not take into account Thurmond's power in the South. Reagan had been able to make no headway with Thurmond.

Before the convention, Nixon sought a meeting with Thurmond to discuss his presidential candidacy. Nixon had little opportunity to apply any oil—instead, he was questioned thoroughly by Thurmond about his stand on the issues. Thurmond's recollection of the conversation was that several areas were discussed. The first was the military. Strom asked Nixon if he would stand for

strong national defense second to none. He
[Nixon] said he would. I asked him how he felt
about appointing judges to the Supreme Court
. . . who . . . were strict constructionists of the
Constitution. He said he would. . . . Then we
discussed about the federal government going
into so many fields of activity and dominating
the states . . . and he felt the same as I did about
it. . . . I told him that I thought it was foolish not
to let children go to the nearest school. . . . I said,
"Why not let them go to the neighborhood
school, if they are not satisfied there, go to any
school they want to, without any discrimination," and he said he would favor a "freedom of
choice in schools without discrimination. . . . He
said, "I do not favor discrimination in any way,
shape or form, but I do favor freedom of
choice."[1]

With all this agreement on substantive issues, Thurmond was
prepared to back Nixon and do whatever he could to get him
elected. Indeed, in his desire to get and hold Thurmond's support,
Nixon agreed to give him a veto of sorts over his selection of
running mate. This veto was to be a powerful weapon in holding
the South for Nixon.

The first thing Nixon needed was to hold the southern delegates
at the convention. In the national convention of 1968, unlike many
recent conventions, no candidate had the election sewn up beforehand. Fewer states had primaries then; more states used conventions to select delegates, and many delegates remained
uncommitted.

These uncommitted delegates were relentlessly stalked before
and during the national convention. Many states with large blocks
of uncommitted delegates caucused (met) during the early days of
the convention. They routinely invited candidates and potential
candidates to meet with them. New York Governor Nelson
Rockefeller and California Governor Ronald Reagan were the
primary caucus-hoppers as the convention began. Nixon set the
tone for his presidency by remaining away from the fray—he
counted on Congressman Gerald R. Ford, the permanent chairman
of the convention, and Senate Republican Leader Everett M. Dirksen
to keep things going his way.

Other flies in the ointment were "favorite son" candidates, Governor George Romney of Michigan, Governor James A. Rhodes of Ohio, and Senator Clifford Case of New Jersey. They used their status to hold their states' delegations for other candidates and to put themselves in the role of kingmaker. Another favorite-son candidacy had a similar purpose. Strom Thurmond of South Carolina was in his second try for the presidency but his agenda was to hold the South for Nixon.

The Reagan strategy was to make an official announcement that would elevate his own favorite-son candidacy into an official challenge. After California Senator William Knowland made a speech proclaiming that there was significant support for Reagan, he did declare—a scant forty-eight hours before the balloting was to take place.

Nixon recognized the threat to his southern strategy, but he had a plan. From the moment he had arrived in Miami Beach, Strom Thurmond was on the phone, cajoling southern delegates into the Nixon corner. When Reagan's announcement was made, Thurmond made personal calls and visits to delegates from Louisiana, North Carolina, and Texas. For wavering delegates, there had even been trips out to the converted sub-chaser that served as "Nixon's navy." Nixon personally met with the delegates from Alabama, District of Columbia, Georgia, Kentucky, Louisiana, Mississippi, Texas, and the Virgin Islands—with Strom Thurmond at his side. (Strom's aide, Harry Dent, overheard many of these southern delegates tell Strom, "If you're satisfied [with Nixon], we are."[2])

When the roll call began, everyone including Nixon wondered if Thurmond could hold the South. The delegate count produced no surprise: the South held for Nixon and Wisconsin's delegates put him over the top. While Nixon's victory literally had a cast of thousands, two Reagan aides put the credit where it belonged: "The essential problem was Strom Thurmond. I don't think anyone knew the extent to which Thurmond had a hold on the South. If we could have shaken loose Mississippi, South Carolina, or Florida we'd still be in there balloting. But Strom had them buttoned up."[3]

With his victory won, Nixon did not forget Strom Thurmond. He was publicly consulted about the vice presidential choice. With southern support, Nixon ended up choosing Maryland Governor Spiro T. Agnew. Nixon's actions were not purely based on gratitude. He knew that to be elected he would also have to carry a large portion of the South in the November election against Hubert Humphrey. These efforts would require the continued support of Strom Thurmond.

Thurmond provided that support, and it proved vital because of the entry of a third-party contender, Alabama Governor George Wallace. Wallace campaigned on the need for a third party: neither major political party, he said, represented the best interests of the South, an argument almost exactly like Thurmond's twenty years earlier when he had taken the plunge.

The irony may have been lost on Thurmond, but in his new role as a "party man," he traveled throughout the South, urging southerners to support Nixon and not to waste their votes on Wallace. In the hotly contested 1968 election, Republicans feared that Wallace's campaign might throw the election into the House of Representatives, which could cost Nixon the election.

As Thurmond launched his "support Nixon, forget Wallace," campaign swing through the South, Hubert Humphrey dubbed his opposition the "Nixiecrats" and declared that "the coalition of Nixon and Thurmond is the old Republican reactionary coalition that would lead America back."[4]

The 1968 presidential election was a close one, with Nixon edging out a victory over Humphrey—principally because he carried several southern states, including South Carolina. Partly because of the efforts of Strom Thurmond, Richard Nixon was elected president. For many in the South, this signaled the real end of something. Allegiance to the Democratic party was lost forever. A Republican president had been elected with their help; southerners looked to him to see what he would do to thank them. Former Thurmond aide Harry Dent moved to Washington to take an active role in cementing Republican ties in the South with a "southern strategy" of his own.

For Thurmond, this election marked another milestone. With a great victory won, the senator again turned his thoughts to himself. He was growing old; and he had no wife or children.

Strom Marries Again

In 1947, when Strom was courting and marrying Jean Crouch, Paul and Julia Moore's daughter, Nancy, was still in diapers. Her father came to Aiken to serve as a chemical engineer with the Savannah River Plant, which Strom had helped to bring into existence.

As Nancy grew up, she set high goals for herself and achieved them. While she was in college, she was elected Miss South Carolina in 1965 and competed in the Miss USA pageant. In 1966 she returned to school at Duke University in North Carolina and graduated. Her next step was to enroll in the University of South Carolina law school.

Whatever her career plans at that point, they were sidetracked when she met Strom Thurmond, some forty-four years her senior. They were introduced in the spring of 1968 at the Grape Festival in York, South Carolina, and at a square dance in nearby Clover. Someone suggested that Strom dance with Nancy "and teach her how."

Their chance meeting at a public function quickly grew into a relationship. Friends of Thurmond were aghast at the possibility of another relationship with a woman so much younger than the senator. As the relationship grew serious, Harry Dent decided to do what he could to end it. Over a two-week period, he met four times with Nancy trying to convince her to call the relationship off. Dent told Nancy that if she loved Thurmond, she would "leave him alone."[5] Describing the meetings, he later said, "We painted every horrible consequence possible, including how their children would be abnormal."[6]

Their concern, of course, was for Thurmond's career, and this time he, too, gave it some thought. But in the end, he rationalized that "normally, for a man to marry a woman that much younger wouldn't help his career. . . but I'd been with Nancy enough to know she had her feet on the ground, she was smart, and I just felt she'd make a good wife and mother. So if she felt she was willing to take the chance, well, I was. We both loved each other."[7]

Strom and Nancy were married at a large church wedding on December 22, 1968. Their marriage was soon blessed with a daughter, Nancy Moore. Over the next few years, the Thurmonds would have three more children: J. Strom, Jr., Juliana Gertrude, and Paul Reynolds. Nancy and the children proved to be a help rather than a hindrance to Strom's career. In addition to her role as mother, Nancy played an active role in Strom's subsequent campaigns and found time to write and carry on other worthwhile activities.

Once again, Strom's unorthodox actions did not bring the predicted dire consequences. Discarding all political wisdom, he had followed his heart once again, without regard for the consequences. Strom Thurmond demonstrated that he may be one of the greatest romantics of our time.

At this point, all was right in Strom's world: he had a new wife and a new president. He was progressing up the seniority and power ranks in his new party and seemed to be heading toward even greater power and prestige than he had ever known. Then he was hit with the closest thing to scandal he had ever seen in his political life. The story broke in *Life* magazine in an article entitled "Strom's Little Acres."

A Hint of Scandal

Back in 1953, Strom and his Aiken law partner, Charles E. Simons, Jr. (later a federal judge), began buying some rough sandy land in Aiken County. Eventually they bought some three thousand acres at a cost of about $14.35 per acre.

In 1966 the highway department began condemnation proceedings on land in Aiken County needed to construct Interstate 20. Included in the land they needed was a sixty-six acre strip through land owned by Thurmond and Simons. The highway department hired three appraisers to set a value on the land, and they appraised it at between $130 and $192 per acre.

At that point, Judge Simons entered into negotiations with the highway department. Most of the other acreage had been purchased for around $200 per acre, but Simons wanted more. First, he asked that a cloverleaf be constructed where the interstate was to bisect a dirt road that ran through the Thurmond-Simons property. Simons then presented three experts who testified that the land was valuable as an industrial site and, as such, was worth between $500 and $550 per acre.

The highway department was uncertain what to do, but as the trial date moved closer, they decided to settle and an agreement was reached to pay Judge Simons and Senator Thurmond $492 per acre. *Life* magazine was following these events with interest, and its reporters asked state Judge Julius B. "Bubba" Ness for information on the purchase. The magazine quoted Ness's reply that he was not "interested in selling copies of *Life* magazine."

Life pursued the story, and on August 29, 1969, interviewed Thurmond about his role. For his protection, Strom had tape recorders and a stenographer to record both the questions and his answers. When asked about the size of the settlement, he said he thought a jury would have awarded them as much as $50,000 if it had gone to trial (rather than the approximately $33,000 they settled for). Remember Strom's success in arranging larger payments for clients back when the Atomic Energy Commission had been condemning property to build their plant in Aiken County.

When the Nixon administration heard of the deal, they decided to launch their own investigation. This investigation was headed by John Erlichman, White House counsel, later known for his role in the Watergate cover-up. None of this affected Thurmond. No charges were brought, and indeed, there was no great hue and cry. Some protested that these men received special treatment because of their position, but there was no apparent wrongdoing. In Strom Thurmond's entire life, no other incident of questionable ethics had ever come to light. For that reason (and because Judge Simon played the lead role in the questionable negotiations), Strom was able to carry off this incident without damage.

A Mellowed Fellow

Despite his repeated insistence that he does not concern himself in other people's races, Strom Thurmond follows some of them closely. In 1969 Republicans were planning a concerted effort to capture the governorship in South Carolina. The man picked to make the attempt was well qualified: Congressman Albert Watson, who represented the Columbia area and had switched from the Democratic to the Republican party with Strom Thurmond.

Many people believed that Thurmond urged Watson to run, but Strom denied that, insisting, "I never advised anybody to run for an office. . . . I told them what I would do if I were in their shoes if they wanted to be Governor. . . . I told them that if I felt the State needed them or if they could run a good service, but Watson, that is a decision that he made himself. . . . I spoke . . . four or five times, I doubt if I spoke over a dozen times for him, but I did speak for him. I felt that he was an abler man, and I felt he was a progressive man, but yet he was sound in his views."[8]

Despite his progressive nature, some aspects of Watson's campaign struck many South Carolinians as racist—so much so, that some Republicans asked him to tone down his rhetoric. The 1970 election pitted Watson against a moderate Democrat, John West, and West was the victor. Thurmond's intervention had failed in two races (Marshall Parker's Senate race and Albert Watson's campaign). Perhaps in these two campaigns, especially Watson's, Thurmond saw the potential for a coalition of moderate whites and blacks that could topple him from his seat, which was coming up for reelection in 1972.

During that time, Strom Thurmond began to try to change his image. His first step was to hire a black, Tom Moss, as a member of his professional staff. According to Strom, his decision had little to do with his upcoming election: "I think the time had come, sometimes you do things too quickly and take a step that will cause a setback, but I felt that the time had arrived that it would be proper to appoint black people to the staff."[9]

After hiring Moss, Thurmond began adding other blacks to his professional and clerical staff, appointing black pages and appointing blacks to service academies.[10] Among southern legislators, Republican or Democrat, Thurmond was the first to appoint a black to his professional staff. Perhaps these efforts were part of his campaign strategy. Possibly, though, Strom did what he did because he genuinely felt that it was time to do so. His efforts did not end with these appointments. In 1976 he sponsored a black attorney, Matthew J. Perry, as a federal judge, and in 1977 he enrolled his daughter Nancy Moore at A. C. Moore Elementary, where half her classmates and nearly half her teachers were black. If Strom was attempting to make a political statement designed for his reelection, he could have stopped short at any time. Instead, he continued to moderate his stance. He voted several times for extending the Voting Rights Act, supported the creation of the Martin Luther King federal holiday, and even made some noise in behalf of statehood for the District of Columbia.

Since then, he has gained support among South Carolina's black voters, and he has rehabilitated himself with some of their leaders. Almost every black educational institution in the state has honored him with a degree of some sort. Most people regard these efforts and the corresponding tributes as political. Thurmond, they say, changed his approach because he was afraid of losing. Yet what about the many instances in Thurmond's long career when he acted contrary to political shrewdness? A lifetime of potentially career-ending "blunders," make a poor case that Thurmond's actions since 1970 have been part of some shrewd plan.

An even more convincing argument can be made for motives other than political self-interest by analyzing the results of the elections. Thurmond began moderating his style between 1970 and 1972. In the 1972 election, he received just 8 percent of the black vote. In the 1978 election, he received just 8 percent of the black vote. Given the lack of success of these efforts, a natural assumption would be that Thurmond would abandon the efforts if their sole purpose was to get black votes. Instead, he continued.

Age and a broader perspective might also have played a role. In a 1988 interview, Thurmond discussed the difference between his stances of the present and the past: "When you are in disagreement with so many things that Lyndon Johnson wanted to do, you naturally are attacking more. . . . You are confronting more, don't you see? Now once you get in the chairman's position, or a position of power, then instead of confronting, you want to pull people in all you can. . . . Times change and people change. . . . You got to meet changing conditions."[11]

Thurmond recognized that a switch from outsider to insider demanded a different role. He may even have seen that arguments in favor of preventing one segment of Americans from participating in all that our nation had to offer were not defensible. Certainly it required no great political courage to make his views on race more encompassing, but a stubborn ideologue never changes, and a master politician changes only when he has to. And as will be seen, Thurmond had nothing to worry about in his next campaign.

The 1972 Campaign

Richard Nixon was running for reelection as president in 1972, and in South Carolina Thurmond was running for reelection, too. Thurmond was still supporting Nixon, but his support had not prevented his giving Nixon fits on occasion. In July of 1970 he had accused Nixon of a "breach of faith" over the school issue when the Justice Department was rather tough in enforcing integration in many southern school districts. He also criticized Nixon because of his willingness to admit the People's Republic of China to the United Nations.

These differences apart, though, Thurmond headed into the 1972 election in fairly good standing with the national Republican leadership and in good shape in South Carolina. Before that year, many Democrats in the state had been certain that a strong challenger could be found to oppose Strom. His support for Nixon had earned him some grief, and his remarriage seemed to rekindle hopes that he could be defeated in his second try as a Republican. But as the months passed, no major challengers appeared.

The Democrats eventually selected as their standard-bearer another state senator much in the image of Bradley Morrah. The sacrificial goat for 1972 was Nick Zeigler, of Florence County. In his effort to unseat Thurmond, Zeigler ran into the same difficulties faced by other Thurmond opponents—Strom hardly acknowledged his presence during the campaign. Thurmond was so unconcerned that he traveled to other states and campaigned for other candidates and for Nixon, neglecting campaign appearances in South Carolina.

Even though Thurmond acted unconcerned, his campaign, under the leadership of Joe Rogers, Jr., of Manning, was working furiously to deliver the vote for Strom. As was the case in 1966, the Thurmond strategy involved two separate organizations: the Re-elect Thurmond Committee, composed of Democrats and independent supporters, and the Thurmond Republican Committee, which worked through the regular Republican state, district, county, and precinct organization. That meant that each county had two Thurmond organizations, but both had the same seven objectives: (1) raise funds; (2) identify every Thurmond supporter; (3) make certain that Thurmond supporters were legally registered to vote in the precinct they resided in; (4) register unregistered supporters; (5) prepare a list of qualified supporters; (6) telephone every Thurmond supporter on election day to get out the vote; and (7) ensure that all votes cast are accurately counted.[12] (Republicans in South Carolina have had to emphasize ballot security because several elections seem to have been lost in the counting process.)

Throughout the campaign, Zeigler tried to engage Thurmond in some sort of dialogue on the issues, and Thurmond ignored him. Thus, Zeigler's campaign message soon was reduced to one issue: "Why won't Strom Thurmond face the people of South Carolina?" or, to paraphrase, Why won't Strom Thurmond debate me? Zeigler even ended one of his "Z-grams" with the appeal, "Tell him [Thurmond] to face Nick Zeigler and the People of South Carolina."[13]

Thurmond, of course, refused to be swayed. Instead, he relied on the standard tactics of incumbents. He reminded the people of the many things he had done for them, especially in the area of constituent service, and he arranged for many testimonials to be published that supported him. In October of 1972 he asked several of his Senate colleagues for a statement than could be run in an ad. One of those solicited was his old friend Barry Goldwater.[14] Goldwater gave him a ringing endorsement that ended: "The Senate cannot afford to lose a man like Strom." In his cover letter, Senator Goldwater let Strom know that he had not forgotten Strom's loyalty in the past. He said, "Anything you want and anything I can do is fine with me."[15]

With his name recognition (which dwarfed Zeigler's) and his record of constituent service (and aided by a huge Nixon win over George McGovern), Thurmond was easily reelected to his second term as a Republican in the 1972 election. The vote was 428,148 to 246,182—not even close.

Strom Marches On

After his reelection in 1972, Strom expected to be able to concentrate on the issues that had been so important to him—looking after veterans and doing what he could to reduce the intrusiveness of the federal government. But events beyond his control shifted his focus, once again, and these issues had to take a back seat.

The first issue before the country in the days after the election was the growing scandal in the national government. At first blush, it appeared to involve only political operatives employed by the Republican party, but as events unfolded, rumors indicated that the scandal might reach into the White House itself. Vice President Agnew was the first to go, and he went quietly. The problem of what to do with President Nixon was another matter. He refused to cooperate with the investigation, and his aides "stonewalled" efforts to get to the truth. Two Congressional committees were intimately involved in these investigations: the House Judiciary Committee, headed by Congressman Peter Rodino of New Jersey, and the Senate Judiciary Committee, headed by Senator Sam Ervin of North Carolina.

Television carried all the later proceedings, and this introduced many Americans to a group of national legislators that many had never heard of. Strom Thurmond was serving as a member of the Senate Judiciary Committee and, as such, was intimately involved in the investigation. Both the House and Senate committees were dominated by Democrats, so Republican Nixon could not expect to get any breaks. Republican legislators naturally stood by the president as long as they could, and Thurmond was one of the last to give up defending Nixon.

President Nixon's resignation and his pardon by Gerald Ford put Republicans everywhere in a bad light. Many areas in the South that were beginning to swing Republican returned to the Democrat fold in the 1974 and 1976 elections. The Republican party, which had not controlled either house of Congress since the 1950s, was certainly on the way to losing the presidency and appeared headed for obliteration.

One southern bright spot occurred in South Carolina when a Republican state senator from Charleston, James B. Edwards, captured the governor's position in the 1974 election. He defeated veteran Democratic Congressman Bryan Dorn (who was the standard-bearer only because the South Carolina courts had ruled a young man by the name of Charles "Pug" Ravenel ineligible after he had won the nomination). South Carolina Republicans exulted in their first governor since Reconstruction.

Meanwhile, in Washington, the policies of Republican President Gerald Ford were not setting well with Strom Thurmond. The issues that raised the hackles of South Carolina's senior senator were unionization of the armed forces and negotiation of a new treaty with Panama for the Canal Zone. If Strom had been relatively quiet since the mid-1960s, he awoke with a vengeance in the 1970s.

Panama Canal negotiations began at the behest of President Nixon and were continued by President Ford, who left former Vietnamese Ambassador Ellsworth Bunker on the job. Bunker's assignment was to negotiate with Panama's strongman of the time, General Omar Torrijos, a settlement that would turn canal operations and sovereignty to the Panamanians over a thirty-year period.

Thurmond (and others) were aware of these negotiations, and as a preventative measure, Thurmond (and Pennsylvania Congressman Daniel Flood) organized members of Congress in opposition to any attempts to "give away" the Canal Zone. Thurmond was successful in these efforts, initially, as he acquired the signatures of thirty-seven senators who declared that they would oppose "any relinquishment of authority" over the Canal Zone. Two-thirds of the Senate must agree to any treaty, so any thirty-four senators can kill an effort like this.

Another item that rose, seemingly from nowhere, was the issue of unionization of U.S. military personnel. On March 5, 1976, Thurmond introduced legislation that would specifically prohibit unionization of the armed forces. He was joined by twenty-four cosponsors when he said that unionization would mean "the end of an effective defense force in this country." Proposed penalties for violating the provisions of the act were severe: Thurmond wanted unions to be fined between $25,000 and $50,000 for attempting unionization activities and individuals to serve prison terms of up to five years.

Thurmond's opposition, which was powerful enough to put a stop to both of these efforts in 1976, proved not to be enough after the 1976 elections. Gerald Ford was barely edged out by Jimmy Carter, and Republicans lost a few more seats in Congress. Senate conservatives were replaced by liberals, and the new Congress was more agreeable to the kinds of proposals that Thurmond was against. At President Carter's urging, the Senate did ratify a treaty transferring the Canal Zone back to the Panamanians. Carter was unsuccessful in pushing some of his other projects, such as military unionization, however.

With the change in Washington came a new hope in South Carolina among the Democrats. If a southern moderate like Jimmy Carter could be elected president, maybe a southern moderate could beat Strom Thurmond. One youthful southern moderate decided to try. The man who opposed Thurmond in the 1978 campaign was Pug Ravenel.

A Tough Campaign: 1978

The campaign for the 1978 U.S. Senate race in South Carolina actually began several years before, in 1974, when Charles "Pug" Ravenel threw himself into the governor's race with a style and vigor that took the state by storm. Using television very effectively, Ravenel's youthful appearance as he talked to groups of South Carolinians about their hopes for the future caught the imagination of the people. In the 1974 Democratic gubernatorial primary, Ravenel easily defeated his rivals (including Lieutenant Governor Earl Morris and Congressman Bryan Dorn) to gain the nomination. Something happened to the Harvard-educated investment banker on his way to the ball, however. The South Carolina courts ruled that Ravenel had not met the necessary residency requirements and disqualified him from the race. The state Democratic Executive Committee then selected Bryan Dorn, who was defeated by Jim Edwards in the November general election.

Ravenel's image remained strong, however, and he was considered an odds-on favorite in 1978 for governor. Others were not certain that Ravenel would run for governor a second time. In Strom Thurmond's long-range planning for the 1978 election, his staff put together a list of nine possible contenders. Included were Republicans Carroll Campbell (who was elected to Congress in 1978 and was elected South Carolina's governor in 1986), Jim

Edwards, and George Dean Johnson (later to become chairman of the S.C. Republican party). The list also contained the names of six Democrats: Congressmen Mendel Davis, Butler Derrick, and John Jenrette and state senators Dick Riley (who was elected as governor in 1978 and reelected in 1982), Tom Smith, and Pug Ravenel.[16]

Indeed, Ravenel's inclusion on the list was astute, as Ravenel wrote to Thurmond in July of 1975 with the news that "you have heard rumors that I may run for your seat in 1978. This is indeed possible but I have made no decision about it and will not before the late fall of 1977. In the meantime I am anxious to see what your plans for the future are." And he closed his letter with, "Respect and admiration for your long and good services to our state."[17] Thurmond answered the letter cordially, and told Ravenel, "As for my plans in 1978, about which you inquired, I definitely plan to run for reelection. I feel that my good health and experience will enable me to serve the people of South Carolina with continuing effectiveness."[18] Ravenel was undaunted by Thurmond's decision to run, and as the campaign got underway, he would seem to forget both his respect and admiration for Thurmond.

Meanwhile, Thurmond was not taking things easy. For the first time as a Senator, he appeared to feel a sense of urgency to run a strong campaign and to win by a big margin. He engaged Allison Dalton as his campaign manager and began gearing up his efforts in the state earlier than usual. This was noted by an old adversary who had mellowed and was now a die-hard Thurmond ally— Solomon Blatt, now speaker emeritus of the S.C. House of Representatives. Blatt wrote to Strom: "From what little I hear Ravenel in all probability will make the race against you and I am delighted to see that you are letting no grass grow under your feet . . . you can rest assured that I shall do everything within my power to get you reelected and I have talked with a number of Democrats who told me they would support you against Ravenel."[19]

By July 25 of 1977 Ravenel had firmed up his plans to run and made his announcement. With the announcement, everyone knew there was going to be a real contest, a contest many thought Thurmond could lose. At seventy-six, he was beginning to show signs of age and some thought he should step aside and give the new fellow a chance.

At the national level, Thurmond once again had a Democratic administration out to get him. On February 1, Vice President Walter Mondale declared that Ravenel was a man "this country needs."[20] Opposition from the administration would be felt again during the campaign—at higher levels.

Ravenel sought to use his Harvard connections (and those he had gained while working in New York) as a way to raise funds. South Carolina newspapers carried pictures of Ravenel at these events, such as the Park Avenue apartment of Peter Frelinghuysen. The message came through to the South Carolina voters: Ravenel was not really one of them—consorting with liberal vice presidents and sipping champagne on Park Avenue were not the kinds of things the people of this state wanted to see. But Ravenel had a lot of support, so Thurmond and his staff stayed on their toes.

As has been his custom, Strom made a late announcement concerning his plans to seek reelection. His press release date was April 6, 1978, and in it he invited everyone in the state to drop by his Columbia home at 13 Waccamaw Avenue, where he and Mrs. Thurmond would be personally greeting guests at the door.

In his message, he reminded the people of the state that he remained in close touch, "whether voting on the issues or in representing you before the ever-growing agencies of the Federal bureaucracy." He closed his statement by reminding the people that he had plenty in common with them: "We must all work together to assure that our children—yours and mine—will continue to live in a nation of freedom and opportunity."[21]

Instead of rhetoric, he sought to put his election on a more personal level. The campaign strategy called for a division of forces, with Nancy and the children touring the urban areas in a caravan known as "Strom Trek" while Strom talked to the older citizens in the rural areas. Strom even resorted to the "just one more time" approach often used by those who are near the end of their political career. This was the only campaign in which he ever allowed such an appeal to be used, and it showed how seriously he took the challenge in that he would resort to this kind of personal appeal.

In June President Carter's press secretary, Jody Powell, attended a fund-raiser in Boston for Ravenel and declared that the president had taken "an extra special interest" in the Ravenel campaign.[22] At news of this, Thurmond fired off an angry note to President Carter. In it, he demanded to know if "you are injecting yourself into the United States Senate race in South Carolina this fall."[23]

Thurmond got no direct reply to this letter but the president made his intentions clear when he came to Greenville, South Carolina, in September (to the residence of Jeff Hunt) to say a few good words about Ravenel. His remarks at the fund-raising occasion were a glowing endorsement of Ravenel, and he said, "For the last four years, I have been trying to get Pug to come to Plains. And he wouldn't cross the Savannah River until after this election. But I think next January, he will be taking a trip. And we will let him come home every weekend or two to let you know what he is doing in the United States Senate, representing you."[24] President Carter had publicly challenged Thurmond and committed another of the gaffes that he became known for. If the president had studied the history of the state, he would have understood the futility of outside endorsements. Instead of helping Ravenel, his endorsement hurt him.

Despite his initial show of respect and deference to Thurmond, Ravenel's message was a bit more strident in this race. One of his stump speeches included the statement that "to defeat Thurmond would be the greatest thing I could do for America." Part of Ravenel's frustrations came from his repeated calls for debates, which Thurmond ignored. On July 26, Ravenel wrote to Thurmond reminding him that he had been critical of Truman's decision not to debate him in 1948. He then asked that Thurmond "continue that tradition by joining with me to debate the critical issues which affect the people of South Carolina."[25] Thurmond chose to not even respond directly to this letter, instead letting Allison Dalton, his campaign manager, to answer it for him: "As you are quite well aware, Senator Thurmond prefers to carry his campaign to the people in his own way. I am sure you are capable of doing the same."[26] For his part, when asked by reporters why he would not debate Ravenel, Thurmond had a prompt reply: "I'm running on my record; let him run on his—if he has one."[27]

As the campaign swung toward its close, many South Carolina Democrats made a decision to come out publicly for Thurmond. Some, no doubt, made their decision to punish Ravenel, who had never been a part of the Democratic organization, but others were certainly motivated by the feeling that Strom was the best person for the job. On August 7, a group of prominent Democrats that included State Representative Tom Mangum went to the people with the formation of a Democrats-for-Thurmond group. And on October 27, in the final days of the campaign, Sol Blatt sent Strom a copy of a statement he had made for the local radio stations in Thurmond's behalf. In his address, Blatt noted that he was "speaking for over 200 Democrats in this immediate area who have supported the Democratic candidates [and] do now pledge our full and complete support and vote to the honorable Strom Thurmond."[28]

The election results were all that Thurmond could have hoped for. He blasted Ravenel by a margin of 351,733 to 281,119. By defeating him, he did more than win an election. He effectively finished Ravenel's political career. Moreover, he added another ring of invincibility around his own already thick trunk.

One postscript to Thurmond's 1978 election involved a telegram from the West Coast. The congratulatory telegram came from one of Strom's supporters: Ronald Reagan.[29] Even though he could not vote for Thurmond, Reagan was interested in the South. His group, Citizens for the Republic, had taken an interest in Strom's race. On his third try for the presidency, Ronald Reagan knew that he must make it. He hoped for that wave of southern support that had been missing in 1968.

Thurmond was looking forward to the 1980 elections too. Perhaps the Republicans could take back the White House. Of course, his independence would reassert itself—as it always had—to Ronald Reagan's disappointment.

The Reagan Revolution and Beyond

In 1980 Strom Thurmond had suffered through the past three years of Jimmy Carter's presidency. With inflation and unemployment at record highs, the Republicans figured on recapturing the White House. Ronald Reagan was the early front-runner, but close behind, especially in the early days, were George Bush and the former Democratic governor of Texas, John Connally, who had joined the Republicans.

Given Thurmond's historical support of conservative candidates and the relative strength of Reagan's campaign, one might assume that the South's most prominent Republican, Strom Thurmond, would support Reagan. But it was at this point, in 1980, that Thurmond began his practice of endorsing secondary presidential candidates. In January of 1980 both Thurmond and South Carolina's former Republican governor James B. Edwards endorsed John Connally. (The Edwards endorsement was especially surprising because he had been one of Reagan's staunchest supporters in the divisive 1976 Republican presidential contest when President Ford had barely won the right to seek the presidency on his own over a tough Reagan campaign.)

In his speech endorsing Connally, Thurmond noted, "At a time in our history when the United States, which I consider the greatest nation on earth, has become known for its vacillation in foreign policy and confusion in domestic affairs, we need John Connally's leadership . . . our next President must fully realize the necessity for returning the flow of power from Washington back to the people at the local and state levels."[30] Obviously, he thought Connally shared his views.

In 1980 the Republican presidential primary in South Carolina was to be held on March 8, three days before the primaries in Alabama, Florida, and Georgia. Connally was counting on a victory in South Carolina to give him momentum going into these three pivotal southern primaries. This was the beginning of Super Tuesday, in which southern Republicans grouped several primaries together so that the South had a significant impact on the selection of the Republican presidential nominee.

In South Carolina, Strom's endorsement (and that of Governor Edwards) carried little weight. Reagan won the primary and the South on his way to the Republican presidential nomination in 1980. (Interestingly, Thurmond risked his political prestige in a presidential race again in 1988 when he endorsed Kansas Senator Robert Dole over front-runner Vice President George Bush. Bush was heavily favored by the Republican leaders in the state and was on his way to a certain victory in the primary when Thurmond made his endorsement. Even in 1988, Thurmond had the courage to continue to speak his mind—even if he knew it would have little impact on events.)

Once Reagan was nominated for president (with George Bush as his vice presidential nominee), Strom immediately got on the Reagan bandwagon. He made speeches throughout the South promoting the Reagan candidacy. When the votes were counted in the November election, the South had gone overwhelmingly for Reagan, as had the nation. Reagan's election had also had coattails: Republicans captured control of the U.S. Senate for the first time since 1954. With this majority (which was fifty-three Republicans, forty-six Democrats) and, Harry F. Byrd, Jr., a Virginia Independent who organized with the Democrats, Thurmond was guaranteed some leadership posts. These would be coveted posts he had never had, and they promised to be powerful.

The highest post Thurmond assumed was president pro tempore of the Senate. This designation generally goes to the senator with the greatest seniority, and the duties are to preside over the Senate during the absence of the vice president. This post also placed Thurmond in line for presidential succession.

The second post Thurmond held was lower in rank but even more powerful—he took the chairmanship of the Judiciary Committee from Massachusetts Senator Edward Kennedy. In an interview immediately after the election, Thurmond said, "We're not going to be arrogant or gloat, but we're going to be determined to bring some changes that ought to be brought," his goal being to "turn the country around."[31] How, exactly, did he intend to do that? His answer included the following items: limiting abortion to cases in which the mother's life was threatened or to incest or rape; opposition to forced busing to achieve racial integration; adoption of a constitutional amendment to require a balanced budget; repeal of the 1965 Voting Rights Act or extension of its provisions into all states, not just the South; easing of the Freedom of Information laws to give greater access to government records; and a "friendlier" charter for the F.B.I.[32]

And in a throwback to his days as a junior, Thurmond wanted to tighten immigration laws: "I don't think people ought to be allowed to come into this country just because they want to come here." Most Asians, Cubans, and Haitians, he argued, are not "political refugees. They are economic refugees. Unless they are political refugees, they should be kept out."[33]

One of his first acts as Judiciary Committee chairman was to establish the Security and Terrorism Subcommittee, headed by Alabama's conservative Senator Jeremiah Denton. The jurisdiction of this subcommittee was "terrorism, espionage and counterfeiting plus oversight of the F.B.I., the Drug Enforcement Administration, and the legal attachés in all U.S. embassies." Thurmond noted, "We had a similar one [subcommittee] years ago. . . . That subcommittee was abolished when Senator Edward Kennedy became Judiciary Committee chairman, I thought it was a mistake to abolish the subcommittee then. We have got to be on guard against those who might be guilty of terrorism and espionage directed from outside this country."[34]

A study of Thurmond's effectiveness as chairman of the Judiciary Committee shows he was unsuccessful in securing passage for any of these measures. Yet his impact on the national government may be felt for many years, long after he no longer serves in the Senate. His impact may well be felt most in the legal arena rather than the political one. As chairman of the Judiciary Committee, Thurmond had input into the appointment of numerous federal judges. These judges, for the most part, had to pass the Thurmond acid test on limiting federal power. The effects of "strict constructionist" judges are just now being felt, and may be felt for many years to come.

When the 1984 elections rolled around, Thurmond found himself running for reelection with President Reagan at the top of the ticket. Strom took the election in stride, this time ignoring any suggestion that it was his last race. His opposition was token, and he easily defeated Melvin Purvis by a margin of 644,814 to 306,982.

In 1986, in the aftermath of the "Iran-Contra" affair, Republicans lost control of the Senate. With their majority went Thurmond's positions as president pro tempore and as Judiciary Committee chairman. At that point, he became the ranking Republican, and he also served as the senior on the Armed Services Committee.

In 1990 Strom declared his health good and reiterated his ability to serve his state and offered for reelection. There was no Republican opposition, and his Democratic opponent was a former Republican who acknowledged that he had no chance of winning. Thurmond was easily reelected.

As an aftermath of the 1990 elections, Strom had to deal with some personal upheaval. In the spring of 1991 the Thurmonds agreed to a separation and, later, to a divorce. The divorce was amicable but, as a result, Strom was again alone.

Some sadness may accompany this failed relationship but relationships have always been tough on Thurmond. Now, as he had done during so much of his life, he was able to devote his attention, single-mindedly, to his work. And South Carolina's "living legend," as he was dubbed in a 1978 poll, has nothing to fear from political opposition. He has made joking references to running again in 1996 when he will be ninety-four-years-old. Who knows? He may just make it.

Chapter 16

THE PUBLIC MAN

From the very beginning, Strom Thurmond was programmed to serve the people. Growing up in the home of Will Thurmond and as a neighbor of Ben Tillman, and becoming a veteran of political stump meetings by the time he was a teenager, Strom had every opportunity to experience (and grow into) the political life. An interesting conclusion one can draw from his early life is that, despite his preteen ambition to be governor, Strom may later have had other career plans. You can almost hear the role-reversing discussion that might have occurred between Strom and his father when Strom decided to become an agricultural teacher. "Strom," Will could have said, "you ought to think about a political career. It'll be mighty hard to run for office while you're teaching school." "But Pa," Strom might have replied, "I really believe I can do some good as a teacher." And at that point, Will would shrug, knowing that parental pressure is sometimes counterproductive.

Later though, as often happens, parental will proved to be a strong force. Young Strom decided to abandon the teaching life for the rough-and-tumble world of politics, making his father very proud in the process. With the zeal of a convert, Thurmond embraced that new world, and with single-minded determination, he has climbed to the very top of his profession. Along the way, he has been the recipient of many favorable breaks, but he has always made the most of them—and he has done what he thought best for his people—without regard for the political consequences.

Thurmond's determination to do what was right sets him apart from many of his colleagues, who have deserved the low opinion of politicians the public holds today. Certainly, it hampered his effectiveness as a legislator. Others have been willing to compromise principle time and again to see their pet legislation enacted or their careers advanced. Thurmond has never been willing to play that game; consequently, few of his proposals have been enacted into law, and he has been somewhat unsuccessful in preventing laws from being passed. (We can be grateful that some of his early campaigns against civil rights legislation failed.)

We can look to Thurmond as an excellent example of personal and political courage. He has always been willing to accept the consequences of his actions—from his run for the presidency in 1948 to his party switch in 1964, through his decision to back Robert Dole for president in 1988 in the face of the certain knowledge that he would not win—Strom Thurmond has never been afraid to tell the people what he believes in and to suffer whatever consequences his actions bring.

For this reason, and this reason alone, my feeling is that those who categorize Thurmond's change of heart on the race question as a "political" decision are wrong—period. Time and time again, Thurmond has done things that purely political animals would avoid. With those types of actions bracketing his change on racial issues, it is probable that the change was genuine. My feeling is that when he had the opportunity to examine the institution of segregation and all of the accompanying attitudes, he eventually realized that it was not justifiable from any standpoint. After having come to that conclusion, he abandoned his defense of those issues and did what he could to correct past mistakes.

This same courage motivated Strom to speak up against other things that he believed to be detrimental to the nation he dearly loves—not as a man might love a car that he has bought specifically to tinker with, but as a boy loves his mother. There is a real affection, devotion, and love of country embodied in Strom Thurmond that is missing from many of the vapid, upwardly mobile politicians of today. An old joke that made the rounds revolved around Strom's practice of dragging the Constitution into every issue. The refrain that was often heard was, "Of course Strom knows a lot about the Constitution; he was there when it was written." Strom Thurmond has been around a long time. When he was born, the Spanish-American War was recent history, and people still relied largely on animals for transportation. His perspective is different from that of almost everyone alive today, and for that reason, some of his stands deserve to be examined in the light of his environment.

Much of the criticism of Strom Thurmond has revolved around a few issues (principally his early civil rights stance) and his personal characteristic of being willing to stand up—stubbornly and all alone, if necessary—for his beliefs. His record shows much to applaud in many areas, from serving his people in South Carolina and to being willing to present to the nation his vision of some of the values that hold America together. What some see as addled idealism, others regard as old-fashioned patriotism. What some see as closed-mindedness, others regard as adherence to principle. Surely there is room for Strom Thurmond's kind of public servant in our nation.

We return, then, to the central theme of Strom Thurmond's life—public service. Though he may not have known it early on, his sole purpose seems to have been to serve his fellow man. Once he accepted this mission, he did what he could to encourage the perception, and he enjoyed the inevitable consequences of his climb up the ladder. One thing cannot be denied, however, and that is that Strom Thurmond has served the people. His every action had been taken under a microscope that was held not by dispassionate scientists but by political enemies who were only too willing to attack him whenever they could. But throughout his career, he has withstood the scrutiny without flinching. Further he has forsaken many of the pleasures that others insist are part of life so that he could serve. Other historians may not be as charitable as this one toward Thurmond, but I have attempted to show that, by evaluating the whole of his career and not just certain aspects, one finds much to admire. And with Thurmond, there appears to be little distinction between himself and his career, so for me, he has become Strom Thurmond . . . the public man.

NOTES

The Strom Thurmond papers, housed at Special Collection of the Clemson University Library, Clemson, South Carolina, are cited throughout as Thurmond Collection. All sources cited are from the Thurmond Collection unless otherwise noted.

Chapter 1: Young Thurmond

1. Untitled story, Camden *Chronicle*, April 2, 1897.
2. Ibid., April 23, 1897.
3. Orville Vernon Burton, *In My Father's House Are Many Mansions: Family and Community in Edgefield, South Carolina* (Chapel Hill, N.C.: University of North Carolina Press 1985), 21.
4. Ibid., p. 98.
5. Ibid.
6. Alberta Morel Lachicotte, *Rebel Senator: Strom Thurmond of South Carolina* (New York: Devin-Adair Co., 1966), 4.
7. Telegram from Will Thurmond to B. R. Tillman, Tillman Collection, Special Collections, Clemson University, May 6, 1902.
8. Jim Naughton, "'Uncle Strom': The Pragmatist's Legacy," Washington *Post*, Style, November 2, 1988.
9. Louise James DuBose, "Governor J. Strom Thurmond of South Carolina, As Seen by His Family and Friends," *South Carolina Magazine*, January 1947: 7.
10. Will Thurmond to B. R. Tillman, Tillman Collection, February 25, 1913.
11. Francis Butler Simkins, *Pitchfork Ben Tillman, South Carolinian* (Baton Rouge: Louisiana State University, 1944), 532.
12. Lachicotte, *Rebel Senator*, 4.
13. DuBose, "Governor J. Strom Thurmond," 7.
14. Ibid.
15. Ibid.
16. Ibid.
17. Ibid.
18. Lachicotte, *Rebel Senator*, 26.
19. DuBose, "Governor J. Strom Thurmond," 8.
20. Lachicotte, *Rebel Senator*, 27.
21. DuBose, "Governor J. Strom Thurmond," 6.
22. Ibid., 7–8.
23. Lachicotte, *Rebel Senator*, 5.

Chapter 2: *Thurmond at Law*

Notes for this chapter are predominantly from the Legal file of the Thurmond Collection.

1. Strom Thurmond to Hanes; *W. O. Carson v. R.J. Reynolds Tobacco Company*, July 24, 1937.
2. Sam B. Craig to Strom Thurmond; *T. A. Brown v. Lowe Transfer Co.*, November 20, 1935.
3. Will Thurmond to Strom Thurmond; *W. P. Yonce v. H. G. Eidson Administrator Estate of J. L. Whaley*, March 7, 1934.
4. Will Thurmond to Gunter and Gunter; *Abney v. Abney et al.*, March 27, 1932.
5. Will Thurmond to Daisy Dortha Mae Floyd; *Floyd v. North American Gold Mines*, March 16, 1934.
6. Will Thurmond to J. A. Hamilton, May 23, 1934.
7. M. L. McHugh to Strom Thurmond, June 20, 1931.
8. Thurmond and Thurmond to George Waters, November 23, 1933.
9. Robert H. Hodges to Thurmond and Thurmond, May 24, 1934.
10. Strom Thurmond to Charles H. Moorefield, January 12, 1932.
11. Ibid.
12. Euguene S. Blease to Strom Thurmond, June 1, 1931.
13. Strom Thurmond bill to Town of Johnston.
14. Thurmond and Thurmond bill to Town of Johnston.
15. Thurmond and Thurmond to Anderson Whatley, August 12, 1933.
16. Will Thurmond to Helton and Belser, July 21, 1932.
17. Strom Thurmond to J. Russell McElvee, January 16, 1936.
18. Strom Thurmond to Henry R. Sims, October 26, 1933.
19. Strom Thurmond to Robert Brooks, August 5, 1939.
20. Strom Thurmond to B. M. Fowler, January 1, 1935.
21. Stewart Walker to Strom Thurmond; *Hooper Adams v. Sarah Mae West*, November 2, 1936.
22. Strom Thurmond to Stewart Walker, November 5, 1936.
23. John E. Johnston to Strom Thurmond; *Ada Bettie et al. v. L. M. Smith*, December 26, 1934.
24. Strom Thurmond to Hicks and Johnston, January 1, 1935.
25. Casebook (the Casebook contained records regarding Thurmond's criminal cases and is included with the Legal file, Thurmond Collection).
26. Strom Thurmond to Robert Mance, Jr., February 25, 1933.
27. Ibid.
28. Strom Thurmond to Governor Ibra C. Blackwood, July 12, 1932.
29. Casebook.
30. Strom Thurmond to Rafe Higgins, November 2, 1935.
31. C. B. Rich to Strom Thurmond, May 15, 1935.
32. Strom Thurmond to Robert H. Hodges, August 31, 1935.
33. Frank G. Tompkins to Strom Thurmond, June 28, 1934.
34. Ibid.
35. Strom Thurmond to Frank G. Tompkins, July 26, 1934.
36. Strom Thurmond to George Bell Timmerman; *Holmes Cosey v. Highway Express Company*, August 10, 1935.
37. *Town of Lexington v. Strom Thurmond/Hugh Corley.*
38. Strom Thurmond to Sam B. Craig, November 29, 1935.

Chapter 3: The Journey Begins

1. "Method of Paying Teachers Rapped by Senate Committee," Columbia *Record*, February 20, 1932.
2. Interview with Strom Thurmond.
3. Ibid.
4. Letter to the editor, Edgefield *Advertiser, Historical Record Book*, vol. I.
5. Unidentified newspaper article, *H. R. B.*, vol. I.
6. Edgefield *Advertiser*, January 10, 1933.
7. Letter to the editor, Columbia *State, H. R. B.*, vol. I.
8. 1937 Legislative Manual, Thurmond Collection.
9. Unidentified newspaper article, *H. R. B.*, vol. I.
10. Ibid.
11. Strom Thurmond to A. J. Beattie, *H. R. B.*, vol. I
12. Thurmond's 1933 desk calendar, State Senate file.
13. Unidentified newspaper article, *H. R. B.*, vol. I.
14. Ibid.
15. Message to the Junior Order of the United American Mechanics, Speeches file, January 1935.
16. Ibid., June 1935.
17. Ibid.
18. "Beer, Wine Tax May All Go to Public Schools," Columbia *Record*, January 16, 1935.
19. "Godfrey Bill Cause of Hot Senate Fight," Greenville *News*, April 19, 1935.
20. Edgefield Attorney file.
21. Strom Thurmond to J. C. Kircher, Legal file, October 17, 1935.
22. Robert Fechner to James F. Byrnes, October 17, 1935.
23. Strom Thurmond to Jackson Davis, November 12, 1935.
24. Strom Thurmond to M. E. Abrams, June 20, 1936.
25. Unidentified newspaper article, *H. R. B.*, vol. I.
26. Sol Blatt to Strom Thurmond, Circuit Judge file, October 15, 1936.
27. Untitled, undated, Johnston *Herald* article, *H. R. B.*, vol. I.
28. John K. Aull, "Edgefield Man for Lt. Governor," Lexington *Dispatch*, July 22, 1937.

Chapter 4: The Judicial Thurmond

1. Unidentified newspaper article, *H. R. B.*, vol. I.
2. Joseph Bryson to Strom Thurmond, Legal file, August 9, 1937.
3. George W. Freeman to Strom Thurmond, August 9, 1937.
4. Edgefield County Bar endorsement, August 10, 1937.
5. Sol Blatt to Strom Thurmond, August 10, 1937.
6. George Bell Timmerman to Strom Thurmond, August 12, 1937.
7. Sol Blatt to Strom Thurmond, August 16, 1937.
8. Ibid., August 23, 1937.
9. Edgar A. Brown to Strom Thurmond, August 17, 1937.
10. Form letters from Strom Thurmond to Rembert E. Dennis et al. and to G. G. Blackmon et al., August 14, 1937.
11. "Thurmond Bids for Judgeship," Columbia *Record*, August 17, 1937.
12. George Bell Timmerman to James R. Bryson, August 21, 1937.

13. "Timmerman Endorsed for Judge by Lexington Bar," Lexington *Dispatch*, August 19, 1937.
14. Strom Thurmond to Katherine Anderson, August 23, 1937.
15. Strom Thurmond to Donald Russell, September 13, 1937.
16. Strom Thurmond to W. L. DePass, Jr., September 13, 1937.
17. Strom Thurmond to John Bolt Culbertson, September 14, 1937.
18. John Bolt Culbertson to Strom Thurmond, September 23, 1937.
19. Strom Thurmond to Mrs. C. Fred Lawrence, December 7, 1937.
20. Lewis H. Gault to Strom Thurmond, December 28, 1937.
21. Strom Thurmond to Lewis H. Gault, January 7, 1938.
22. Kathleen B. Watts to W. W. Fuller, January 7, 1938.
23. "Believe Speech Blasted Hopes of Timmerman," Anderson *Daily Mail*, January 16, 1938.
24. Eugene S. Blease to Mrs. J. William Thurmond, January 13, 1938.
25. L. R. Booker to Strom Thurmond, January 14, 1938.
26. Strom Thurmond to J. P. Coates, January 19, 1938.
27. Sol Blatt to Strom Thurmond, January 15, 1938.
28. Unidentified newspaper article, *H. R. B.*, vol. I.
29. Strom Thurmond to Virginia McKeithen, February 11, 1938.
30. Unidentified newspaper article, *H. R. B.*, vol. I.
31. Ibid.
32. L. D. Lide to Strom Thurmond, July 1, 1938.
33. Strom Thurmond to L. D. Lide, July 5, 1938.
34. Strom Thurmond to Julian S. Wolfe, July 12, 1938.
35. Strom Thurmond to L. D. Lide, August 26, 1939.
36. L. D. Lide to Strom Thurmond, August 31, 1939.
37. Strom Thurmond to Robert McFigg, Jr.
38. Unidentified newspaper article, *H. R. B.*, vol. I.
39. Charles R. Witt to Strom Thurmond, October 31, 1938.
40. "Holds Corrupt Politics enemy," Greenwood *Index-Journal*, December 8, 1938.
41. "Thurmond Stresses Home Influences," Anderson *Independent*, February 6, 1939.
42. Albert D. Betts to Strom Thurmond, May 1, 1939.
43. Burnet Maybank to Strom Thurmond, September 8, 1939.
44. Strom Thurmond to Burnet Maybank, September 9, 1938.
45. Wilton Hall to Strom Thurmond, July 10, 1939.
46. Stephen Nettles to Strom Thurmond, January 3, 1940.
47. Unidentified newspaper article, *H. R. B.*, vol. I.
48. War Department to Strom Thurmond, January 27, 1940.
49. Strom Thurmond to War Department, February 3, 1940.
50. "Thurmond Cites Need for Home Detention for Young Men, 17–25," Anderson *Independent*, March 13, 1940.
51. Strom Thurmond to James W. Crain, December 7, 1940.
52. Gordon Baker to Strom Thurmond, April 8, 1941.
53. Strom Thurmond to Reuben Long, January 18, 1941.
54. "Yesterday at the Courthouse," Columbia *State*, May 27, 1941.
55. Unidentified newspaper article, *H. R. B.*, vol. I.
56. Interview with Strom Thurmond.

Chapter 5: He's in the Army Now

1. Strom Thurmond to Senator Williams, January 10, 1942.
2. Milledge L. Bonham to Strom Thurmond, March 12, 1942.
3. "Captain Thurmond," Yorkville *Enquirer*, April 23, 1942.
4. "SC Judge Pleads Case for Albany Army Wife," Knickerbocker *News* (Albany, New York), June 8, 1942.
5. "Doomed Negro Gets New Trial," Columbia *Record*, July 6, 1942.
6. Strom Thurmond to S.C. Probation and Parole Board, September 12, 1942.
7. Clemson University Library Exhibit — "Strom Thurmond: Soldier."
8. First Army Headquarters to Strom Thurmond, September 29, 1942.
9. Strom Thurmond to J. B. Westbrook, November 23, 1943.
10. Ibid., January 24, 1944.
11. Harry L. Coles and Albert K. Weinberg, *Civil Affairs: Soldiers Become Governors*, Office of the Chief of Military History, Department of the Army: Washington, D.C., 1964, 722–724.
12. Ibid.
13. Strom Thurmond to J. F. Ouzts, Jr., May 14, 1944.
14. Unidentified newspaper article, *H. R. B.*, vol. I.
15. Ibid.

Chapter 6: A Soldier Becomes a Governor

1. "State Officials Warned of Peace-Time Dangers," Columbia *State*, January 23, 1946.
2. Press Release (1946 gubernatorial campaign), May 15, 1946.
3. "State Candidates Open Long Drive in Primary Race," Orangeburg *Times & Democrat*, June 12, 1946.
4. Irby J. Koon, "Candidates for Governor, Other Offices, Open Campaigns," Columbia *State*, June 12, 1946.
5. Unidentified newspaper article, *H. R. B.*, vol. I.
6. Ibid.
7. "Scott Continues Tirade Against Judge Thurmond," Charleston *News & Courier*, June 22, 1946.
8. Jack Foster, "Barnwell Hears Candidates Hit at 'Ring Rule,'" Columbia *Record*, June 26, 1946.
9. Anti-Ring speech, Speeches file.
10. Unidentified newspaper article, *H. R. B.*, vol. I
11. James Banks, *Strom Thurmond and the Revolt Against Modernity*, thesis, Kent State University, 1971.
12. Brim Rykard, "Under Capitol's Dome," Anderson *Independent*, November 17, 1946.
13. "Thurmond Works on New Plan for Control of Liquor," Florence *Morning News*, November 30, 1946.
14. Thurmond inaugural address, Speeches file.
15. "5000 Attend Inauguration of Thurmond," Anderson *Daily Mail*, January 21, 1947.
16. "Thurmond's for Election of Trustees," Columbia *Record*, April 12, 1947.
17. "Governor Declares Eisenhower Is Not Interested in Politics," Sumter *Daily*, April 8, 1947.

18. "Governor Hits Wallace Views," Anderson *Independent*, April 19, 1947.
19. Press Release, February 8, 1947.
20. "Civic Courage Shown in Key South Carolina Trial," New York *Times*, May 18, 1947.
21. "Buzhardt Now on Clark's Hill Body," Columbia *Record*, July 1, 1947.
22. "Governor Thurmond Urges Total Mobilization," Rock Hill *Evening Herald*, July 15, 1947.
23. "Claims Thurmond Made Profit," Charlotte *Observer*, October 15, 1947.
24. "Thurmond Says Story Is Untrue," Augusta *Chronicle*, October 15, 1947.
25. *SC Club Woman* magazine, October 10, 1947.
26. "SC White Primary Illegally Affirmed," Charlotte *Observer*, December 31, 1947.

Chapter 7: Thurmond and His Bride

1. Lachicotte, *Rebel Senator*, 12.
2. Ibid., 13.
3. Ibid.
4. Ibid., 14.
5. Ibid.
6. Ibid., 15.
7. Jean Crouch to Strom Thurmond, Jean Crouch Thurmond file, April 10, 1947.
8. Ibid., April 29, 1947.
9. Ibid., May 14, 1947.
10. Ibid., May 21, 1947.
11. Lachicotte, *Rebel Senator*, 24.
12. Jean Crouch to Strom Thurmond, June 19, 1947.
13. Lachicotte, *Rebel Senator*, 24.
14. Jean Crouch to Strom Thurmond, August 25, 1947.
15. Ibid., August 26, 1947.
16. Ibid., August 29, 1947.
17. Strom Thurmond to Jean Crouch, September 13, 1947.
18. Jean Crouch to Strom Thurmond, September 13, 1947.
19. Lachicotte, *Rebel Senator*, 20–22.
20. Ibid., 22.
21. Jean Crouch to Strom Thurmond, August 26, 1947.
22. "Capital Rumor Says Governor to Wed Jean Crouch," Charleston *Evening Post*, October 2, 1947.
23. Lachicotte, *Rebel Senator*, 33.
24. Ibid., 46.

Chapter 8: Thurmond for President

1. Unidentified newspaper article, *H. R. B.*, vol. VI.
2. Ibid.
3. Brim Rykard, "Johnston Backs Two State Conventions," Anderson *Independent*, February 29, 1948.
4. "SC Democratic Committee Votes to Recommend Party Oppose Truman Nomination," Charleston *News & Courier*, March 2, 1948.

5. "Southernors Primed for Convention Walk," Charleston *News & Courier*, March 2, 1948.
6. "Dixie Governors Oppose Truman," Greenville *News*, March 14, 1948.
7. "Thurmond Raps Court Decision," Orangeburg *Times & Democrat*, April 22, 1948.
8. "Thurmond Given Rebuke for Criticism of Court," Charlotte *Observer*, April 23, 1948.
9. "Wright Is Heard on Eve of Conference," Greenville *News*, May 10, 1948.
10. "States' Rights Keynoter Sounds Southern Meeting Call for United Action," Jackson (Miss.) *Daily News*, May 10, 1948.
11. "Thurmond Frees SC Delegates in Favor of Ike," Greenwood *Index-Journal*, July 3, 1948.
12. "Thurmond Appeals to Truman to Withdraw," Columbia *Record*, July 9, 1948.
13. "SC Delegates Stand Solid Against Truman; Governor Shouts Down Crowd's Boos," Sumter *Daily* Item, July 15, 1948.
14. Lachicotte, *Rebel Senator*, 41.
15. Ibid., 43.
16. "Dixiecrats Spurn Aid of Gerald L. K. Smith," New York *Times*, July 19, 1948.
17. Undentified newspaper article, *H. R. B.*, vol. VIII.
18. Greenville *Piedmont*, October 5, 1948.
19. "Tough Soviet Policy Urged by Thurmond," Washington *Post*, October 4, 1948.
20. "The Viewpoint of a Negro," Roanoke *Times*, August 2, 1948.
21. James A. Hagerty, "Dewey and Warren Appear Sure to Win," Charlotte *News & Observer*, October 26, 1948.
22. "South Prefers to Go Down Fighting, Senator Brown Writes Democratic Official," Columbia *Record*, October 14, 1948.
23. Unidentified newspaper article, *H. R. B.*, vol. VIII.
24. Ibid.
25. Ibid., November 27, 1948.

Chapter 9: Governor Again

1. William L. Davey, "People Should Know Colonels—Culberston," Greenville *Piedmont*, May 25, 1949.
2. "Britton Charges Thurmond Fails on His Promises," Gaffney *Ledger*, July 7, 1949.
3. "AF of L Calls Thurmond's Labor Stand Impartial," Newberry *Ledger*, August 5, 1949.
4. "Ex-Thurmond Backer Says Not Sincere," Anderson *Independent*, January 18, 1950.
5. "Byrnes Can Do as He Damn Pleases, Truman Declares," Columbia *Record*, January 19, 1950.
6. Unidentified newpaper article, *H. R. B.*, vol. X.
7. "Culbertson Predicts Johnston Would Sweep State in Senate Race Against Gov. Thurmond," Columbia *State*, February 22, 1950.
8. "Warren Nominated as Keynote Speaker for Demo Convention," Columbia *Record*, April 11, 1950.

9. Unidentified newspaper article, *H. R. B.*, vol. X.

10. Ibid.

11. Lachicotte, *Rebel Senator*, 72.

12. "Johnston Gives Thurmond His Time at Sptbg Meeting," Columbia *State*, July 1, 1950.

13. Lachicotte, *Rebel Senator*, 74, 75.

14. Unidentified newspaper article, *H. R. B.*, vol. XI.

15. Ibid.

16. Ibid.

17. Ibid.

18. Ibid.

19. Lachicotte, *Rebel Senator*, 76.

20. Unidentified newspaper article, *H. R. B.*, vol. XI.

21. Ibid.

22. Ibid., vol. X.

23. Ibid.

24. Ibid.

Chapter 10: Thurmond at Large

1. "Press Praised by Thurmond for Support," Orangeburg *Times & Democrat*, January 13, 1951.

2. Manning Harvey, "Thurmonds Settle Down at Aiden," Columbia *Record*, April 12, 1951.

3. "Jury Hikes Land Price in Aiken," Augusta *Chronicle*, October 4, 1951.

4. James Walker, "Thurmond Calls for Armed Might to Meet Communism," Greenville *News*, May 30, 1951.

5. "GOP Poll Lists Taft as 1952 Choice; MacArthur Is Second," Columbia *State*, September 10, 1951.

6. "Kennedy Case Goes to Jurors Today," Augusta *Herald*, October 17, 1951.

7. Edith Bell Love, "Mrs. Kennedy Given Verdict of Acquittal," Augusta *Herald*, October 18, 1951.

8. "Thurmond Sees Ike Nomination," San Antonio *Evening News*, July 11, 1952.

9. Tom Gallant, "Thurmond Warns UN Treaties Endangering US by Superseding Constitution," Chattanooga *News & Free Press*, February 18, 1953.

10. Unidentified newspaper article, *H. R. B.*, vol. XII.

11. "Strom Thurmond Backs Stevens in Senate Probe," Boston *Globe*, June 16, 1954.

12. Frank Van Der Linden, "Treat Reserve Officers Right, Thurmond Urges," Greenville *News*, July 21, 1954.

13. Ned Ramsaur, "Move On to Name Edgar Brown to Senate by Committee," Greenville *News*, September 3, 1954.

14. "Maybank Rites Today," Charleston *News & Courier*, September 3, 1954.

15. Ashley Haley, Jr., "Dixiecrat in Washington," *Saturday Evening Post*, October 8, 1955.

16. R. E. Grier, "Committee Hands Brown Nomination," Columbia *State*, September 4, 1954.

17. "Thurmond Denounces Backing Given Brown," Columbia *Record*, September 10, 1954.
18. Unidentified newspaper article, *H. R. B.*, vol. XIII.
19. "Byrnes Says Committee Should Call Primary," Columbia *State*, September 15, 1954.
20. William Jennings Bryan Dorn, *Dorn: Of the People, a Political Way of Life* (Columbia: Bruccoli Clark Layman, 1988), 157–158.
21. "Bennett Pledges Fight, Columbia *Record*, September 16, 1954.
22. Weyman Busch to Edgar Brown, Edgar A. Brown Collection, Special Collections, Clemson University Library.
23. Edgar Brown to Weyman Busch (Brown Collection), September 20, 1954.
24. Anderson *Free Press*, September 16, 1954.
25. E. C. Watson, Jr., to Olin Johnston (Brown Collection), September 22, 1954.
26. Brown statement (Brown Collection), October 30, 1954.
27. "Mitchell Says Mechanics of Write-in to Beat Thurmond," Columbia *State*, October 6, 1954.
28. "Thurmond Scores Mitchell's Bird-in-Hand Statement," Charleston *News & Courier*, October 7, 1954.
29. Speech (Brown Collection), October 13, 1954.
30. Unidentified newspaper article, *H. R. B.*, vol. XIII.
31. Salley statement (Brown Collection).
32. Byrnes statement (Brown Collection), October 23, 1954.
33. Ibid.
34. "Thurmond Says Brown Deserted Party in 1948," Columbia *State*, October 27, 1954.
35. Greenville *News*, October 29, 1954.
36. Ned Ramsaur, "Brown Put O.K. on Strom's 1948 Candidacy," Charleston *News & Courier*, October 31, 1954.
37. Telegram, Perry A. Shumpert to Edgar A. Brown (Brown Collection), November 3, 1954.
38. Edgar Brown to J. Carl Kearse (Brown Collection), November 3, 1954.

Chapter 11: Thurmond Goes to Washington

1. Frank Van der Linden, "Strom Expected to Again Enter National Spotlight," Greenville *News*, January 1, 1955.
2. "Thurmond Claims South Belongs to Neither Political Party," Orangeburg *Times & Democrat*, January 15, 1955.
3. Unidentified newspaper article, *H. R. B.*, vol. XIV.
4. Ibid.
5. Frank Van Der Linden, "Would Bar Men from Party Meet," Greenville *News*, April 20, 1955.
6. Essel Thomas, "Strom Aids the G.O.P. on Marine Showdown," Florence *Morning News*, June 25, 1955.
7. Unidentified newspaper article, *H. R. B.*, vol. XIV.
8. "Thurmond Pledges Efforts to Maintain Segregation," Greenville *News*, July 17, 1955.
9. "S.C. Solons are Indignant," Anderson *Independent*, January 6, 1956.

10. Carlton Truax, "States' Rights Crusade Begins," Columbia *Record*, January 27, 1956.
11. Thurmond's Manifesto draft, February 6, 1956.
12. Ibid.
13. Final draft: Southern Manifesto.
14. Ibid.
15. "Thurmond Charges Racial Disorder Communists' Aim," Charleston *News & Courier*, March 27, 1956.

Chapter 12: Back to the Senate

1. "Johnston and Thurmond Flay Civil Rights Bill in Senate," Florence *Morning News*, July 12, 1957.
2. Greenville *News*, August 29, 1957.
3. Unidentified newspaper article, H. R. B., vol. XVI.
4. "Thurmond's Bill Seeks Exam of Constitutional Powers," Charleston *News & Courier*, January 24, 1958.
5. "Country Drifting Away from Constitution," Greenville *Observer*, May 21, 1959.
6. Frank Van Der Linden, "Kennedy Loses in Bid to Repeal Loyalty Oath," Greenville *News*, July 24, 1959.

Chapter 13: A Personal Tragedy . . . and Moving On

1. Lachicotte, *Rebel Senator*, 143.
2. Ibid., 144.
3. Ibid., 150.
4. Ibid., 152.
5. Ibid., 153.
6. Ibid., 155.
7. Frank Van Der Linden, "Goldwater Given Outside Chance," Greenville *News*, April 3, 1960.
8. "Thurmond Replies to Hollings, Explains Uncommitted Stand," Columbia *Record*, September 2, 1960.
9. Mike Karrelan, "Senate Coalition Lauded by Thurmond at Sumter," Charleston *News & Courier*, November 23, 1960.
10. Congressional Record, February 2, 1961.
11. Washington *Post*, July 21, 1961.
12. Congressional Record, August 4, 1961.
13. Ibid.
14. Lachicotte, *Rebel Senator*, 163.
15. Congressional *Record*, September 2, 1961.
16. Unidentified newspaper article, H. R. B., vol. XXVII.
17. Ibid.
18. Ibid.
19. George Ball to Senator Stennis, March 29, 1962.
20. Edited speech 100, SPIS (Senate Preparedness Investigating Subcommittee) file.
21. Edited speech 31, SPIS file.
22. Lachicotte, *Rebel Senator*, 184.
23. Ibid., 169.

Chapter 14: The Winds of Change

1. Lachicotte, *Rebel Senator*, 220.
2. Ibid., 225.
3. Ibid., 227–228.
4. Ibid., 231.
5. Ibid., 233.
6. Ibid., 234.
7. Television address, September 16, 1964.
8. Memorandum (Goldwater campaign), September 24, 1964.
9. Strom Thurmond to Drake Edens, November 25, 1964.
10. Ibid., December 3, 1964.
11. Willie C. Williams to Strom Thurmond, February 1, 1965.
12. Harold L. George to George L. Murphy, January 4, 1965.
13. Dolly Hamby to Strom Thurmond, April 27, 1966.
14. Ibid., May 19, 1966.
15. Ibid., June 27, 1966.
16. Press release, August 1, 1966.
17. Unidentified newspaper article, *H. R. B.*, vol. XLII, Part 1.
18. Ibid.
19. Ibid.
20. Greenville *News*, October 13, 1966.
21. Elliot Hall, Jr., to J. Fred Buzhardt, November 4, 1966.
22. Undated Morrah campaign memo (author unknown).

Chapter 15: Thurmond Becomes a Statesman

1. Southern Oral History Program #4007 A-166, University of North Carolina, 14–15.
2. "Eyeball to Eyeball with Strom," *Newsweek*, 19 August 1968, 27.
3. Ibid.
4. Ibid., 26.
5. Don Oberdorfer, "Ex-Democrat, Ex-Dixiecrat, Today's 'Nixiecrat,'" *New York Times Magazine*, October 6, 1968, 62.
6. "How Strom Thurmond Does It." *Newsweek*, September 13, 1971
7. Nina Totenberg, "How Strom Thurmond Would Like to Change America," Washington *Post* (*Parade Magazine*), February 15, 1981, 23.
8. Southern Oral History, 16–17.
9. Ibid., 19.
10. Ibid., 19–20.
11. Jim Naughton, "'Uncle Strom': The Pragmatist's Legacy," Washington *Post*, Style Section, November 2, 1988.
12. Undated 1972 campaign memo (author unknown).
13. Zeigler Z-Gram.
14. Strom Thurmond to Barry Goldwater, October 4, 1972.
15. Barry Goldwater to Strom Thurmond, October 11, 1972.
16. Undated 1978 campaign memo (author unknown).
17. Charles Ravenel to Strom Thurmond, July 29, 1975.
18. Strom Thurmond to Charles Ravenel, August 6, 1975.
19. Sol Blatt to Strom Thurmond, June 6, 1977.
20. "Mondale Says Country Needs 'Pug' Ravenel," Charleston *News & Courier*, February 1, 1978.

21. Undated Thurmond press release.
22. "Carter Press Aide Powell Stumps for Ravenel," Columbia *State*, June 23, 1978.
23. Strom Thurmond to Jimmy Carter, June 23, 1978.
24. Speech by Jimmy Carter, June 23, 1978.
25. Charles Ravenel to Strom Thurmond, July 26, 1978.
26. Alison Dalton to Charles Ravenel, July 28, 1978.
27. Unidentified newspaper article, *H. R. B.*, vol. XLIV.
28. Democrats for Thurmond press release, August 7, 1978.
29. Ronald Reagan to Strom Thurmond, November 8, 1978.
30. "Thurmond Endorsement Boosts Connally," *Conservative Digest*, February 1980, 13.
31. Ed Magnuson "The Conservatives Are Coming," *Time*, November 24, 1980, 14–16.
32. Ibid.
33. Author unknown, "Abortion, Busing, Crime: Strom Thurmond Speaks Up," *U.S. News & World Report*, March 33, 1981, 41–42.
34. Ibid.

INDEX

Alcohol, 37, 78, 80, 83, 85, 173, 190–91
Agnew, Spiro T., 232, 240

Ball, George, 207–8
Baker, Bobby, 167
Baker, Gordon, 63, 77, 84, 179
Barnwell Ring, 27, 43, 48, 79–81, 157
Baskin, William P., 106
Beattie, A. J., 36, 79, 80
Benedict College, 122
Bennett, Neville, 57, 155, 158–59, 160–61
Blackwood, Ibra C., 25
Blatt, Solomon, 17, 27, 43, 48–50, 53, 54, 79, 80, 81–82, 243, 245
Blease, Cole, 6
Blease, Eugene S., 6, 21, 53, 179
Bobo, Jesse S., 155
Bonham, Milledge L., 69, 163
Booker, Leonard R., 54, 151
Britton, Earle R., 129
Brockington, Heyward, 158
Brown, Edgar A., 17, 27, 43, 48–50, 53, 79, 80, 82, 90, 92, 118, 150, 155, 157–65, 166, 168, 177
Bryson, James R., 50
Bryson, Joseph R, 48
Bush, George H. W., 246, 247
Butler, John M.
Buzhardt, J. Fred, 28, 58, 90, 179
Byrd, Harry F., 106, 112, 175, 176, 192, 247
Byrnes, James F., 17, 26, 133, 134, 140, 142–43, 146, 149, 150, 152, 154, 158–59, 163–64, 171, 179, 201, 219

Calhoun, John C., 35, 175, 201
Callison, T. C., 24, 48, 131, 155
Campbell, Carroll, 242
Cantrell, E. W., 90
Carter, A. F., 62
Carter, Jimmy, 242, 244–45, 246
Civil Rights Act, 185–88, 198–200, 211–13
Civilian Conservation Corps, 41, 61–62
Clayton, Faith, 128, 131
Clemson University, 8–10, 32, 36
Cleveland, Grover, 33
Coates, J. P., 54
Coleman, Francis F., 149, 156
Connally, John B., 246–47
Conner, Eugene, 113
Conner, Loretta, 167
Cooke, H. Kemper, 36
Crawford, Leon, 179
Crouch, Horace, 96, 97
Crouch, Inez Brezeale, 96
Crump, Edward H., 112
Culbertson, John Bolt, 27, 51, 127–29, 135, 148, 222
Cullen, H. R., 115

Dalton, Allison, 243, 245
Daniel, Charles E., 156, 166–67
Daniel, John M., 91
Daniel, Price, 176
Daniel, William L., Jr., 86
D-Day, 71, 72–74
Democratic National Convention, 5, 31, 42, 105, 108–10, 147–49, 171, 177, 178, 200–1, 216
Democratic Party, 30–31, 33, 57, 79, 93, 105, 106–9, 113, 117, 119, 121,

265

135, 147–50, 154, 157, 158, 160–62, 164, 168, 178, 179, 193, 215–19, 220
Dennis, Rembert, 155
Dent, Harry, 167, 187, 188, 217, 219, 220, 223, 232, 233, 234
DePass, W. L., Jr., 51
Dewey, Thomas E., 90, 103, 117, 119, 120–21
Dirksen, Everett M., 224, 231
Dole, Robert, 247, 251
Dorn, William Jennings Bryan, 154, 156, 158, 242
Douglas, Paul, 188
Drum, Hugh A., 70
Dusenberry, Richard, 167

Eastland, James, 112, 174, 212
Eddings, Inez, 223
Edens, J. Drake, 220
Edwards, James B., 241, 242–43, 246
Eisenhower, Dwight D., 72, 76, 87, 106, 109, 148, 149–50, 151–52, 153, 157, 160, 162, 167, 169–70, 171, 172, 173, 178, 180, 182, 183, 184, 185, 188, 200
Elmore, George, 93
Epps, Carl B., 79–80, 82
Equal Rights Amendment, 170
Erlichman, John, 236
Ervin, Sam, 176, 240

Farmer, James, 211
Featherstone, C. C., 55
Fishbourne, Edward L., 63
Folsom, Jim, 91, 100, 105
Ford, Gerald R., 231, 240, 241, 242
Fox, Sara, 145
Freeman, George W., 48
Fulbright, William, 176, 203–4, 205

Gault, Lewis H., 52
George, Walter, 146, 176, 177
Goldwater, Barry, 187, 189, 192–93, 200, 201, 205, 216–18, 239
Graham, Frank P., 138
Grant, Wilbur, 54, 125
Greneker, Thomas B., 29, 48, 50, 152
Gressette, Marion, 27, 155, 186

Haig, Alexander, 76

Hall, Wilton, 61, 158
Hamby, Dolly, 223
Harlan, John M., 170
Harris, Will, 1–2, 5
Haynsworth, Clement, 184
Herbert, R. Beverly, 200
Hinton, J. M., 93, 106
Holdridge, Herbert C., 112
Holland, Spessard, 176
Hollings, Ernest F., 174, 201, 221, 224, 226, 227
Hoover, Herbert, 30, 33, 169
Hope, Dorothy C., 167
Huggins, F. Mildred, 60–61
Humphrey, Hubert H., 110, 115, 150, 212, 216, 230, 233

Immigrants, 248

Javits, Jacob, 192
Jester, Beauford, 105
Johnson, Lady Bird, 197, 217
Johnson, Lyndon B., 119, 168, 172, 177, 183, 184, 186, 188, 191–92, 193, 198–200, 212, 213, 215, 216, 219, 220, 225, 229–30, 238
Johnston, Olin D., 41–42, 43, 52, 53, 57, 78, 79, 81, 92, 105, 106, 118, 123, 124, 125, 130, 131, 136–37, 139–40, 159–60, 170, 179, 186, 219, 221
Jones, Ira B., 6
Junior Order of United American Mechanics, 12, 38–39, 52, 146

Kennedy, Edward, 248
Kennedy, John B., 146–47
Kennedy, John F., 169, 190, 192–94, 198, 200–1, 207–8, 209–10, 212
Kennedy, Margie, 146–47
Kennedy, Robert F., 212, 226, 230
Kennedy, Robert M., 131–32, 164, 179
King, Martin Luther, Jr., 211
Knowland, William, 187, 232
Ku Klux Klan, 37, 61, 63, 126, 129, 142

Labor, organized, 63, 126, 138–39, 190, 193, 220–21
Lane, Preston, 105

Laney, Ben, 105, 107, 110, 111, 112
Leevy, I. S., 87–88
Lide, Lanneau D., 54, 56–57
Liquor, see Alcohol
Logue, Joe Frank, 12, 65–66
Logue-Timmerman Feud, 64–67
Long, Earl K, 113
Long, John D., 79, 80
Long, J. Reuben, 64
Lybrand, Dorcey, 144

Manning, Wyndham M., 154
Mansfield, Mike, 211
Marchant, Preston S., 156
Marshall, Thurgood, 88
Maybank, Burnet R., Jr., 57, 60, 92,
   138, 148, 152, 154, 155, 156, 162
McCarthy, Joseph, 153
McFall, T. Carr, 129
McGrath, Howard J., 105, 112, 139
McKinney, John L., 129
McLeod, James, 79, 80, 90
McMillan, Claud R., 90
McNair, Robert F., 221, 222, 226,
   227
McNamara, Robert, 204–5
Means, William M., 91
Mims, M. Hanford, 41, 54
Mitchell, Clarence, 187
Mitchell, Stephen, 157, 161, 171
Morrah, P. Bradley, Jr., 222, 224–27
Morse, Wayne, 168, 177, 187
Moss, Tom, 237
Mundt, Karl E., 205, 224

NAACP, 88, 110, 136, 172–73, 187,
   200
Nicholson, B. E., 57
Nixon, Richard M., 167, 169, 181,
   198, 201, 224–25, 230–33, 238,
   240

O'Neal, Dell, 79, 80

Parker, John J., 93
Parker, Marshall, 222–23, 226, 236
Parris, Jeff D., 40
Pattison, Jenny, 15
Pearson, Drew, 127, 134, 138
Pepper, Claude, 138
Perry, Matthew J., 237

Plowden, William C., Jr., 225
Poll tax, 85, 133
Pope, Tom, 87
Powell, Adam Clayton, 171
Powell, Jody, 242
Proxmire, William, 188
Purvis, Melvin, 249

Quarles, Jean, 167

Ramage, C. J., 45–46, 47–48
Ravenel, Charles R., 242–46
Rayburn, Sam, 171, 177
Reagan, Ronald W., 230, 231, 246,
   247, 249
Reid, James J., 91
Republican National Convention,
   230–32
Republican Party, 3–4, 30, 33, 107,
   127, 146, 162, 215–20, 221, 224,
   227–28, 247
Reserve Officers of America (ROA),
   145–46, 148, 151, 152–53, 171
Reynolds Tobacco Company, R. J., 16
Rhodes, James A., 232
Rockefeller, Nelson, 230, 231
Rogers, Joe, Jr., 239
Rogers, Joseph O., 223
Romney, George, 232
Roosevelt, Eleanor, 148
Roosevelt, Franklin Delano, Jr., 30,
   33, 42, 103, 105, 148–49
Russell, Donald S., 17, 26–27, 51,
   154, 221, 222
Russell, Richard B., 110, 146, 168,
   176, 191–92, 199, 202, 205, 212,
   224

Salley, Alex S., 163
Sawyer, Ben, 41–42
Schlesinger, Arthur M., Jr., 202–3
Scott, Roger W., 79, 80
Secret ballot, 133
Simons, Charles E., Jr., 144, 235–36
Sims, Henry, 97
Smith, Gerald L. K., 113
Smith, Howard, 176
Smith, Margaret Chase, 127, 206
Sobeloff, Simon E., 172
South Carolina Highway Commission,
   42, 43, 50, 90

Southern Manifesto, 173–81
Southern Railway Sysrem, 25–26, 28
States' Rights Party, 102, 103, 111,
 113–14, 115, 116–17, 119, 120–21,
 127, 129, 149
Stennis, John, 176, 206, 224
Steppe, Sarah Jones, 167
Stevenson, Adlai, 148, 178–79, 180
Stone, Marcus, 79, 80, 81, 158

Taft, Robert, 119
Talmadge, Herman E., 113, 119, 224
Taylor, John C., 41
Taylor, John R., 79, 80
Thompson, Frank R., 178
Thompson, M. E., 105
Thurmond, Allan George, 7
Thurmond, Eleanor Gertrude
 Strom, 2, 5, 7, 190
Thurmond, George Washington, 3
Thurmond, Gertrude, 7
Thurmond, J. Strom, Jr., 234
Thurmond, Jean Crouch, 96–102,
 143, 144, 152, 167, 187, 188, 195–98
Thurmond, John William, Sr., 1–2,
 5–7, 8, 9, 14, 17–19, 22, 26, 29,
 152, 250
Thurmond, John William, Jr., 7
Thurmond, Juliana Gertrude, 234
Thurmond, Martha, 7
Thurmond, Mary, 7
Thurmond, Nancy Moore (wife),
 233–34
Thurmond, Nancy Moore (daughter),
 234, 237, 244
Thurmond, Paul Reynolds, 234
Tillman, Benjamin R., Sr., 1, 4, 5–6,
 32, 36, 250
Tillman, Benjamin R., Jr., 29, 31–32
Timmerman, George B., Sr., 17,
 27–28, 48, 49, 50, 178
Timmerman, George B., Jr., 17, 140,
 152, 170, 177, 179, 180, 181, 183

Townsend, Joel, 89
Truman, Harry S, 87, 102, 103, 104,
 109, 115–16, 118, 119, 120–22,
 134–35, 139, 145–46, 148, 150,
 151, 161–62, 170, 179,
Tuck, William M., 104,

University of South Carolina, 19,
 37, 58, 100

Vaughn, Harry, 161–62

Walker, Edwin A., 208–9
Wallace, George, 233
Wallace, Henry A., 87, 103, 108–9
Waring, J. Waites, 93
Warren, Earl, 90
Warren, George, 108, 149
Watson, Albert, 219, 221, 223, 226,
 236
Watts, Kathleen B., 52
West, John, 236
Westbrook, J. B., 70, 71, 74
Westmoreland, William C., 76
Williams, Ashley H., 117
Williams, Ransome J., 77, 79, 80,
 162–63
Williamson, J. S., 90
Wilson, Woodrow, 6, 33
Winthrop College, 43, 44, 54, 60, 85,
 97, 197
Wofford, Thomas A., 89, 177, 180, 225
Wolfe, Julian S., 57
Wood, A. L., 79, 80
Workman's Compensation Act, 45
Wright, Fielding, 90, 106–7, 110,
 111, 112, 134, 178
Wrighten, John W., 88
Wyche, Cecil C., 26–27, 145

Yarborough, Ralph, 213–14

Ziegler, Nick, 238–39